the **Fates** of **African Rebels**

the **Fates** of **African Rebels**

Victory, Defeat, and the Politics of Civil War

Christopher Day

LYNNE
RIENNER
PUBLISHERS

BOULDER
LONDON

Published in the United States of America in 2019 by
Lynne Rienner Publishers, Inc.
1800 30th Street, Boulder, Colorado 80301
www.rienner.com

and in the United Kingdom by
Lynne Rienner Publishers, Inc.
Gray's Inn House, 127 Clerkenwell Road, London EC1 5DB

Library of Congress Cataloging-in-Publication Data
Names: Day, Christopher, 1973– author.
Title: The fates of African rebels : victory, defeat, and the politics of
  civil war / Christopher Day.
Description: Boulder, Colorado : Lynne Rienner Publishers, Inc., 2019. |
  Includes bibliographical references and index.
Identifiers: LCCN 2018047285 (print) | LCCN 2018048397 (ebook) | ISBN
  9781626377943 (e-book) | ISBN 9781626377615 (hardcover : alk. paper) |
  ISBN 9781626377646 (pbk. : alk. paper)
Subjects: LCSH: Civil war—Africa. | Insurgency—Africa. | Political
  violence—Africa. | Africa—Politics and government—1960–
Classification: LCC DT30.5 (ebook) | LCC DT30.5 .D385 2019 (print) | DDC
  322.42096—dc23
LC record available at https://lccn.loc.gov/2018047285

British Cataloguing in Publication Data
A Cataloguing in Publication record for this book
is available from the British Library.

Printed and bound in the United States of America

The paper used in this publication meets the requirements
of the American National Standard for Permanence of
Paper for Printed Library Materials Z39.48-1992.

5   4   3   2   1

To Connie

Contents

Acknowledgments

It was a long walk to finish this book. My research, writing, and revising all featured a motley assortment of friends, family, colleagues, and misfits to whom I will always be grateful.

The book really began years ago in the field, which provided the raw material of on-the-ground experience and an environment for the gestation of ideas. As an aid worker with Médecins Sans Frontières (MSF)—in Sudan, Ethiopia, Nigeria, Sierra Leone, Kashmir, Côte d'Ivoire, and Uganda—I learned how to navigate the politics of rebellion in order to help deliver relief to populations in crisis. Unbeknownst to me at the time, I fell into what would later become a research agenda, having spent ample time up-close-and-personal with a lively assortment of African rebels. These experiences connected me to key networks and taught me the basic logistics of fieldwork and how to be "all terrain." I have never really lost my MSF identity or shed the values I acquired over nine missions. In fact, my ongoing connection to the organization became a key component of my scholarly research, as MSF field teams provided a soft landing and indispensable home bases in Sierra Leone, South Sudan, and Central African Republic. Special thanks go to Tunis Mansarray, Gibril Massaquoi, Mike Lamin, Chris Lockyear, and Martin Braaksma. In addition, while working in northern Uganda in 2004 I befriended the then colonel Dick Olum of the Ugandan national army. Now a brigadier, he and his wonderful family have made me one of their own and have hosted me on recurring Uganda field trips.

Research began during my years at Northwestern University. I would not have ended up at Northwestern if not for the wise counsel and loyal friendship of Will "Mr. Williams" Reno. Also at Northwestern, Jim Mahoney and Hendrik Spruyt generously encouraged my research with a mixture of grace and tough love. Other Northwestern faculty members whom I always considered to be on my team include Risa Brooks, Tim Earle, Ed Gibson, Brian Hanson, Jeff Rice, Rachel Riedl, Andrew Roberts, Kathleen Thelen, Butch Ware, and Jeffrey Winters. Thanks also go to David Easterbrook and Esmeralda Kale and Northwestern's great Herskovitz Library. I also thank Wayne Steger and David Barnum, who invited me to teach part-time in DePaul University's Political Science Department and gave me office space to develop the early manuscript.

My time in Evanston would not have been so meaningful without the sharp minds and good humor of colleagues Toby Bolsen, Marissa Brookes, Ross Carroll, Jennifer Cyr, Valerie Freeland, Carlos Freytes Frey, Miklos Gosztonyi, Rick Hay, Olivier Henripin, Patrick Johnston, Andrew Kelly, Moses Khisa, Erin Kimball, Kendra Koivu, Natacha Lemasle, Jesse Dillon Savage, Larkin Terrie, Doug Thompson, and Ariel Zellman. Add to this group my extended family in Evanston: the Frays, the Knakes, the Cohens, the Silversteins, and the good people at Fonseca Martial Arts.

Of course, field research does not get completed and books do not get written without institutional support. I am grateful to the National Science Foundation, the United States Institute of Peace, and the Social Sciences and Humanities Research Council of Canada. The Buffett Center of International and Comparative Studies was likewise very good to me, providing funding, a chance to participate in the Chieftaincy Working Group, and above all allowing me to run the ENGAGE Uganda Summer Study Abroad Program for two years. Northwestern University's Graduate School and the Kellogg School of Management's Dispute Resolution Research Center also provided generous funds for travel to Africa and elsewhere. The College of Charleston has also been generous with support, providing a number of small grants that all meaningfully added up. Thanks to Jerry Hale and the School of Humanities and Social Sciences; David Cohen and the School for Languages, Cultures, and World Affairs; and to the good faculty R&D folks.

The Center for Basic Research became my research home in Uganda, and I am grateful for its resources and the camaraderie of its staff and scholars. I am also indebted to Sister Rosemary Nyirumbe and her sisters in Gulu, who provided a safe and loving home on more than one occasion. And special thanks go to all my counterparts in the field who facilitated my research—especially Jimmy Otim and Hippo Twebase in Kampala, Mother Gina and Kamilo Tafeng in Juba, and Igor Acko in Bangui.

The College of Charleston provided a suitable life anchor for the final stages of writing and revising. Not only am I a College of Charleston alumnus (1995), but it is also important to point out that way back in between MSF missions I worked as an adjunct instructor in the Department of Political Science; those good folks encouraged me to pursue a PhD. I am most fortunate to have such a terrific group of colleagues who have cheered me on during my writing and revising process: John Creed, Claire Curtis, Andy Felts, Lynne Ford, Hollis France, David Hinton, Phil Jos, Kevin Keenan, Guoli Liu, Mark Long, Jordan Ragusa, Kendra Stewart, Annette Watson, and Claire Wofford. In addition, the College of Charleston's African Studies Program is populated with fellow travelers and worthy sparring partners: Abdellatif Attafi, Meg Goettsches, Simon Lewis, Jack Parson, Rebecca Shumway, and of course the late, great Tim Carmichael. Special thanks also go out to my favorite students—you know who you are.

A key step in developing the manuscript was a rock-star workshop in September 2013, which featured Ana Arjona (Northwestern), Stathis Kalyvas (Oxford), Zach Mampilly (Vassar), and Will Reno (Northwestern). This was one of the most humbling and intellectually exhilarating experiences of my life, and I am grateful to these brilliant folks for their guidance and support. Funding for the workshop came from Pete Calcagno and the Center for Public Choice and Market Process (CPCMP), which has also helped fund research trips to Uganda and Central African Republic.

Additional scholars and practitioners who have helped me along the way with friendship and support include Kasper Agger, Sareta Ashraph, Ron Atkinson, Adam Branch, Matthew Brubacher, Ledio Cakaj, Noelle Carmichael, Cara Delay, Marc Dubois, Rebecca Golden, Kimberly Howe, Buddhika Jayamaha, Ben Kauffeld, Peter Lewis, Sacha Lezhnev, Louisa Lombard, Romain Malejacq, Dipali Mukhopadhyay, John Prendergast, Alphonze Sesay, Nick Rush Smith, Paul Staniland, Vic Tanner, Jacob Steere-Williams, Mike Woldemariam, and Jen Wright.

Above all I thank my immediate family—my wife, Jessica; our son, Samuel; and my father and mother, Richard and Sharron. Please forgive any omissions. All mistakes are my own.

1

Exploring the Fates
of African Rebels

*In revolutionary warfare, the mere fact of an insurgent surviving and
not being eliminated is in itself a success.*

—Yoweri Museveni,
National Resistance Army/Movement

On 19 January 2002, government motorcades roared past crowds packed
into Wusum Sports Stadium in Makeni, Sierra Leone.[1] Only a few hun-
dred yards from my office, President Ahmed Tejan Kabbah came to com-
memorate the Joint Declaration of End of War alongside Issa Sesay,
interim leader of the Revolutionary United Front (RUF), a rebel group
that had fought Sierra Leone's government for over a decade. The RUF
was probably best known for its contributions to Africa's iconic war
imagery—blood diamonds, the vacant gaze of stoned child soldiers, and
the amputated limbs of bewildered peasants. Beyond this snapshot, the
rebel group was part of a broader regional conflict and an extension of a
power axis rooted in Liberia that supplied rebels with arms and ammunition in exchange for precious gems. The RUF fought a series of weak
regimes that faced threats from within their own military, regimes that
also relied heavily on patchy outside support from regional African
armies, United Nations (UN) peacekeepers, and British troops. By mid-
2001, despite massive international intervention to prop up various unstable regimes, the RUF had come to control large parts of Sierra Leone,
mining alluvial diamonds and gold, controlling illicit cross-border trade,
looting everything lootable, and preying savagely on ordinary people. In
fact, there were several times during its rebellion that the RUF seemed
capable of victory. At the very least, over the course of the conflict, and
at the behest of regional and international actors, the rebel group was
offered more than one power-sharing opportunity with the government.

1

I had arrived in Makeni, the largest city in the Northern District, when it was the seat of the RUF's high command. Its fighters strutted around in Tupac T-shirts. They manned checkpoints with no traffic save for our Toyota Land Cruisers and the charred remains of roadside vehicles. As an aid worker at a nongovernmental organization (NGO), I maintained an air of friendly deference toward the RUF Big Men. When sober, the jovial "humanitarian coordinator," Gaskin Amara, was my official counterpart (no self-respecting rebellion goes without a "humanitarian" wing). Colonel Augustine Gbao, chief of security, always reassured me of my safety as he held court over 555 cigarettes, his brand of choice, and ranted about revolutionary politics (I eventually gave him my Che Guevara T-shirt). Multiple-gold-chained John "Bokello" Bangura was Sesay's main diamond commander, childhood friend of my local logistician, and buyer of rounds of Guinness. And of course, there was Sesay himself—"General Issa"—at whom I nervously winked once and received a strikingly boyish smile in return.

But now in Wusum Stadium, as Sesay delivered a contrite speech ahead of a symbolic arms-burning ceremony, things were different. The war was over and the RUF had neither won nor exactly lost. The group's leaders had squandered their chance to join the government, and any remaining "peace process" merely extended UN peacekeeping and state authority throughout the country. Most RUF rank and file had begun handing in their arms, breaking ranks, and rejoining civilian life as best they could via underfunded reintegration programs that promised vocational training. Although they were granted amnesty, most of these fighters anonymously walked away with nothing else.[2] Some left to fight in Liberia and Côte d'Ivoire, while a small number unsuccessfully struggled to transform the RUF into a political party.

Emblematic of the RUF's threadbare condition was the implosion of Makeni's Big Men. Chased out of the eastern city of Kono by stick-wielding civilians, Gaskin kept only the shirt on his back. Gbao habitually stopped me in the street to beg for a sack of rice. Bokello carefully rationed his remaining diamond dollars by drinking the local palm wine instead of Guinness. Sesay remained paranoid about his security and was eventually bundled off to face an indictment for war crimes. After a conflict that had claimed an estimated 200,000 lives in Sierra Leone and Liberia, that had displaced upward of 2 million, the RUF collapsed around its leaders and basically vanished as a rebellion. And I watched it happen.

Years later, as I worked on my graduate studies, the question of the RUF's fate came into sharper relief when I was doing preliminary fieldwork in Uganda. An investigation into newspaper articles on armed groups in the country from 1986 until 2002 yielded a hefty list of almost fifty of them. Some were merely "briefcase rebels"—rebels in name alone who appeared only fleetingly to talk to the press. But many were quite real and quite violent, dragging the Ugandan government into several simultaneous conflicts.[3] Aside from the obvious question of why there were so many rebellions, a closer look at how each of them had ended showed a remarkable amount of variation. The Uganda People's Democratic Army (UPDA) and the Uganda People's Army (UPA) fought briefly but intensely until signing peace accords and joining ranks with the Ugandan government. As the West Nile Bank Front (WNBF) fragmented internally, the army killed or arrested its fighters while a related but separate group, the Uganda National Rescue Front II (UNRF II), signed an accord and secured government sinecures. A clutch of small rebel groups—the National Army for the Liberation of Uganda (NALU), the Uganda Muslim Liberation Army (UMLA), and the National Democratic Army (NDA)—was roundly trounced on the battlefield. Their scattered remnants formed the core of the Allied Democratic Front (ADF), which fought for a decade until it fragmented and imploded much like the RUF, only to rebound later.

As I was doing this research, Uganda's most notorious rebel group, Joseph Kony's Lord's Resistance Army (LRA) was alive and well, carving a path of terror through the lightly governed hinterlands between Uganda, South Sudan, and the Democratic Republic of Congo (DRC). Internationally arranged peace talks based in Juba, the capital of South Sudan, limped forward (and eventually failed) alongside ongoing Ugandan military action against LRA fighters in the bush (that also failed), and the group's fate has remained up in the air (it still is). Years earlier, when I was an aid worker in northern Uganda, I had seen the LRA's handiwork while running humanitarian programs for its civilian victims, and I was deeply and personally invested in seeing this war over. Surely the fates of all of these other groups could illuminate something about which path this persistent rebellion might follow after having fought so brutally and for so long.

The Puzzle

My goal here is to explain the fates of rebels in Africa's contemporary civil wars, which can vary considerably, and sometimes unexpectedly. A look at the fates of the RUF and Uganda's myriad rebels shows that they do not quite correspond with conventional views of conflict outcomes. These tend to focus on the victory, defeat, success, or failure of states or armed groups, or on the middle path of peace agreements often brokered by external actors. As shown by many cases beyond those in Sierra Leone and Uganda, this depiction of how conflicts end does not always explain what happens to individual rebellions as they move through civil wars and eventually end in one way or another. The tendency to focus on this victory-defeat dichotomy and on the external orientation of peace accords misses the complex dynamics shaping many recent rebellions and does not meaningfully capture a potential range of fates beyond success or failure, rebellion or nonrebellion.

To be sure, there are clear wins and losses in conflict. For instance, the Rwandan Patriotic Front (RPF) is emblematic of Africa's few victorious rebellions, keeping company with Uganda's National Resistance Army and the Ethiopian People's Revolutionary Democratic Front (EPRDF).[4] In contrast, after years of civil war, the government of Sri Lanka eventually wiped out the Liberation Tigers of Tamil Elam (LTTE). The União Nacional para a Independência Total de Angola (UNITA) rebellion limped to defeat following the death of its leader, Jonas Savimbi, in 2002 and has since transformed itself into Angola's second-largest political party. Similarly, Colombia's M-19 rebellion was defeated militarily but its members were allowed to contest politically in the late 1980s.

But other rebels may achieve a sense of "victory" through a peace accord or political settlement. El Salvador's Farabundo Martí National Liberation Front (FMLN) ended this way, as did the fifteen-year civil Resistência Nacional Moçambicana (RENAMO) rebellion against Mozambique's Frente de Libertação de Moçambique (Frelimo) regime. In contrast, the RUF in Sierra Leone suffered from a sort of "self-defeat"— neither winning nor losing to the national army, nor entering into a durable political settlement via massive international intervention despite having numerous chances to do so.

In explaining distinct rebel fates as variants of conflict outcomes, I have drawn on evidence from Africa to address a novel question within the broader literature on civil wars and insurgent violence. Based on original research and fieldwork, I have developed an argument that attributes rebel fates to their historical role in regime politics.

The Argument

To explain the fates of African rebels, I propose the following: Rebel groups are organized by their degree of political embeddedness in state authority structures. Although these structures can be formal, they are largely informal and based on patronage networks. This means that some groups may be composed of disparate political outsiders, whereas others contain key insiders from the fragmented networks of the prevailing political establishment. It is these variations in embeddedness that predict different rebel fates.

Politically embedded rebel groups cohere around disenfranchised elites—insiders—who once played either formal or informal roles in state institutions. These elites maintain prewar patronage networks that bring organizational endowments into rebellion, which either increase the likelihood of winning outright or facilitate their reentry into regime politics by way of a political settlement with incumbents. Alternatively, groups composed of political outsiders are already marginalized from the existing political system. Although these outsiders may have alternative sources of organizational cohesion, such as ethnicity or class, they will lack the access to political networks granting entry to authority structures, unless they replace them entirely. Short of victory, these groups are more likely to lose militarily or unravel on their own.

In addition, although I rule out military capacity as a major factor in explaining rebel fates, I do consider the parity of rebels with state military forces, elsewhere described as the "technology of rebellion."[5] In other words, rebels can fight in irregular wars that are asymmetrical, using guerrilla tactics against a more conventional state military. Or, as in many cases, rebels fight in contexts where irregular warfare is symmetrical, where rebels and state militaries are more or less evenly matched. Either way, although one would expect that a rebel group's capacity relative to a state adversary would make for stable forecasts, a key insight here is that political embeddedness mediates capacity and is a better predictor of rebel fates.

Why Rebel Fates Matter

In 1980, Gurr noted, "The outcomes of violent conflict are problematic and intrinsically worthy of study."[6] Yet since then, the broader literature on civil war has focused on its causes, conduct, and patterns of violence.[7] My work here contributes to the expanding scholarship on the organization and behavior of rebellions in civil war,[8] engaging in dialogue with the more limited literature on conflict outcomes.[9] Examining the puzzle of rebel fates expands the conceptualization of these outcomes to be more in line with "win, lose, or draw" but considers these as variations of victory and defeat.[10] This dovetails with Staniland's

observation that there are alternative ways to think about conflict outcomes that capture the fine-grained dynamics of civil wars.[11] Additionally, this study provides a corrective to views of conflict outcomes as
endgames that are "resolved" by outsiders, lending key insights into the
larger industry of policy-oriented research on intervention and conflict
resolution.[12] More important, the research in this book signals a key
conceptual shift from generic conflict outcomes to the distinct fates of a
conflict's main actors—in this case, rebel groups—which is a new
direction of inquiry that contributes to the broader comparative literature on civil wars and insurgent violence.

In a more general sense, I interrogate the extent to which the win-
ners or losers of Africa's civil wars can potentially shape the broader
nature of politics and society on the continent. Studying the fates of
rebels casts light on the politics of weak states and has implications for
wider-ranging issues related to political order and stability. To be sure,
rebellion in Africa bears witness to the imperfect monopoly of violence
held by many African regimes over their territories. This study therefore
provides further insight into the projection of state authority, particularly in the context of state-society relations in environments with weak
formal institutions and where governance functions largely through
patronage networks and elite coalitions. A key theoretical contribution
here is the observation that rebellions do not necessarily occur peripheral to or distinct from the regimes they fight but can arise from the
very political networks that sustain regime authority.

In this vein, my focus on rebellion in weak states takes up the call
from Kalyvas to explore the understudied and less understood phenomena of symmetrical, irregular wars that play out in contexts such as
Africa.[13] This means looking at conflicts where both rebel groups and
state armies adopt similar strategies in fighting one another against the
backdrop of weak or failing state institutions. For instance, for most of
Sierra Leone's civil war, RUF rebels fought a poorly trained, undisciplined army that exploited disorder for personal gain, ushering in the
phenomenon widely described as "sobels"—soldiers by day and rebels
by night.[14] In addition, in expanding our knowledge of symmetrical,
irregular wars, examining the fates of rebels who fight in these conflicts
can contribute to a broader understanding of how rebel organizations
are developed, maintained, or unwound in violent environments.

Finally, studying the fates of rebels has important policy implications. As a former aid worker, I have seen firsthand the tremendous
human costs of civil wars in Africa and South Asia. They cause economic and political instability in regions already saddled with weak

institutions. Millions are killed, many from direct violence but most from conflict's downstream consequences of displacement, disease, and malnutrition. Research into the inner workings of rebel groups and their corresponding fates can provide practical advice on how to ultimately solve and possibly prevent such conflicts and more effectively mitigate their humanitarian consequences. For example, foisting peace agreements upon regimes that compel elites to incorporate certain types of rebel groups into state politics may not work out as planned. Equally, counterinsurgency strategies that ignore the complex political networks that are the wellsprings of rebellion can turn out to be much more grueling affairs than expected. More nuanced responses require policymakers and practitioners to take more seriously the full range of forms and possible fates that characterize contemporary rebel groups in weak states and the regions in which these wars occur.

Prevailing Approaches

What factors explain the fates of African rebels? As mentioned above, the lion's share of research on civil war and rebellion tends to focus on their causes and their myriad processes. Like much of this literature, the more limited, albeit growing work on conflict outcomes deploys large-N, cross-national studies and casts a wide net around a range of state-level variables such as state weakness, natural resources, or geography. This work explores the key questions of why some conflicts last longer than others, what conditions are necessary for them to end, and why some civil wars are more difficult to resolve than others. If rebel fates can be considered distinct variants of conflict outcomes, it makes sense then to situate things in the broader literature of conflict duration and termination, which casts these phenomena as conceptual cousins.

From this literature, we can identify two dominant conceptual binaries. One sees conflict outcomes as a matter of incumbent victory versus rebel victory and examines the ability or willingness of rebels and/or incumbents to fight and win. The other pits conflict resolution versus failed conflict resolution and examines the ability or willingness of rebels and/or incumbents to negotiate. This approach straddles conceptual terrain, framing successful conflict resolution as a variant of conflict termination, and its failure in terms of conflict duration.

In seeking to understand the causal wellsprings of conflict duration and termination, scholars have developed a sizable literature on bargaining in civil wars.[15] Most of this work begins with the assumption that fighting is costlier than not fighting, and that both rebels and incumbents would prefer to get what they can from negotiations. A more Clausewitzian view recognizes that conflict onset, duration, termination, and even the downstream consequences of civil war can all be folded into a process of bargaining between rebels and incumbents.[16]

Walter helpfully breaks down bargaining into three key components.[17] First, bargaining is possible when actors overcome information asymmetries about the capabilities and resolve of their adversaries—not an easy task. Second, a major obstacle to reaching any resolution comes from the problem of credible commitments. This involves judging whether or not an adversary will back out of a deal, which becomes a thorny issue because bargaining exposes hidden weaknesses and brings forth vulnerabilities associated with disarming. Finally, bargaining must bear in mind the political and economic stakes of a settlement, which can often be indivisible.

This notion that bargaining is the crux of ending civil wars has generated a veritable industry of conflict-resolution scholarship and practice.[18] Here, third-party intervention, guarantees by outside mediators, and promises of power sharing are seen to undergird any successful negotiation in order to overcome any "barriers" to peace (i.e., ongoing fighting). Conflict termination thus becomes a story of bargaining success, and conflict duration is a story of bargaining failure.

If bargaining is indeed the crux of conflict duration and termination, there are surely multiple factors that shape the willingness or capacity of rebels and/or incumbents to bargain at all. These factors slot into two broad categories: the motives that drive rebels or incumbents, and the means that support them. Although valuable, this work suffers from several problems.

Motive-based explanations assert that conflict termination and duration are rooted in the goals and interests of the actors, and by extension, their *willingness* to bargain based on these goals and interests.[19] Indeed, Kirschner observes that if negotiations are to be successful, actors must look beyond past transgressions and overcome their fear of uncertain time horizons through the mechanism of *trust*.[20] Yet Wucherpfennig et al. argue that reaching a political settlement is much more difficult when conflicts are based on ethnic identity, which are also inclined to be more intractable as the stakes of divisible political spoils tend to be higher.[21] In this vein, perhaps because such rebels are more intransigent, Mason, Weingarten, and Fett add that they tend to be the victors of "ethnic conflicts"—but they also claim that secessionists are more likely than ideological "revolutions" to settle with incumbents, which is a counterintuitive claim, considering the more indivisible stakes of terri-tory.[22] In addition, because civil wars often involve many actors, Cun-ningham maintains that the multiple, overlapping interests of too many "veto players" render them more difficult to resolve.[23]

However, although some rebel groups do organize around ethnic identity, ideology, or territorial identity, there are many other tools of recruitment and allegiance. A closer look shows that rebel motives are wide ranging, can change over the course of conflict, and say little about what fates they experience in civil war. And the main problem with tying motives such as ethnicity to rebel fates is that they are most often only a proximate factor that aggregates a wide range of individual motives. Ethnicity, for example, is not so much a driver of rebel fates per se, but acts as a marker for more salient structural issues that histor-ically situate these groups within political society and its institutions.[24]

Above all, though some rebel leaders certainly wish to rule, not all of them fight to become regime leaders or heads of state.[25] Instead, many groups "derive from blocked aspirations and in some cases from reactive desperation"[26] and "rage against" the dysfunctional institutional machinery of the state.[27] In other words, a rebellion can be as much about damaging, discrediting, or integrating into the state as it is about replacing it. This means that in addition to measurement problems, con-ventional views of the willingness of rebel groups to bargain often make incorrect assumptions about what they ultimately want. Above all, motive-based arguments break down once it becomes empirically clear that groups with similar motives may follow contrasting paths, and those with different motives can experience the same fate.

Means-based explanations consider how the material capacities of rebels or incumbents matter to conflict outcomes. This suggests that access to resources—particularly the fungible, lootable variety—can bolster capacity, prolong fighting, and reduce incentives to bargain.[28] On the incumbent side of the ledger, Rouen and Sobek claim that the increased bureaucratic effectiveness of the state, along with its simply having a bigger army, likely leads to rebel defeat.[29] In contrast, Lyall and Wilson argue that incumbents lose wars more frequently because of the mechanization of national armies, which inhibits more fleet-footed counterinsurgency strategies against shadowy rebel chal-lengers.[30] External intervention that provides material support for either rebels or incumbents can shift material capacities and affect conflict outcomes.[31]

Whereas such work tends to consider the victory-versus-defeat con-ceptualization of conflict termination, other means-based arguments factor capacity into bargaining models. For instance, Cunningham, Gleditsch, and Salehyan look at the strategic interaction between "strong" and "weak" adversaries, not in terms of military victory or defeat but as a basis for incentives to negotiate.[32] In other words, rebels and incumbents may talk only after sizing one another up. This means that raw material capacity to fight and win plays a lesser role than *perceptions* of such, which plays into estimating the odds of winning or losing. Above all, uncertainty of relative means matters during stalemates. Where the conventional view holds that a "mutually hurting stalemate" increases the likelihood of actors' willingness to negotiate,[33] Findley points out that stalemates are often too rife with ambiguity for stable settlements.[34] This means that stalemates may push adversaries to bargain, but only in the short term. Once negotiations are under way, previously obscured information about capacity and resolve is made available through joint interactions, which may incentivize a return to fighting and the prolonged duration of conflict.

This observation underscores a key problem with means-based explanations for conflict outcomes: there is a disconnect between assumptions of perfect information when estimating the capacity of adversaries and the recognition that actors can misestimate or misrepresent capacity, particularly during negotiations.[35] As will become clear in Chapter 2, this is not to say that resource endowments do not matter at all to conflict outcomes, but they are neither a sufficient nor a necessary factor for predicting the fates of rebels. In many cases, there are things that happen off the battlefield that are more important in shaping rebel trajectories than the number of guns and gumboots at their disposal, or even perceptions of such things.

Although such motives or means-based bargaining literature has provided numerous key insights into conflict outcomes, it suffers from additional shortcomings. First, shoehorning rebels and incumbents into game theoretic models tends to impute a rather one-dimensional intentionality to things and brings overarching validity problems in inferring the motives of actors and estimates of their means. This is particularly difficult when considering that most conflicts consist of more actual fighting than bargaining.[36] And as Findley has observed, even if rebellion is viewed as a violent extension of bargaining, there are still multiple stages that unfold where learning occurs and preferences shift.[37] Moreover, civil war is not just about dividing the political pie—as this book will show, incumbents may simply choose to completely foreclose any bargaining opportunities with rebel groups by pursuing their elimination. Alternatively, rebels may prefer ongoing conflict to any sort of resolution. Second, most studies do not disaggregate rebel fates from broader conflict outcomes and tend to conflate the factors behind civil war onset, duration, and termination.[38] This conceptual blurring, plus the fixation on conflict dyads as the unit of analysis, can obscure the more distinct puzzle of rebel fates.

Above all, the prevailing approaches to conflict outcomes are remarkably agnostic about the political context in which they occur and do not always account for unintended consequences in the highly contingent environments of civil war and rebellion. As Thyne has observed, even small variations within regime politics can influence the dynamics of bargaining.[39] To be clear, I do not necessarily seek to explicitly engage in bargaining models of conflict duration or termination. But I do seek to contribute to the broader literature on conflict outcomes in several ways.

First, this study reconceptualizes how civil wars end as distinct rebel fates. These fates are viewed from the vantage point of rebel groups and are essentially reworked variants of "victory" and "defeat." Here a "victory" can be viewed as replacing incumbents militarily or joining them politically. "Defeat" can occur at the hands of incumbents or can be self-inflicted. In portraying rebel fates in this way, this approach deliberately sidesteps the concept of conflict duration, which it treats as a separate phenomenon called "rebel persistence," addressed in Chapter 6.

Second, I introduce the concept of political embeddedness as the key factor guiding the calculations of rebels and incumbents alike, and it bends the trajectories of rebel groups toward their respective fates in civil war. In this sense, what predicts rebel fates remains a game of perception in terms of what behavior rebels and incumbents expect from one another. But unlike the motives or means predicting bargaining and negotiation, political embeddedness is a structural feature of African state institutions. Thus, the game is placed in the broader environment of African patronage politics and how regimes deal with different elements of political society that challenge their authority. In this context, the rules of the game are shaped by both formal and informal institutional patterns, where the cost-benefit calculus of incumbents varies by the nature of the threat posed by the rebellion, which is a function of where the rebellion sits within political society. Rebellion becomes a way to either replace or negotiate into prevailing state authority networks—most rebels seek total victory if they can get it, partial victory if they cannot. Incumbents seek to maintain hegemony over prevailing political networks one way or another and can achieve this through a variety of means.

Scope Conditions

To proceed, it is important to draw boundaries around the distinct political terrain that holds the characteristics salient to rebel fates. I expect my theory to apply to civil wars where rebel fates are definitive. That is, ongoing rebellions such as the Lord's Resistance Army, whose fate is not yet known, are not considered here. Moreover, the argument relates best in cases where rebel groups fight the armed forces of weak, fragmented states, and sometimes across contentious regions. Recall that this category of civil war is further refined along the dimensions of the "technology of rebellion," or the joint military tactics of both states and rebels engaged in armed conflict.[40] In this regard, the cases considered in this study occur primarily within the context of symmetrical, nonconventional conflict, where the military capacity of both the state and the rebel group is low and more or less equivalent. Correspondingly, the approach here does not consider the structural anatomy of African rebels to be overly complex or very high-tech. The ability of some groups to survive for considerable periods of time in the bush, the widespread use of small arms such as the Kalashnikov rifle, and the ease of its use by even children are illustrative of this point. In this sense, my argument stands in contrast with Staniland's observations of armed groups that fight much more capable regimes and often in the context of more conventional warfare.[41]

Methods, Empirics, and Moving Forward

My objective is to explain how variations in political embeddedness make some rebel groups more likely to experience certain fates over others. In doing so I make a general argument but test it against evidence from Africa, which falls suitably within the study's scope conditions and provides a large reservoir of representative cases. A detailed look at a smaller set of these cases is designed to sharpen similarities and differences between them in order to determine each rebel group's degree of political embeddedness, the technology of warfare, configurations of which specify the causal pathways to each particular fate.

I approach rebel fates by looking at patterns of relationships within Africa's wider political fabric and draw on a historical institutional analytical approach. Rebellion is, after all, a political act, albeit writ violent. It is structured by the distributional conflicts between different political actors and the asymmetries of power associated with the origins, operation, and development of state institutions and the state systems they occupy. It is these institutions—both formal and informal—

that distribute power and status unevenly across social groups, giving some disproportionate access to decisionmaking processes, promoting some actors while demobilizing others.[42]

My research for this study included extensive fieldwork in Uganda, Sudan, and Sierra Leone from 2007 until 2013, and in Central African Republic in 2015. Original data are based on visits to current and former war zones and upon multiple and repeated field interviews with former rebel leaders, ex-combatants, military personnel, national scholars, civil society leaders, and government and NGO officials. Interviews provided detailed, on-the-ground narratives and insights into the internal strategic debates and decisionmaking of rebel and military leaders. Questions focused on the political origins of the rebellion's membership, the biographies of leaders, and their prewar roles in the state's political establishment. Where possible, primary documents and newspaper archives from each country augmented the testimony of these participants, reconstructing and confirming narratives, and pointing to patterns of events during the trajectory of each rebel group.

To summarize, rebel fates can be viewed as an issue separate from conventional views of conflict outcomes, prompting us to ask why different fates occur. Using the methodological overview outlined here, the rest of the book is arranged as follows. Chapter 2 focuses on developing a theory of rebel fates rooted in an understanding of regime politics in Africa. It begins by establishing rebel fates as their own units of analysis, surveying the organizational characteristics of African rebels in particular. It then builds a theory from Africa's domestic political context, which shapes political embeddedness and creates rebellions composed of either political insiders or outsiders. I then consider the technology of rebellion, exploring how differences in symmetrical or asymmetrical warfare configure with political embeddedness to push rebels down different trajectories. Taken together, the elements of Chapter 2 provide a new set of theoretical and conceptual tools for analyzing rebellions as civil wars unfold and as they meet their respective fates.

The central portion of the book is divided into three empirical chapters that tackle the problem of rebel fates through several frames of comparison. In Chapter 3, Uganda provides an opportunity for a controlled subnational comparison of nine rebel groups. Taken together, Uganda's insurgencies represent a near complete inventory of the theory's outcomes. Holding the state constant, these cases provide variation across rebel fates within a defined geographic area and a compact time span. This chapter also showcases the inductive development of the book's theoretical argument. Data for this chapter was gathered from an investigation into Ugandan newspaper articles that covered armed movements from 1986 until 2006 and fieldwork conducted in Uganda from 2007 until 2016.

In Chapter 4, two cases provide cross-national and within-case comparisons that test the argument elsewhere in Africa. Here I examine two cases of politically embedded rebel groups, or "insiders." The first case is the Sudan People's Liberation Army (SPLA), whose political settlement in 2005 was a direct outcome of political embeddedness, a factor often overlooked by many observers. The SPLA survived twenty-two years of civil war despite changes in its external resource linkages and in its relations to incumbent regimes' political networks. Data for both cases was gathered from primary sources and the newspaper *Africa Confidential,* and fieldwork in South Sudan was conducted for the SPLA case. The second case study examines the slow path to victory of Côte d'Ivoire's Forces Nouvelles. A composite of several armed groups beginning in 2002, the Forces Nouvelles fought its way to a negotiated settlement by 2007, only to renew fighting in 2011 after the settlement collapsed around highly contested elections.

In Chapter 5, two additional cross-case and within-case comparisons consider the fates of "outsiders." First, Sierra Leone's Revolutionary United Front is a case of defeat via disintegration, which occurred in spite of access to resources. The RUF factionalized and imploded over an eleven-year civil war even after entering into an internationally brokered peace agreement with Sierra Leone's incumbent regime. Second, the Séléka rebellion in Central African Republic (CAR) is illustrative of outsider victory. Although the Séléka alliance's disparate members had previously negotiated with the incumbent regime, this failure set the scene for renewed rebellion and ultimate victory. The Séléka case, however, contains key implications for postconflict political order and stability, as its consolidation of a postvictory regime was unsuccessful. Research for these cases was based on secondary sources and fieldwork in each country. Information was also gathered from an investigation into *Africa Confidential* and *West Africa* magazine, Trial Chamber Judgment Reports from the Special Court on Sierra Leone, as well as Sierra Leone's Truth and Reconciliation Commission (TRC) report.

In Chapter 6, I summarize the study's main claims and reinforce the significance of its contributions to the literatures on civil war, insurgent violence, and African politics. I then extend my framework and consider several key implications of rebel fates not entirely captured by the book. First, I present a broader discussion of rebel persistence. What factors explain why rebel groups such as the LRA continue fighting in spite of peace and reconciliation efforts or superior (or inferior) state military capacity? Looking at these cases from the perspective of political embeddedness can shed light on why rebel groups abandon a political settlement or fail at a bid for incorporation, illuminating spoiler issues and explaining why peace accords fail. Second, I revisit rebel capacity and look specifically at proxy warfare as a potential factor in shaping rebel fates. Rather than simply looking at capacity as a material element of rebellion, the cases under consideration here raise interesting questions about the politics behind those resources and ask to what extent different rebel groups become beholden to the imperatives of their sponsors. Although arguments in the book downplay the role of capacity and resources for rebel fates, there are some instances where trajectories are tempered by the strategic priorities of political actors outside their own states.

Chapter 6 concludes with potential directions for future research on the political stability of African states, which includes a discussion on the viability of peace operations and counterinsurgency, and the factors that lead to postconflict political order. The observation that political insiders are more likely to be incorporated into regimes has direct implications for the effectiveness and stability of negotiated settlements, which is an unsettled question in the broader study of peace accords. The stability of settlements also raises questions about the utility of rebellion and its likelihood to cause political change, where civil war often serves to preserve a political order rather than change it, suggesting nonviolent options ought to be more effective.

Notes

1. "Kabbah's Presence in Makeni Manifests Peace—Gen. Issa Sesay," *Standard Times* (Freetown), 23 January 2002.

2. Douglas Farah, "'They Fought for Nothing, and That's What They Got,'" *Washington Post*, 1 September 2001.

3. Day, "The Fates of Rebels."

4. Young, "The Victors and the Vanquished," p. 178.

5. Kalyvas and Balcells, "International System and Technologies of Rebellion."

6. Gurr, "On the Outcomes of Violent Conflict," p. 245.

7. Kalyvas, *The Logic of Violence in Civil Wars*.

8. For an excellent overview of the current literature on civil war and rebellion, see Woldemariam, *Insurgent Fragmentation in the Horn of Africa*; Arjona, *Rebelocracy*; Balcells, *Rivalry and Revenge*; Krause, *Rebel Power*; Adunbi, *Oil Wealth and Insurgency in Nigeria*; Cohen *Rape During Civil War*; Roessler, *Ethnic Politics and State Power in Africa*; Staniland, *Networks of Rebellion*. For a snapshot of literature that inspired this current scholarship, see Wickham-Crowley, *Guerrillas and Revolution in Latin America*; Petersen, *Resistance and Rebellion*; Wood, *Insurgent Collective Action and Civil War in El Salvador*; and Reno, *Warlord Politics and African States*.

9. O'Connor, "Victory in Modern War."

10. Mason, Weingarten Jr., and Fett, "Win, Lose or Draw."

11. Staniland, *Networks of Rebellion*, p. 245.

12. Walter, "The Critical Barrier to Civil War Settlement"; Stedman, "Spoiler Problems in Peace Processes"; Licklider, *Stopping the Killing*; Carroll, "How Wars End"; Stedman, Rothchild, and Cousens, *Ending Civil Wars.*

13. Kalyvas, "Civil Wars."

14. Keen, *Conflict and Collusion in Sierra Leone*; Abraham, "State Complicity as a Factor"; Kandeh, "What Does the 'Militariat' Do When It Rules?"

15. Schelling, *The Strategy of Conflict;* Wagner, "Bargaining and War"; Pillar, *Negotiating Peace*; Powell, "Bargaining Theory and International Conflict"; Powell, "War as a Commitment Problem"; Reiter, "Exploring the Bargaining Model of War."

16. Reiter, "Exploring the Bargaining Model of War."

17. Walter, "Bargaining Failures and Civil War."

18. Crocker, Hampson, and Aall, *Taming Intractable Conflicts*; Walter, *Committing to Peace*; Toft, *Securing the Peace*; Fortna, *Does Peacekeeping Work?*; Regan, "Third-Party Interventions and the Duration of Intrastate Conflicts"; Howard and Stark, "How Civil Wars End."

19. Fearon, "Why Do Some Civil Wars Last So Much Longer than Others?"

20. Kirschner, *Trust and Fear in Civil Wars.*

21. Wucherpfennig, Metternich, Cederman, and Gleditsch, "Ethnicity, the State, and the Duration of Civil War."

22. Mason, Weingarten, and Fett, "Win, Lose or Draw."

23. Cunningham, "Veto Players and Civil War Duration."

24. Gilley, "Against the Concept of Ethnic Conflict," p. 1159.

25. Johnston, "The Geography of Insurgent Organization and Its Consequences for Civil Wars," pp. 119–120.

26. Clapham, *African Guerrillas*, p. 5.

27. Bøås and Dunn, eds., *African Guerrillas*, p. 10.

28. Collier, "Rebellion as a Quasi-Criminal Activity"; Fearon, "Why Do Some Civil Wars Last So Much Longer?"; Ross, "What Do We Know About Natural Resources and Civil War?"; Ross, "A Closer Look at Oil, Diamonds, and Civil War."

29. de Rouen Jr. and Sobek, "The Dynamics of Civil War Duration and Outcome."

30. Lyall and Wilson III, "Rage Against the Machines."

31. Shirkey, *Joining the Fray.*

32. Cunningham, Gleditsch, and Salehyan, "It Takes Two."

33. Zartman, *Ripe for Resolution.*

34. Findley, "Bargaining and the Interdependent Stages of Civil War Resolution."

35. Mason and Fett, "How Civil Wars End"; Mukherjee, "Why Political Power-Sharing Agreements Lead to Enduring Peaceful Resolution of Some Civil Wars, but Not Others?"; Elbadawi and Sambanis, "External Interventions and the Duration of Civil Wars."

36. Fearon, "Fighting Rather than Bargaining."

37. Findley, "Bargaining and the Interdependent Stages of Civil War Resolution."

38. Hegre, "The Duration and Termination of Civil War"; Collier, Hoeffler, and Söderbom, "On the Duration of Civil War."

39. Thyne, "Information, Commitment, and Intra-War Bargaining."

40. Kalyvas and Balcells, "International System and Technologies of Rebellion."

41. Staniland, *Networks of Rebellion*, pp. 10–11.

42. Hall and Taylor, "Political Science and the Three New Institutionalisms"; Thelen, "Historical Institutionalism in Comparative Politics."

2

A Theory of Rebel Fates

Who rebels? Who rises in arms? Rarely the slave, but almost always the oppressor turned slave.

—Emile M. Cioran

To outside observers, the end of civil war can seem unambiguous, with declared conquerors and devastated also-rans. But for many rebels, the termination of war does not always equal these outcomes. Peace agreements can become face-saving exercises in which rebels humble themselves before magnanimous incumbents who dole out government posts in response to international pressure. And as noted elsewhere, "an insurgency could effectively be over without either side realizing it had won or lost for several years."[1] A "victory" may simply mean a set of conditions that provide opportunities for some actors and place constraints on others.[2] "Defeat" can be total or partial, externally exacted or self-inflicted. Depending on the vantage point, outcomes that are otherwise thought of as similar can actually be quite different. Moreover, the termination of war is often subjectively ambiguous and does not correspond to the fluidity of war aims over the course of conflict.[3]

Focusing on rebel fates clarifies how wars end. This focus requires a fresh look at the complex dynamics shaping many recent rebellions and the patterns of political interaction with the states they fight, which, as argued here, are situated within their historical institutional context. The question of rebel fates provides a new direction of inquiry within the broader comparative literature on civil wars and insurgent violence and contributes a distinct theoretical statement about the nature of regime politics and the exercise of political authority in civil wars.[4]

In this chapter, I lay the theoretical groundwork for explaining how rebellions end as a function of their political relationships with incumbent regimes. My first objective is to conceptually recalibrate conflict outcomes into different rebel fates. I then develop a theory that explains this variation. After surveying the development of regime politics associated with the African context, I delineate the organizational characteristics of rebellion within an explanatory framework and connect this to a theory of rebel fates that explains how variations in "political embeddedness" play out against the backdrop of symmetrical or asymmetrical warfare.

Whose Fates? Civil Wars and Their Outcomes

At this point, a short discussion of unit-of-analysis issues is in order. Kalyvas defined a civil war as "armed combat within the boundaries of a recognized sovereign entity between parties subject to a common authority at the outset of the hostilities."[5] For the purposes here, this definition provides a suitable conceptual anchor amid ongoing searches for an operational definition of a complex phenomenon and a rapidly expanding research agenda.[6] Conceptual debates about civil wars have been useful. They have, for instance, exposed the uncritical assumptions and incomplete data behind the false distinction between "old" and "new" civil wars.[7] Other debates have highlighted the difficulties in establishing the coding rules that classify civil wars as a distinct category of violence or armed conflict and have raised questions about the utility of baseline definitional thresholds such as the number of deaths per given time frame (battle vs. civilian deaths?) or the magnitude of violence.[8]

This push for conceptual refinement is no doubt tied to a surge of fresh research on civil wars and rebellion in recent years, which has moved away from the traditional preoccupation with civil war onset attributed to factors such as state weakness, economic agendas, or identity.[9] Newer scholarship pursues a range of research questions related to the microdynamics of conflict and the joint interactions of its main actors.[10]

However, as this research has expanded in different directions, and despite the push toward microlevel analysis, most studies of conflict outcomes have not shaken the modal orientation toward the civil war as the primary unit of analysis. Very seldom are the fates of individual armed groups disaggregated from the treatment of conflict outcomes. As Staniland correctly points out, most measures of these outcomes focus on state-rebel dyads, which means any attention to the distinct trajectories of insurgents in these conflicts is not explicitly considered.[11]

This tendency to look at a civil war or the country in which it occurs as the primary unit of analysis is especially apparent in large-N, cross-national studies. To be sure, databases such as the Uppsala Conflict Data Program (UCDP) and the Correlates of War Project (CWP) have been quite worthwhile in gathering and warehousing information on a large number of conflicts worldwide. However, there remains a lot of ambiguity in the coding and measuring of how these conflicts end. For instance, UCDP database outcomes of "cease-fire agreement" and "peace agreement" are not sufficiently defined as conflict outcomes per se, and the distinction between them is unnecessary at best. Moreover, the categories of "low activity" refer to too large a number of cases to not demand a more sophisticated conceptualization.

Even those large-N studies identifying individual rebel groups in their data sets run into additional coding problems. For instance, the UCDP's older Conflict Termination Dataset treats several Ugandan armed groups as a single observation collapsed into one Ugandan civil war. The CWP identifies and consecutively numbers different civil wars that occur within the same country, but it applies this method inconsistently when it comes to individual rebel groups, coding Liberia's Liberians United for Reconciliation and Democracy (LURD) and Movement for Democracy in Liberia (MODEL) rebellions together as part of a single civil war, and repeating this pattern with Côte d'Ivoire's Mouvement Patriotique de Côte d'Ivoire (MPCI), Mouvement pour la Justice et la Paix (MJP), and Mouvement Populaire Ivoirien du Grand Ouest (MPIGO) insurgencies. This overaggregation misses key distinctions among these individual rebellions, misunderstands their complex dynamics, and oversimplifies how each conflict ends.

Rebels Rebel

> *This is a rebellion, isn't it? I rebel.*
> —Jyn Erso

This is a study of rebels, a term used interchangeably with insurgencies, rebellions, and rebel groups, which are armed organizations that rebel against state authority. There have been roughly 150 such rebel groups in modern Africa.[12] A more detailed discussion of their key dimensions follows later in this chapter, but here some conceptual clarification is in order. The category distinguishes rebels as a type of armed actor but is sufficiently broad to include a range of subtypes that seek to challenge or replace the authority of state elites in one way or another.[13] In other words: rebels rebel.

Although not explicitly addressed in the case studies that follow, Africa's liberation movements provide a suitable historical bookend for this study, and they do so despite the legal and conceptual distinctions between the colonial and the independent African state. They are relatively few in number, but there was nevertheless substantial variation in the fates of these groups. Anticolonial rebels such as Amilcar Cabral's Partido Africano da Independencia da Guiné e Cabo Verde (PAIGC) helped dislodge Portuguese rule from Africa and established sovereign regimes.[14] Whereas Kenya's Mau Mau rebels, although they had a lasting political impact, were militarily unsuccessful and by some measures became a study in effective, albeit repressive counterinsurgency.[15] Similarly, majority rule rebels that purged the last traces of white domination from Africa such as Rhodesia's Zimbabwe Africa National Union (ZANU) fall well within this study's scope conditions.[16]

The study also applies to separatist movements and their various fates. Sudan's Anya-Nya rebellion fought its way to 1972's Addis Ababa Agreement that broadened South Sudan's political autonomy.[17] Following their defeat in Nigeria's civil war in the late 1960s, Igbo fighters of the Biafran secessionist movement were "retired" from government positions, but separatist leader Ojukwu was eventually permitted to reenter Nigerian politics. In addition, the theoretical framework presented here applies to the more abrupt cases of military coups d'état. McGowan counts 188 African coups that took place from 1956 to 2001—80 successful and 108 failed, as well as 139 plots.[18] Only half a dozen African states have escaped coups that range from the multiple "coups of descending order" in Benin, Burkina Faso, and Nigeria to coups of sheer luck, like twenty-seven-year-old Captain Valentine Strasser's seizure of Freetown's Executive Mansion in 1992.[19]

Omitted from this study, however, is the category of militias.[20] Somalia's kaleidoscopic armed groups, operating in various and shifting combinations of clan loyalties and linkages to external actors, have had until recently no functioning state against which to rebel. Alternatively, militias can serve as auxiliaries of state militaries, which recruit and arm groups like Sudan's Janjaweed or Uganda's Arrow Boys to fight actual rebellions. Elsewhere, militias take the shape of "home guards," as with Congo's Mayi Mayi or Sierra Leone's Kamajors.[21] Such groups, often quite violently, defend their communities against perceived threats that can take the form of state militaries, rebels, or even other militias. CAR's anti-Balaka militias rallied against the victorious Séléka rebels with help from ousted government elites and army officers.

Which Fates?

An investigation into Africa's many rebellions shows a striking amount of variation in their fates. A quick and dirty distillation of large-N cross-national studies shows that only about 10 percent of insurgencies in Africa that were not coups d'état have ever achieved victory, nearly 40 percent ended in a cease-fire or peace agreement, and 30 percent met some variant of defeat. The other 20 percent of African rebels are still engaged in ongoing conflicts, cases that are not addressed in this book, as their fates are not yet known. However, understanding the causal factors behind the fates of other rebels can shed light on the potential trajectories of those rebellions currently under way, a subject I address in Chapter 6. The next section presents a reconceptualization of conflict outcomes into distinct rebel fates that go beyond victory and defeat.

Victory Domination. When rebels win, they capture and dominate state institutions in whole or in part. Some victors, particularly in coups d'état, may adopt a "balance-wheel model" of incorporating existing bureaucrats in order to run the day-to-day operations of governing.[22] For instance, following their coups, Samuel Doe's People's Redemption Council (PRC) relied on Liberian government technocrats, and Idi Amin actively courted members of Uganda's political intelligentsia even as he purged ethnic Acholi and Langi officers who dominated the armed forces.

But victory domination often involves the wholesale replacement of regime elites. In 1986, Uganda's National Resistance Army pushed the incumbent Uganda National Liberation Army (UNLA) junta from the capital, Kampala. The coalition of the Ethiopian People's Revolutionary Democratic Front became the ruling regime in 1991 after overthrowing the communist Derg junta. In 1994, the Rwandan Patriotic Front marched to Kigali after nearly four years of insurgency, supplanting the Hutu-dominated regime and stopping genocide against ethnic Tutsi. Eric Young noted that these cases constituted a "new type" of African insurgency—the victorious. On balance, this has been a rare outcome for African rebels.[23] The historic overthrow of Libya's Muammar Gaddafi in the summer of 2011 and the Séléka rebellion's 2012 takeover of the Central African Republic are the first of such outcomes in Africa in well over a decade. A close look at the factors behind victory domination makes a difference in how we understand the current trajectories of ongoing conflicts around Africa.

Victory Incorporation. Incorporation means the transformation of an armed actor into a political actor through a political settlement with an incumbent regime. The negotiation and implementation of a peace agreement is commonly associated with rebel leaders acquiring official status and their fighters being absorbed by the national armed forces. For example, the 1992 Rome General Peace Accords ended a fifteen-year civil war between Resistência Nacional Moçambicana rebels and Mozambique's Frente de Libertação de Moçambique regime. Similarly, the 2003 Accra Comprehensive Peace Agreement brought a negotiated end to Liberia's second civil war. The settlement brought a handful of rebel leaders into the government and disarmed and demobilized fighters from the conflict's two main rebellions, Liberians United for Reconciliation and Democracy and the Movement for Democracy in Liberia. Examining incorporation takes into account that many rebels do not necessarily seek to overthrow or replace a regime but instead wish to use rebellion as a means to negotiate into prevailing authority networks. Exploring this fate challenges assumptions in the civil war literature that settlements are a function of the rebels' capacity to force the government to negotiate rather than a function of their organizational origins within political society.

Defeat Elimination. Elimination captures the more classic form of rebel defeat, in which a state military exerts sufficient pressure or delivers enough shocks to undermine and break the basic functions of rebellion. Leadership is decapitated, fighters scatter, and the group disappears because it cannot adapt and recover. Angola's União Nacional para a Independência Total de Angola fought for decades, only to crumple following the death of its leader, Jonas Savimbi, in 2002. Namibia's Caprivi Liberation Front (CLF) was barely noticed before being crushed by the state, with its remaining members tried for treason.

Defeat Disintegration. Some rebel groups that appear to have lost have in fact fallen apart on their own. All rebel groups experience organizational pressure, but disintegration occurs when a rebel group succumbs to fragmentation because of infighting between rival leaders who compete with one another over resources and strategies. This leads to uncoordinated actions in battle and high rates of desertion and defection until control over the entire rebel organization unravels. Deep factions within Sierra Leone's Revolutionary United Front over a decade of civil war led to its ultimate implosion. In some cases, fragments of rebel groups spin off and form their own rebellions or merge into other groups. These are then new groups with fresh structural configurations that send them down a new trajectory. For instance, after Côte d'Ivoire's Mouvement Populaire Ivoirien du Grand Ouest and Mouvement pour la Justice et la Paix were purged of Liberian and Sierra Leonean mercenaries, their remaining few Ivorian fighters were consumed and incorporated by the more mainstream Mouvement Patriotique de Côte d'Ivoire, which collectively became the Forces Nouvelles within months and followed a different path.

African Rebels and African States

A theory of rebel fates must be rooted in an understanding of how political authority works in the African context. Bøås and Dunn correctly identified African rebellions as "rational responses to the composition of African states and their respective politics."[24] I approach rebel fates in a similar fashion by looking at rebel organization and patterns of relationships within Africa's wider political fabric. This draws on a historical institutional analytical approach. Rebellion is, after all, a political act, albeit writ violent. It is structured by the distributional conflicts among different political actors and the asymmetries of power associated with the origins, operation, and development of state institutions and the state systems they occupy. As introduced in Chapter 1, it is these institutions—both formal and informal—that distribute power and status unevenly across social groups, giving some disproportionate access to decisionmaking processes, promoting some actors while demobilizing others.[25] These factors are reflected in the organizational bases of rebel groups and their relationships with regimes, which shape rebel fates.

Rebellion and Fragmented Politics:
The Roots of African Regimes

The fates of rebels play out within the political arena of the contemporary African state, a concept that has already been examined in elegant detail.[26] For the purpose of using the African state to build a theory of rebel fates, I use Young's conceptualization of the state as "a complex symbiosis of the normative state, the legacy of the colonial state, and the customary precepts of social reciprocity and more personalized concepts of rule."[27] I also draw on the observation that comparatively, the historical institutional development of the African state is quite distinct, particularly in terms of its fragmented politics. By *fragmented* politics, I mean the institutionalization—formally and informally—of traits salient to the differentiation of groups within political society. For colonial states, the deliberate creation of fragmented politics facilitated domination on the cheap. For independent African rulers, consolidating and maintaining fragmented politics continued to serve the purpose of internal control.

The rickety, unambitious colonial state routinized asymmetries of accumulation and control along highly fragmented lines. Young has argued that the colonial state was able to gain almost complete hegemony over its African subjects through the use of force, the co-optation of African elites, and the imposition of legal codes.[28] The lack of legitimacy required vis-à-vis African populations meant there were few imperatives to construct robust state institutions other than those resulting from the prerogatives of small, weak administrations set up to extract resources and sustain limited bureaucracies. Herbst adds that the main problem of colonial rule—a problem that has also plagued African rulers since independence— was their inability, or even unwillingness, to project authority over distances that contain low population densities or, more simply, to control diverse populations with scarce resources.[29] Accordingly, common strategies of rule followed a pattern of delegation that marked out and hardened distinct ethnic and regional boundaries among groups within colonial territories. Mamdani identified in some cases the establishment of two parallel legal systems, in which urban classes were considered "citizens" and rural peasants were seen as "subjects."[30] For instance, the British in Uganda played a large role in shaping ethnic Acholi identity, particularly because of their dominance in the colonial army, the King's African Rifles.[31] Separate administrations in the British colonial state in Sudan erected institutional divisions that solidified identities and divisions between northerners and southerners.[32] And Belgium's administrative reification of Tutsi and Hutu had severe downstream political consequences in postcolonial Rwanda and Burundi.[33]

Upon independence, many African regimes replicated this kind of politics, developing their own strategies of internal control behind the inherited structural ramparts of their new states. African regimes have reinforced fragmentation by holding on to customary law and through other strategies of maintaining authority, including single-party systems and military rule. Where the colonial state had created legally based identities without rights, postcolonial law made group identity the basis for political identity and used that as a basis for domination.[34] By extension, any impetus to build inclusive, functioning state institutions would require regimes to dedicate scarce resources to their maintenance, which could simultaneously provide channels through which rival political power bases could undermine them. In other words, the benefits of fragmentation eclipsed the opportunities for African regimes to legitimately engage a range of groups within political society, as there have been few mechanisms to constrain the exercise of power and many to enable it to be enforced.[35]

In this context, the management of fragmented politics is the purview of elites. Elites are those who are able, by virtue of their strategic positions in the state, to affect political outcomes regularly and substantially.[36] High office is generally restricted to a small, identifiable group of elites who maintain a monopoly on decisionmaking positions. Anyone who wishes to gain access to state allocations must channel demands through these actors, who penetrate, circumvent, overturn, or manipulate institutions in their favor.[37] Elites command a disproportionate amount of resources due to their position of state privilege. Hence, domination is equated with accumulation, which further fuels the engine of neopatrimonial authority.[38]

In Africa, the political realm is not structurally differentiated, or "emancipated" from the rest of society.[39] Instead, the "big man" at the center of regime authority interacts vertically with an extended retinue, "from the highest reaches of the presidential palace to the humblest village assembly."[40] Here, the right to rule is held by a person rather than given to an office. This person maintains concentrated authority through personal patronage rather than through ideology or law. Seldom is there a distinction between private and public resources. Chabal and Daloz have referred to these dynamics as the "informalization of politics," where dominant state actors minimize the flow of society-wide resources (and personal favors) and distribute them down vertical networks in exchange for personalized political support.

By their nature, these complex, multifunctional chains of relationships are competitive.[41] Elite "instrumentalization of disorder" ensures power can be extended within the weak institutionalization of political practices.[42] This reproduces patterns of factionalism and fragmentation among competing, mobilized networks, each of which seeks to secure the available resources for its members at the expense of the rival network.[43] As elites and rival political entrepreneurs compete, institutional manipulation, segregation, and coercion all act to eliminate, co-opt, or demobilize rival bases of power while limiting the successful management of conflict among different groups within the sphere of competitive, formal institutions.[44] It is within this arena that rebellion takes place, where fragmented political authority lowers the opportunity costs for organizing rebellion as a feasible option for redress.[45]

Characteristics of African Rebels

As mentioned earlier, much of the prevailing literature focuses on explaining the roots of African wars. Williams, for instance, identifies the "ingredients" as including neopatrimonial politics, control over resources, self-determination, and ethnic and religious identity.[46] Although certainly comprehensive and quite parsimonious, such approaches tend only to categorize types of conflicts, and by extension they characterize rebellion as manifestations of these causes. As a result, they can erroneously attribute rebel fates to these factors.[47] The key observation here is that once a rebellion begins and is set in motion, the factors that explain its onset cannot always be laid directly at the same door as its fate.

Instead, the fates of African rebels depend largely on essential characteristics. In order to identify those that are most salient to rebel fates, this study requires a firm understanding of the wide-ranging characteristics of African rebels, which can vary from case to case and across time. Although the notion of "characteristics" may be intuitive, it nevertheless requires some differentiation, as some traits matter more than others. Moreover, prevailing efforts to categorize these characteristics suffer from some shortcomings.

Clapham and Reno have marked out different historical types of African rebellions that are defined by their particular goals.[48] Liberation insurgencies were historically concerned with throwing out colonial or minority rulers. Separatist insurgencies were guided by ethnic or regional differentiation within the state that bred ambitions to either gain autonomy or secede territorially. Reform insurgencies were undergirded by revolutionary ideology and sought a "new kind of state." And warlord insurgencies sought to overthrow an incumbent to appropriate the patrimonial state apparatus for personal gain, or they carved out their own fiefdom within collapsed states. Reno further breaks down liberation insurgencies into *anticolonial* and *majority-rule* rebels, also adding the category of parochial rebels, or those who fight to protect their communities. Additionally, Bøås and Dunn unfurl a wide range of characteristics that are both distinct to rebels and linked to their broader political context.[49] For instance, they point to the decline of ideological drivers and the increased salience of authoritarian rule, economic breakdown, and poverty to contemporary African rebels.

To be sure, Clapham observes that rebel effectiveness, and by extension rebel "success," derives from how leaders relate to groups within political society and how organizational coherence maintains discipline and articulates goals. He also acknowledges that a rebellion's place within its regional political environment has a significant bearing on its resource networks.[50] In addition, Reno shows why some kinds of rebels occur in some political contexts and not in others. And Bøås and Dunn expand the scope of rebel characteristics that recognize changes in their internal and external political environments.

The key problem with all of these categories is that they tend to focus on the nonstructural characteristics of rebels, or those associated with rebel preferences or identities, which cannot necessarily explain rebel fates. In what follows, I interrogate which characteristics matter and map out the structural characteristics salient to rebel fates, which refer to the organizational dimensions of rebellion that arise from the institutional fabric of regime politics.

The Role of Organization in Rebel Fates

Understanding rebel fates begins with a rudimentary understanding of how rebels organize. Recent scholarly work into the microfoundations of rebellion has illuminated key aspects of insurgent organization. Some scholars have taken deductive models from economics and applied them to rebels. Johnston, for instance, deploys "U-form" and "M-form" organizations to explain variations in rebel military effectiveness.[51] Weinstein demonstrates how variation in resource endowments predicts corresponding levels of internal order, where resource abundance creates conditions of indiscipline that allow less-committed members to commit violence against noncombatants, and where resource-scarce groups must cultivate loyalty and stronger ties to civilian populations.[52] In contrast, Staniland uses a social institutional model to show how different configurations of political and social networks lead to different levels of organizational cohesion, which has consequences for how resources are used.[53] Sinno connects different modes of rebel organization to incentive structures, strategic choices, and how rebels are able to outlast rivals, where the availability of safe havens mitigates the effects from centralized or decentralized power structures.[54] Although such scholarship is valuable, to date few scholars have explicitly pursued the problem of how rebel organization makes a key difference in producing a range of rebel fates.[55]

Moreover, many scholars have recognized that rebel organizations are not necessarily monolithic, coherent entities but "shifting coalitions of groups with malleable allegiances and at times divergent interests."[56] These insights have been very useful in understanding important conflict processes. The argument presented here acknowledges that rebel groups have more than one moving part, but it also identifies that rebel groups do tend to cohere around distinct organizational structures with recognizable boundaries that are salient to their ultimate fates.

In fact, the argument here asserts that the structural anatomy of rebellions, at least in the African context, is *not* overly complex. The ability of groups like the Lord's Resistance Army and Nigeria's Boko Haram to survive for considerable periods in the bush, the widespread use of small arms such as the Kalashnikov rifle, and the ease of its use by even children, illustrate this point. Thus, to simplify the conceptualization of rebel organization for the purposes of this study, here I identify three categories of rebels and discuss each in turn: *followers, leaders*, and *cadres*.

To date, there is a range of explanations for why people are more or less likely to join and to become followers within a rebel organization.[57] Followers join willingly or are coerced. They can be drawn from ethnic or identity-based groups, peasants, workers, or crosscutting alliances among groups that share a common economic precariousness or degree of political marginalization. Politically conscious members of society such as students and activists may participate, but a high correlation has been observed between rebellion and young, unemployed men in a society.[58] Here I assume that followers compose the bulk of any rebellion and their ability to act collectively matters. But the goal is not to make a novel argument for why people join rebellions beyond the key observation that their motivations can vary substantially and cannot on their own be a reliable predictor of rebel fates.

The role of rebel leadership is less understood from a scholarly perspective and is often attributed to social class, political ideology, or even charisma, in that a leader may "seize the task that is adequate for him and demand obedience and a following by virtue of his mission."[59] Here I assert that leaders are the key actors who marshal forward rebellion, interpreting and translating its "means of revolutionary action" in capturing and dominating state institutions.[60]

The most important category is that of the cadres, which have a key role in rebel organization. Cadres occupy the upper ranks of a rebellion's hierarchy. They reliably obey and augment the authority of leaders, serving as an organizational lynchpin in the cohesion of a rebel group. Acting as the nonbureaucratic equivalent of staff, cadres facilitate interactions between leaders and followers that surpass face-to-face interaction.[61] The key observation is that the bonds between leaders and cadres matter most for rebel organizations. As will be made clear in the following pages, the personal authority of leaders is derived from what is rooted in prewar relationships between leaders and cadres and the corresponding power resource endowments they bring to rebellion's organizational capacity before war actually begins.

Cohesion, Status, and Prewar Networks: Insiders vs. Outsiders

How does rebel organization shape rebel fates? A more precise conceptualization requires a look at how rebels are organized both internally and vis-à-vis state institutions and regime authority. First, one must ask, how internally cohesive is the rebellion? Indeed, the study of rebel cohesion and fragmentation is becoming a dominant trend in the broader literature on civil war and rebellion. Bakke, Cunningham, and Seymour argue that rebel cohesion varies along several key dimensions: A cohesive rebellion will have a smaller set of organizations that are based on sub-identities, a higher level of institutional ties between these organizations, and a hegemonic distribution of power.[62] In contrast, rebels with a large number of organizations, weak coordinating institutions, and dispersed power distributions tend to fall into infighting, which can lead to organizational fragmentation. Here, rebel cohesion broadly refers to the ability to build and reproduce structures that perform the basic tasks of rebellion and meet the range of challenges Weinstein has elsewhere presented as recruitment, control, governance, violence, and resilience.[63]

Second, it is important to ask how rebel organization structures the strategic environment in which rebellion takes place. Where an insurgency is situated within a state's status hierarchy is a key dimension of its organization and an explanatory factor for its fate. Yet the concept of *status* is a less studied dimension of rebel organization.[64] It refers to how the relative positions of elites and their retinues play out within *hierarchies* of state authority. Political power, economic power, and prestige confer corresponding levels of *status* within a hierarchy and consolidate control of critical resources.[65] Woven into this kind of politics is the social psychological perception that "one's group is located in an unwarranted subordinate position on a status hierarchy."[66] This may occur through dramatic shifts or reversals in intergroup hierarchies, when insiders suddenly find themselves to be outsiders. Alternatively, *expectations* of acquiring insider status may be blocked in some way. The group that occupies political authority "will be the group perceived as farthest up the . . . status hierarchy that can be most surely subordinated through violence."[67]

In the African context, rebel groups can and often do organize around ethnic identity in order to exit from, capture, or gain access to the state on behalf of a larger group. Certain groups may very well have an explicit ethnic dimension rooted in shared historical grievances and perceived collective damages in the face of state domination. This study explicitly acknowledges the salience of ethnic boundaries to African politics but considers it a marker for the structural issues that historically situate these groups within political society and its institutions.[68] This theoretical premise dovetails nicely with Roessler's observations that regimes in Africa must constantly balance between the threats posed by co-opted ethnic political constituencies on the inside, which can threaten coups, and those posed by excluded groups on the outside, which can threaten rebellion.[69] Roessler identifies this key distinction, and it serves to explain civil war onset. Here, the differences between insiders and outsiders are used to explain rebel fates.

In sum, getting at the question of how rebel organization predicts rebel fates requires an examination of how cohesion and status are derived from a rebellion's structural linkages with state institutions and regime politics. Some scholars have already observed this relationship. Reno, for instance, suggests that Africa's different types of insurgent movements reflect the character of the states they fight.[70] And Mampilly observes further that certain aspects of rebel organization can vary in tandem with the state's "penetration" into society.[71] The argument here follows Staniland's important insight that in many cases, rebel organization is very much a function of prewar politics.[72] Bringing things back to the rudimentary model of rebel organization, it becomes clear that the personal authority of leaders and their relationship to their cadres is derived from their prewar relationships and the corresponding power resource endowments they bring to rebellion's organizational structure before war actually begins. The key point is this: whereas standard accounts of rebellions usually portray them as entirely distinct from the states that they fight, rebellion can arise from the fragmented political networks that sustain the authority of some regimes in African states. A rebel group's organization and its corresponding fate are considered here a function of where leaders and cadres are situated within political society. Some insurgencies can be composed of disparate political outsiders—those who have never walked the corridors of regime authority. Other groups will contain key former insiders from the fragmented political networks of the prevailing political establishment. In the following section, I develop a conceptual framework that considers the implications of this distinction between insiders and outsiders to the fates of rebels.

Political Embeddedness

Following from the previous discussion, another conceptualization is in order. Political embeddedness takes into account the structural histories behind the emergence of armed groups that extend into their basic organization.[73] It builds on Korpi's idea of how coercive, remunerative, and normative power resources, viewed in relation to other actors (i.e., regime elites), are derived from patronage networks and invested in rebel organization.[74] This conceptualization differs somewhat from Staniland's notion of embeddedness, which refers to a rebellion's relationship with social bases that are measured in terms of vertical links among key actors and horizontal links with these key actors' broader communal structures.[75]

Casting African rebels in the same light as ethnic or broad-based social movements, popular uprisings, or revolutions is problematic because in the African context, civilians matter much less to rebel organizations, let alone to the outcomes they experience in civil war.[76] A close look at Africa's rebels shows that shared social structures, mass sentiments, and norms tend to be overdetermining factors for their fates because of the difficulty in identifying the precise level of support required for rebels to follow different trajectories.[77] As Kalyvas points out, civilian control and collaboration are more often functions of violence than of mass mobilization, and local officials are more likely to be targets of violence than conduits for reciprocity arrangements between rebel leaders and communities.[78] Tying rebel fates to social bases also neglects the mass flight associated with civil wars. Those who remain behind are most often the most vulnerable, and they collaborate primarily out of fear.[79]

In contrast, the argument here focuses on a rebel group's historical institutional linkage to the state and regime authority and the associated patronage networks. Rather than characterize rebel groups and their leadership by the extent to which they claim to represent broad sections of society, the salient feature here is the extent to which they reflect, or do not reflect, the political elites they seek to displace. A rebel group's degree of political embeddedness varies with the degree to which its own political networks interact with those of the preexisting milieus, locales, and micro-arenas of Africa's state institutions and the status hierarchies of its regime politics.[80] Those would-be rebel leaders who come from prevailing authority structures tend to have more-concentrated power resources, which they then invest in the creation of rebel organization and convert into authority within it. As Korpi notes, "investments intended to develop routines and institutions to facilitate the mobilization of power resources can decrease the costs of mobilization and augment the effectiveness of power resources by increasing their liquidity."[81] In turn, rebel organizations create order and sets of expectations that facilitate the further mobilization and application of power resources.

Using this concept, we can say that variations in political embeddedness reflect the level of cohesion in rebel groups—how they are led, followed, and organized—by tracing out the historical institutional origins of their leadership and whether cadres do or do not cohere around these distinct actors. Political embeddedness also captures a rebellion's status, or the historical institutional distance between its leaders and the prevailing political order, and is a measure of whether rebel leaders do or do not come from established group hierarchies that find themselves standing outside the purview of state privilege.

For politically embedded insiders, closer historical linkages to domestic state institutions shape how leaders solve collective-action problems—or facilitate group cohesion—before conflict even begins. Politically embedded rebellions are able to mobilize preassembled networks of leaders and cadres that together inject key power resource endowments into the organization of rebellion, features such as personal authority, aptitudes, and organizational skills acquired by virtue of experience with state institutions. Thus, the by-products of institutional proximity include having already addressed large fixed organizational costs, and having developed longer time horizons, stable routines, and adaptive expectations.[82] Rebel leaders draw on these intact bonds with cadres, the preexistence of which provide a foundation for building cohesive, internal hierarchies of rebellion and facilitate organizational reproduction and maintenance.

Of course, there are alternative wellsprings of a rebellion's organizational cohesion. Balcells and Kalyvas, for instance, point to Marxist ideology as a source of more highly organized and disciplined insurgents.[83] Yet political embeddedness endows rebellions with a distinct trait beyond cohesion that provides them with incentives to make strategic calibrations that will give them durable advantages within more institutionally dense environments. Again, as Korpi argues, "the distribution of power resources between parties is reflected and 'built into' these institutions and structures and . . . the parties may have unequal gains from their operation."[84]

The strategies of insiders are shaped by the degree to which they maintain a historically perceived "right of control" over state hierarchies. Within hierarchical power shifts or behind blocked expectations, key actors from prewar state institutions may continue to articulate relationships between rebellion and the state. Recall that these actors, disenfranchised members of the political establishment, often possess institutional residues that are previous activations of power resources—material endowments, education, technical knowledge, and military skills, which serve as conduits for leadership and organization. More important, they bring into rebellion well-established, foundational, and durable networks of cadres based on personal authority and on shared experiences of patronage played out within state institutions. Those with closer ties to state authority will have had more opportunities to build a larger, more cohesive network with elites who maintain an ongoing role in state politics during a civil war. Insiders-cum-rebels do necessarily seek to seize control of the state, but they aim to hijack these networks through rebellion in order to renegotiate their place within existing political hierarchies.

Following from this, a rebellion's political historical proximity to state privilege acts as negativity bias,[85] where the greatest weight is given to the damaging experience of the loss or denial of status and power. Insecurity and resentment born of a loss or denial of status provides an instrumental "switch" that frames the rebellion and helps elites maintain strategic control over cadres by a promise of future rewards.[86] With the cadres' backing, leaders persuade and mobilize followers to participate in violence against the state,[87] where a claim to state authority becomes a key source of strategic control and cohesion for the wider network commanded by the leaders and serves as basis for interaction with the incumbent regime.

Alternatively, a nonembedded rebellion of political outsiders will have very few historical relationships to formal and informal elements of state authority and institutions. Its leadership will be composed of perpetual outsiders, or those who never walked the corridors of state power. Although still a product of fragmented authority, their strategies will nevertheless be less dependent on structural linkages to the state. Fewer prewar linkages mean fewer or smaller clientelistic network nodes derived from state authority, which impacts the extent to which these groups can marshal forward networks of other perpetual outsiders to rebel. As mentioned above, there are multiple sources of group cohesion, and political outsiders may well possess one or more. Yet such groups will not to the same extent draw on preexisting political networks that facilitate entry into the prevailing political establishment.

A final note on the concept of time: to some extent, political embeddedness follows the contours of path dependence, or the institutional processes of positive feedback that render political organizations self-reinforcing over time. Under normal institutional conditions, organization becomes more and more difficult and costly to adjust as time unfolds, leading to an equilibrium where the trajectory is "locked in," even if it is inefficient.[88] Yet over the period of a civil war, rebels face a number of challenges and exogenous contingencies by virtue of having to exist in fundamentally violent environments. Because of this, rebellion's organizational core can be degraded through battlefield deaths, surrenders, and even internal executions. Gradually, the political significance of an embedded rebellion can fade as insider cadres exit and are perhaps replaced by followers who came from outside the political establishment. This observation does not necessarily come with an assertion of how much time must specifically pass in order for political embeddedness to degrade, but it is nevertheless a consideration.

In sum, political embeddedness shapes the fates of rebels by identifying rebel leaders and their strategies according to their independent or interdependent political networks, which sometimes blur the lines between those that sustain domination. The structural linkages between rebellions and regime authority, which are derived from their broader political fabric, say much about rebel organization, both in terms of cohesion and how they are able to negotiate a path into these networks. This latter point is a key component in building a theory on rebel fates, to which I now turn.

Regime Strategies: A Theory of Political Embeddedness

War to End by the Sword
    —Yoweri Museveni, *Sunday Vision* headline

To paint a more detailed picture of political embeddedness and why it matters to rebel fates, consider the following example. The Lord's Resistance Army is one of Africa's longest-running rebel movements and has spent the better part of the last three decades carving a path of violence through at least five countries, killing more than 100,000 civilians and displacing hundreds of thousands more. The group was incubated in the late 1980s within another rebellion, the Uganda People's Democratic Army. This group was composed of members of the Acholi-dominated military regime overthrown by current president Yoweri Museveni's National Resistance Army in 1986. The UPDA's leaders were therefore members of Uganda's military "ethnocracy," some of whom were known personally to Museveni and his brother and consigliore, Salim Saleh. Although the UPDA suffered a string of military defeats in northern Uganda, Museveni was able to use the Pece Peace Accord of 3 June 1988 to peel off its main leaders—politically embedded insiders—and incorporate them into his regime.

By the early 1990s, the nature of rebellion in northern Uganda changed. A new rebel group emerged as a hybrid of two factions: the first contained the intransigent remnants of the more conventional UPDA force commanded by an ex-military leader, Odong Latek. The second was a "cosmological" faction led by Joseph Kony, a self-appointed spiritual medium who mobilized young men through appeals to Acholi identity. After Latek's death in 1989, Kony asserted authority over the group, surrounding himself with cadres based on the UPDA's military template, while refashioning the rebellion around his absolutist vision that sought to "purify" Acholi society through extreme violence. By 1993, the group was being called the Lord's Resistance Army, a force that raided villages for resources and recruits. Kony's LRA launched a program to heavily militarize northern Uganda and conducted halfhearted peace talks that made extensive use of ex-UPDA members as interlocutors. These talks broke down once Museveni issued a one-week ultimatum to surrender, signaling his unwillingness to do business with Kony.

Although Museveni had resisted accommodating Kony, by the mid-1990s the LRA had metastasized into a more formidable foe as the Sudanese government upped its game by providing weapons, training, and far-flung bush sanctuaries in southern Sudan. As conflict intensified in northern Uganda, the LRA tried to reposition itself within Ugandan political society by paying close attention to ongoing peace efforts and electoral politics. When members of the Acholi diaspora, known as the Kacoke Madit, convened in London to discuss prospects for peace, the LRA sent a delegation. When Acholi presidential candidate Paul Ssemogerere framed his campaign around the war in the north, Kony latched on, declaring cease-fires and holding rallies to declare the LRA as a manifestation of long-standing Acholi status-related grievances. Yet such efforts had very little impact on the war. Museveni consistently refused to speak to Kony directly as he expanded his counterinsurgency strategy to contain the entire Acholi population. The Ugandan army forcibly displaced civilians into "protected villages," which drained the countryside and kept guns trained on the Acholi while calling that activity "protection."

Following a Uganda-Sudan rapprochement and lull in violence, 2002's Operation Iron Fist allowed 10,000 Ugandan soldiers into southern Sudan to capture or kill Kony. While the mission overran the LRA's base camps, in response the group opened up a new wave of brutal attacks in the north and east of Uganda. This fresh conflict drove hundreds of thousands into squalid displacement camps that were often the targets of LRA massacres, prompting UN official Jan Egeland to call northern Uganda home to "the world's most neglected humanitarian crisis." A renewed effort on the part of the Ugandan army killed scores of LRA fighters and inspired key ex-UPDA cadres such as Kenneth Banya and Sam Kolo to accept a government amnesty. Above all, the 2005 Comprehensive Peace Agreement (CPA) that ended Sudan's civil war pushed the LRA from southern Sudan. Faced with the closure of its operational spaces in northern Uganda and southern Sudan, the LRA shifted to the hinterlands of the Democratic Republic of Congo.

Around the same time, the internationally brokered Juba Peace Process marked a final effort to draw the LRA from the bush and settle with the Ugandan government. The talks were marred by cease-fire violations, walkouts, and the disproportionate role of LRA "diplomats"— Acholi exiles with no connection to the LRA command structure who used the talks to gain government sinecures. By September 2008, after Kony repeatedly failed to sign the accord, Museveni finally had grounds to launch Operation Lightning Thunder, which was designed to deliver a final knockout blow in the LRA's hideout in DRC's Garamba Forest. Although the maneuver failed, it bookended a renewed regional military strategy for dealing with the LRA, by which Museveni no longer had to pretend to be interested in doing business with Kony.

Although the group still possesses a certain level of cohesion based on Acholi identity, the LRA's place far outside Ugandan political society has been unambiguously cemented. Kony remains at the helm of the group, and its inner core of ex-military cadres has degraded over time, only to be replaced by youths abducted over the course of the insurgency. In the view of many observers, the LRA now operates only in "survival mode," persisting as a collection of semiautonomous groups in DRC and CAR, while Kony cools his heels in the Kafia Kinji region of South Darfur.

The LRA episode reflects a distinct pattern that reveals how rebel leaders must navigate the constraints of incumbent regime politics. To be sure, the rebellion unleashed madness upon northern Uganda and beyond. But its most egregious sin was having a leader who was a primary-school dropout and onetime Catholic altar boy, a man who showed no interest in playing by conventional rules.[89] Although the group's core had once included several key insiders, the early decision to elevate Kony as the primary voice of the LRA foreclosed any opportunity for meaningful rapprochement with Museveni's regime, beyond surrender. Even worse was the group's extreme violence against civilians, which attracted widespread international recrimination and repeatedly embarrassed Museveni for his army's inability to bring the LRA to heel. Despite multiple rounds of negotiations over nearly two decades and international pressure to settle the LRA matter peacefully, it is unlikely Museveni ever intended to pursue any strategy beyond the group's military elimination. This single observation is symbolic of how incumbents deal with different types of rebellions and why political embeddedness matters to the fates of rebels.

The Institutional Limits of Rebel Fates: African Regimes and Their Strategies

In his essential work, *The State in Africa: The Politics of the Belly*, Bayart establishes the elegant principle of "elite accommodation." Bayart argues that to maintain political order and regime hegemony, incumbents identify rivals to their own power bases and incorporate them into their patronage networks. Incumbents constantly seek to manage these rival sources of power to provide for their own security and survival.[90] They do so through their informal domination of fragmented political networks beyond the reach of weak bureaucratic institutions. This strategy enables incumbents to influence directly otherwise autonomous dynamics of interaction, negotiation, resistance, and incorporation between states and rival political forces.[91] Elsewhere, Reno has referred to the "shadow state" to describe elite control of markets that also facilitates processes of elite accommodation.[92]

As Reno has also observed, this picture is analogous to how African incumbents deal with violent challenges to their authority. Most portrayals of African military responses see them as clumsy extensions of unstable regimes, often too weak to project power in any meaningful way. Yet African regimes tend to operate in a very Clausewitzian manner, where warfare becomes politics by any other means, where strategies for dealing with rebels are in many ways the politics of the ordinary. In this regard, the counterinsurgency strategies of many African regimes reflect the degree of a rebel challenger's political embeddedness. This means that the ways in which rulers manage rebellion correspond to the ways they deal with different levels of threats to their authority from corresponding segments of political society. Counterinsurgency, therefore, is not always about military doctrine or winning wars. It is about bringing recalcitrant factions of political society—insiders or outsiders—into the orbit of state control, co-optation, or conquest.

But because not all rebels are politically embedded, some regime strategies for dealing with rebels provide potential opportunities for accommodation, whereas others do not. Either way, the fundamental objective of regimes remains the same: managing rival sources of power and authority. These states usually feature factionalized and sometimes violently divided domestic political networks that leaders manipulate to assert authority. Controlling the patronage networks and associated resources of rivals allows incumbents to maintain hegemony. Most African states that face rebel challengers do not possess the state capacity necessary to carry out strategies that compete with rebels to "outgovern" one another. In a context where regimes lack the means to control the exercise of violence directly or the capacity to mobilize the population, they instead pursue the politics of negotiation, selective targeting, and playing off local power brokers against one another to dominate and incorporate rebels when they can and eliminate them if they must.

The key observation is that variation in political embeddedness is matched by variation in the perceived political threats that rebel groups pose to incumbents. Rebels with closer ties to state authority possess intact, complex, state-interdependent networks and pose a higher threat to incumbents. This requires a strategy of *control*, which involves signaling, bargaining, negotiation, and accommodation with rebel leaders. Political outsiders pose fewer threats and present fewer risks to pursuing a policy of *elimination*, which involves military action that targets insurgent resources and vulnerabilities on the battlefield. Alternatively, regimes may combine elements of the two strategies. For instance, a militarily weakened adversary may be more pliable and riper for co-optation, or issuing a general amnesty can strip away fighters from a rebel group that is also being hunted militarily. But in general, the dominant observation is that regime strategies tend to settle into one pattern or the other.

Table 2.1 provides the basis for an explanatory framework that situates rebels within their broader political context. The political embed-

Table 2.1 Regime Strategies

Political Embeddedness	Internal Threat	State Strategy
Low	Low	Rebel elimination
High	High	Rebel control

dedness of rebels predicts regime strategies, which in turn circumscribe the range of strategic action available to rebel leaders. The strategy of control presents opportunistic linkages for savvy rebel leaders who are elites of groups with high embeddedness, who may decide to welcome accommodation by the state. Alternatively, a strategy of elimination largely closes this off to those non-embedded outsider leaders, who will likely face a more hostile regime.

The Technology of Rebellion

Their biggest weapon was sanctuary.
—Salim Saleh

In the early 1990s, the LRA was a resource-scarce rebellion. Yet after the failure of the 1993 peace talks, the group shifted to southern Sudan, emerging a year later as a proxy of the Sudanese government. The LRA, along with other Uganda-based rebellions, was recruited as muscle against the Sudan People's Liberation Army and to attack its chief sponsor, Uganda.[93] By the mid-1990s, LRA leader Joseph Kony was keeping an office in Juba and was treated like a senior officer in the Sudanese Armed Forces, while key LRA cadre Cesar Acellam coordinated resource transfers with Sudanese officers Lieutenant Colonel Tajadin Hassan and Juma Abud.[94] The LRA now had sophisticated weapons, fresh uniforms, and even land mines.[95] Thousands of LRA fighters received training in jungle warfare and gained battlefield experience fighting the SPLA alongside the Sudanese army. Above all, base camps in Eastern Equatoria's Magwi County and Imatong Mountains were far outside the reach of the Ugandan military, serving as sanctuaries to consolidate the LRA's organizational structure and teaching fighters how to survive in peripheral borderlands.

It is clear that Sudanese resources bolstered the LRA's fighting capacity, intensified conflict in northern Uganda, and were perhaps a reason for the Ugandan army's inability to summarily defeat the group.[96] This resource linkage, however, was inconsistent because of logistical constraints and the limited capacity of the Sudanese regime in Khartoum, the country's capital city.[97] Above all, there were divergent goals between Kony and his Sudanese handlers, who redirected the LRA's cross-border offensives into Uganda against the SPLA in Eastern Equatoria, part of southern Sudan.[98] But the LRA's failures against the SPLA led to their support getting cut off, [99] with Kony placed under house arrest in Juba.[100] Because of this intermittent access to Sudanese support, the LRA was compelled to diversify its resource acquisition strategies, carefully maintaining military stockpiles while creating autonomous, self-sustaining agrarian communities in the bush sanctuaries of southern Sudan.[101] Periodic raids into northern Uganda were designed to gather food, to broadcast their presence, and to recruit and train abductees.

But the LRA never overthrew the regime in Uganda, nor was it ever successfully incorporated via political settlement. Instead, it has experienced a slow but steady decline. Geopolitical shifts in the subregion, which culminated in the 2005 CPA and the subsequent collapse of the Juba Peace Process, pushed the LRA from its sanctuaries in Sudan and substantially diminished its resource link with Khartoum. Since then, the LRA has persisted as a threadbare collection of semiautonomous groups that barely subsist on seasonal rivers, a network of boreholes used for water supply, and temporary farms supplemented by hunting, knowledge of wild foods, and healing herbs.[102] Scattered across Garamba National Park, eastern CAR, and Sudan's Kafia Kinji region, LRA fighters now rely on looting, shifting cultivation, and petty trading as their resource base. Kony has begun exploiting ivory, diamonds, and gold,[103] with Kafia Kinji providing markets to offload them. The LRA, its number estimated at 200, is only a shadow of what it was, as its attacks and abductions decline, defections rise, and the African Union-Led Regional Task Force (AU RTF), until recently, hunted its members daily. But the group has persisted for nearly three decades, and it has done so across periods of both resource abundance and scarcity, which raises questions about the relationship between rebels and resources.

Resources and Rebellion

The LRA case is again instructive, this time in illuminating the limited role of resources as a dimension of rebel trajectories. To be sure, rebellion runs on resources—weapons, ammunition, material, logistics, and financial wherewithal. Yet most of Africa's rebels cannot tax and bor-row to the extent states can to pay for wars. Within these constraints, how rebels acquire and use resources can vary. For instance, those groups identified by popular ideology or ethnic solidarity may exploit a guerrilla war economy, in which resources come from grassroots ties with the wider population. Alternatively, predatory war economies are associated with rebels that seek short-term material gain, similar to those that chase gems, timber, minerals, or plantation crops, and the fungible prizes of an enclave commercial war economy.[104] Moreover, diasporas may contribute significant financing and political and organizational support. Or rebels may exploit a humanitarian war economy, for example, one in which refugee populations provide "humanitarian cover" for military operations.[105] Other forms of support include solidarity with like-minded revolutionary groups in other countries, religious organizations, wealthy individuals, and NGOs.

In line with the LRA case, one of the more significant sources of rebel support comes from foreign alliances, particularly neighboring states that serve either as direct resource providers or as low-cost resource conduits. In the African context, intact boundaries do not stop outsiders from meddling clandestinely in the affairs of their neighbors by sponsoring, or in some cases creating, armed movements as a way of projecting power across their borders to achieve an outcome favorable to their own interests. Because rebels will seek externally what they cannot find internally, bad neighbors in turn foment and exploit them to destabilize border regions and manage threats that emanate from the lightly governed hinterlands.[106] One study has shown that from 1991 to 2001, forty-four out of seventy-four insurgencies received state sponsorship that provided tangible resources critical to fighting.[107] Sponsors also provide territorial safe havens from which to prepare, operate, and convalesce, far outside the reach of the regimes rebels fight.

Yet the impact of resources more generally on rebel fates remains indeterminate. Much of the thinking about the relationship between resource flows and rebel organization is located within the broader political economy of conflict literature,[108] which has developed models that see private gain as the prime mover of war and central to how rebels choose their strategies. But as Staniland points out, there are competing claims within this world, and resources may only be as good as how they are used.[109] From one perspective, external resources ostensibly bolster the capacity of rebel groups, sustain armed campaigns, and deprive state militaries a rapid victory over rebel challengers.[110] Yet an alternative view holds that external resources are destructive,[111] rendering some rebels beholden to sponsors whose strategies may eventually diverge from those of the rebels they once used.[112] Often, as occurred in the LRA case, resources do not flow from a steady stream, and rebels must make do with intermittent access to them. This ambiguity suggests that the role of resources might be an overdetermining factor for rebel fates.

None of this denies that resources matter for a rebellion's organizational maintenance and its ability to fight. In many cases, foreign support can imbue rebel groups with organizational power resources and impose a degree of internal order and cohesion. As a regional analog to political embeddedness, cross-border resource networks between rebel groups and neighboring regimes can be considered a structural feature of Africa's regional institutional context. And because proxy warfare is not uncommon in the African conflict and plays a role in many of the case studies that follow, I will address that issue in Chapter 6. It is not the intention of this study, however, to draw a straight line between resources and rebel fates. Recall that a central claim here is that means-based explanations are insufficient for explaining rebel fates and risk falling down the rabbit hole of measuring the relatively static indicators of military effectiveness.[113] As I will explain, the resource endowments of rebel groups relative to those of the states they fight can only slightly augment, and do not supplant, political embeddedness as the primary driver of rebel fates.

Symmetrical vs. Asymmetrical Warfare

A fuller conceptualization of rebellion is now required. In getting at the question of how rebel capacity matters to their fates, I collapse things into the broader analytical framework—the technology of rebellion—developed by Kalyvas and Balcells.[114] (See Table 2.2.) This disaggregates civil wars into several categories that measure the parity between rebels and state militaries. Conventional civil wars are essentially analogs of their international counterparts, with formal front lines, large battle sets, and a general recognition that rebels and states are fighting on the same plane. In irregular or "guerrilla" war, there is a distinct asymmetry in relative capacity, which sees rebels avoiding direct confrontation with state armies. Instead, they launch fleet-footed attacks from rural peripheries and attempt to bleed their adversaries over time through attrition. Finally, the understudied symmetrical, irregular wars are fought between both threadbare rebels and state militaries alike, where one is likely to see both sides equipped with small arms—AK-47 rifles, also known as Kalashnikovs; RPGs, or rocket-propelled grenades; and the odd tank abandoned in a ditch that no one really knew how to operate.

Table 2.2 Technologies of Rebellion

		State Military Capacity	
		High	*Low*
Rebel Capacity	*High*	Conventional	n/a
	Low	Irregular	Symmetrical irregular

The study of this last category, characteristic of most of Africa's internal conflicts, is a major contribution of this book.

Whether a civil war is symmetrical or asymmetrical, it is nearly always irregular in the African context, with few exceptions. Under symmetrical irregular conflict, where there is parity between rebels and state militaries, this increases the likelihood of both insiders and outsiders winning outright. But once state capacity changes, as it often can with outside support, insiders find their path limited to incorporation, and outsiders then face the possibility of disintegration as well as elimination.

Kalyvas and Balcells have suggested that the technologies of rebellion can have effects on the duration and outcome of civil wars. However, they do not determine the distinct fates of rebels. Instead, they exogenously shape the strategic environment in which rebellion takes place. Here, technologies of rebellion provide an important, simplified conceptual catchall for relative rebel capacity and for analyzing its relationship with political embeddedness. In this regard, it is crucial to understand that political embeddedness fundamentally mitigates the effects of capacity on rebel fates. In pursuing their possible paths, rebels must still navigate the institutional architecture of regime politics and their place within political society.

The Fates of African Rebels

It is now time to configure the dimensions of political embeddedness and the technology of rebellion into a theory of rebel fates. To summarize these dimensions: Political embeddedness takes into account where rebellion sits vis-à-vis neopatrimonial networks and the fragmented institutions of regime authority. Politically embedded rebellions will have more cohesion around disenfranchised former insiders who have played a historical role in state politics. These elites bring to rebellion distinct organizational endowments and prewar networks of cadres. In addition to cohesion, political embeddedness highlights rebel vulnerability to incentives provided and constraints erected by incumbents, predicting the degree of subordination to which they are prepared to subject themselves in order to reenter the political establishment rather than overturn it.[115] The technology of rebellion exogenously captures rebel capacity relative to its adversary.

Circling back to the potential fates of rebels presented at the beginning of this chapter, these include victory domination, victory incorporation, defeat elimination, and defeat disintegration. It is important to note that the predictions made in this scenario are not deterministic. A key observation is that there are several paths a rebel group may take, paths that are not always easily anticipated. Moreover, changes in these dimensions may occur over the course of a conflict, redirecting rebellions down different paths than their original trajectory. As Table 2.3 shows, victory and defeat remain broad outcomes, but the distinctions between rebel groups along lines of political embeddedness and technology of rebellion distribute them into different fates.

This study predicts the following: In cases of symmetrical irregular conflict, domestically embedded political insiders are likely to achieve either victory by domination or by incorporation, whereas in asymmetrical irregular conflict, politically embedded insiders are likely to meet victory by incorporation. The logic is as follows: Politically embedded groups will have more cohesion surrounding disenfranchised elites that have played a historical role in state politics, during which time they occupied positions on the state's status hierarchy before forming a rebellion. Leaders and cadres bring with them distinct power resource endowments. Insider leaders draw on prewar networks of cadres that are mobilized around political membership in a status group, providing a

Table 2.3 Fates of African Rebels

		Political Embeddedness	
		Insiders	*Outsiders*
Technology of Rebellion	*Symmetrical irregular war*	Victory domination Victory incorporation	Victory domination Defeat elimination
	Asymmetrical irregular war	Victory incorporation	Defeat elimination Defeat disintegration

foundation on which to build cohesive, internal hierarchies of rebellion. Political and military skills acquired while operating within the state serve as conduits for leadership and organization, further nourished by the negativity bias that accompanies the ouster from or denied entry into the state's status hierarchy. In the context of symmetrical irregular warfare, where the rebels are more or less evenly matched by a state military, such groups, if they are lucky, can achieve victory through domination.

Insiders fighting in both symmetrical and asymmetrical contexts face the same set of opportunities presented by the regimes they fight. Regime strategies take into account the status dimension of political embeddedness and lead to the likelihood of victory incorporation. Even in asymmetrical conflict when insider-led rebellions are more militarily vulnerable, they nevertheless pose high political threats associated with their historical role in state authority, and perhaps command a sizable portion of opposition within the broader context of the segment of political society they ostensibly represent. This prompts a strategy of insurgent control, which entails attempts at negotiated settlement and an accommodation with rebels, under which leaders receive governmental posts and cadres and fighters are absorbed into the state military. Even in cases of insider intransigence, amnesty and ongoing negotiations peel off followers and perhaps disgruntled cadres, while a military campaign is waged with the goal of weakening the rebellion through force and doing business with what is left. In most cases, politically embedded insiders can be induced to reestablish a relationship with incumbents who control the status hierarchy. There is an ongoing allocative importance of state authority and holding a position somewhere in the status hierarchy, which means access to and control of at least some resources, which the rebel leaders may be able to offer to those beneath them within the context of the prevailing political order. In other words, accepting incorporation becomes a form of victory unobtainable by force.

Alternatively, during symmetrical irregular conflict, outsiders may achieve victory by domination or suffer defeat by elimination, whereas in asymmetrical irregular conflict outsiders will meet defeat by elimination or by decomposition. Again, the logic: Political outsiders are of little significance and pose relatively low threats to incumbents, possessing small networks by virtue of their historical distance from state institutions. Such groups therefore immediately face the major constraint of their broader political environment, meaning that the regimes they fight are far less likely to provide an opportunity for accommodation and will seek the elimination of the rebellion. Thus, the only way into the political establishment is to upend and replace it entirely through victory domination, which rebels can achieve in contexts of symmetrical irregular warfare. More often than not, however, these rebels face outright defeat. In the case of asymmetrical warfare, outsiders will likely experience one of the variants of defeat.

These fates take into account the organizational foundations of non-embedded rebellions. To be sure, it is possible for outsiders to forge cohesion from sources outside political embeddedness and to marshal this toward victory domination. However, most outsiders start rebellion from the distinct disadvantage of having narrower time frames between group formation and rebellion. Ad hoc organizational structures cannot identify, develop, and invest power resources into cohesion. They do not draw on preexisting, shared institutional linkages among leaders, cadres, and state authority that would have otherwise forged organizational networks before rebellion. Instead, cohesion is based on shaky coalitions of small networks whose only commonality is the shared objective of total military victory over incumbents, which for outsiders is the only realistic path.[116] Rebels can be defeated outright through elimination, or organizational fragility creates conditions for fragmentation and defeat disintegration.

Conclusion

A man's character is his fate.
—Heraclitus

As noted, the overall objective in this study is to explain why some rebels achieve different types of victory (domination, incorporation) or defeat (elimination, disintegration). The key argument is that politically embedded rebel groups are more likely to meet different variants of victory (domination or incorporation) than those that are not embedded. This occurs irrespective of resource endowments, and rebel groups are products of where they are situated within state institutions and regime politics. Incumbents respond to rebellions depending on the nature of the threat they pose. The fates of rebels therefore lie in these responses, which provide levels of political accommodation with former insiders and seek the elimination of outsiders.

At a fundamental level, civil wars in Africa are struggles to gain access to the state, either by replacing regimes wholesale or at the very least by using rebellion to negotiate into prevailing authority networks. By gauging the threats posed by rebellions composed of political insiders or outsiders, incumbent regimes determine their strategy. They can control the threat through accommodation and incorporation. Alternatively, they will eliminate the threat entirely. In this chapter, I have provided an explanatory framework for how this process plays out and how political embeddedness shapes rebel cohesion and demarcates the options available for rebel leaders within a set of institutional constraints.

The following chapters examine the experiences of a range of Africa's rebellions. The focus of Chapter 3 is the varied fates of Uganda's armed groups and the outlier among them, the Allied Democratic Front. In Chapter 4, the investigation shifts the frame of comparison to consider the fates of two rebellions composed of insiders: the Sudan People's Liberation Army, which ended with a political settlement; and Côte d'Ivoire's Forces Nouvelles, which achieved victory by domination following a period of failed settlements. Chapter 5 presents two cases of outsider rebellions that met divergent fates: Sierra Leone's Revolutionary United Front met defeat by disintegration, whereas Central African Republic's Séléka rebels achieved victory by domination.

These cases vary considerably. To clarify how these wars ended, I have crafted in this current chapter a rudimentary toolkit for navigating the complex environments of Africa's myriad rebellions. Although cases vary in their complexity, how political embeddedness plays out against the backdrop of the technology of rebellions remains generalizable in most cases. So long as the nature of regime politics is characterized by neopatrimonial networks and status hierarchies of authority, political embeddedness will matter to the fates of rebels.

Notes

1. Connable and Libicki, *How Insurgencies End*, p. xiii.
2. Howard, "When Are Wars Decisive?"
3. Mandel, "Defining Postwar Victory."
4. Staniland, "States, Insurgents, and Wartime Political Orders."
5. Kalyvas, *The Logic of Violence in Civil War*, p. 5.
6. Kalyvas, "Civil Wars."
7. Kalyvas, "'New' and 'Old' Civil Wars."
8. Sambanis, "What Is Civil War?"
9. An old-school overview of this literature can be found here: Zartman, *Collapsed States*; Reno, *Warlord Politics and African States*; Fearon and Laitin, "Ethnicity, Insurgency, and Civil Wars"; Collier and Hoeffler, "Greed and Grievance in Civil War"; Berdal and Malone, *Greed and Grievance*; Keen, "The Economic Functions of Violence in Civil Wars"; Ross, "What Do We Know About Natural Resources and Civil Wars?"; Kaufman, *Modern Hatreds*; Walter and Snyder, eds., *Civil Wars, Insecurity, and Intervention*; David, "Internal War"; Brubaker and

Laitin, "Ethnic and Nationalist Violence"; Posen, "The Security Dilemma and Ethnic Conflict"; Horowitz, *Ethnic Groups in Conflict*.

10. Day, "Civil War and Rebellion."
11. Staniland, "States, Insurgents, and Wartime Political Orders," p. 245.
12. Uppsala Universitet Department of Peace and Conflict Research, UCDP Actor Dataset, http://ucdp.uu.se/#.
13. Englebert, *Africa*, p. 168.
14. Cabral, *Revolution in Guinea*.
15. Bennet, *Fighting the Mau Mau*.
16. Reno, *Warfare in Independent Africa*, pp. 85–98.
17. Poggo, *The First Sudanese Civil War*; Rolandsen, "A False Start."
18. McGowan, "African Military Coups d'État, 1956–2001."
19. Schraeder, *African Politics and Society*, p. 204; Zack-Williams and Riley, "Sierra Leone: The Coup and Its Consequences."
20. Jentzsch, Kalyvas, and Schubiger, "Militias in Civil Wars."
21. Muana, "The Kamajoi Militia"; Ferme and Hoffman, "Hunter Militias and the International Human Rights Discourse in Sierra Leone and Beyond."
22. Schraeder *African Politics and Society*, p. 206.
23. Young, "The Victors and the Vanquished," p. 178.
24. Bøås and Dunn, *African Guerrillas*, p. 19.
25. Hall and Taylor, "Political Science and the Three New Institutionalisms"; Thelen, "Historical Institutionalism in Comparative Politics."
26. Bayart, *The State in Africa,* p. 1.
27. Young, *The Postcolonial State in Africa*, p. 35.
28. Young, *The African Colonial State in Comparative Perspective*, pp. 35–40.
29. Herbst, *States and Power in Africa*, p. 11.
30. Mamdani, *Citizen and Subject*.
31. Atkinson, *The Roots of Ethnicity*.
32. Johnson, *The Root Causes of Sudan's Civil Wars*.
33. Mamdani, *When Victims Become Killers*.
34. Mamdani, "Beyond Settler and Native as Political Identities," p. 661.
35. Ibid., p. 654.
36. Burton, Gunther, and Higley, "Introduction: Elite Transformations and Democratic Regimes," p. 8.
37. Clapham, *Private Patronage and Public Power*, p. 24.
38. Eisenstadt, *Traditional Patrimonialism and Modern Neopatrimonialism*.
39. Chabal and Daloz, *Africa Works*, pp. 4–16.
40. Bratton and van de Walle, "Neopatrimonial Regimes and Political Transitions in Africa," p. 459.
41. Clapham, *Private Patronage and Public Power*, p. 7.
42. Chabal and Daloz, *Africa Works*, p. 13.
43. Clapham, *Private Patronage and Public Power*, pp. 10–11.
44. Huntington, *Political Order in Changing Societies*; Przeworski, *Democracy and the Market*.
45. Chabal and Daloz, *Africa Works*, p. 13.
46. Williams, *War and Conflict in Africa*.
47. Englebert and Dunn, *Inside African Politics*, pp. 268–279; Brooker, *Modern Stateless Warfare*; Sobek and Payne, "A Tale of Two Types."
48. Clapham, *African Guerrillas*, pp. 6–7; Reno, *Warfare in Independent Africa*.
49. Bøås and Dunn, *African Guerrillas*, pp. 15–36.
50. Clapham, *African Guerrillas*, pp. 9–16.

51. Johnston, "The Geography of Insurgent Organization."
52. Weinstein, *Inside Rebellion.*
53. Staniland, *Networks of Rebellion.*
54. Sinno, *Organizations at War.*
55. A recent exception to this is the excellent work by Krause, *Rebel Power*, which looks at power distributions within rebel organizations.
56. Pearlman and Cunningham, "Nonstate Actors, Fragmentation, and Conflict Processes"; Bakke, Cunningham, and Seymour, "A Plague of Initials."
57. Gurr, *Why Men Rebel*; Lichbach, "What Makes Rational Peasants Revolutionary?"; Humphreys and Weinstein, "Who Fights?"; Alison, "Cogs in the Wheel?"; Viterna, "Pulled, Pushed, and Persuaded"; Wood, *Insurgent Collective Action and Civil War in El Salvador;* Gates, "Recruitment and Allegiance"; Petersen, *Resistance and Rebellion.*
58. Collier, *Economic Causes of Civil Conflict and Their Implications for Policy.*
59. Weber, "The Sociology of Charismatic Authority," p. 246.
60. Greene, *Comparative Revolutionary Movements*, p. 26.
61. Schlichte, "With the State Against the State?" p. 248.
62. Bakke, Cunningham, and Seymour, "A Plague of Initials," p. 266.
63. Weinstein, *Inside Rebellion*, p. 12.
64. Day, "The Fates of Rebels."
65. Benoit-Smullyan, "Status, Status Types, and Status Interrelations."
66. Petersen, *Understanding Ethnic Violence*, p. 40.
67. Ibid., p. 25.
68. Gilley, "Against the Concept of Ethnic Conflict."
69. Roessler, *Ethnic Politics and State Power in Africa.*
70. Reno, *Warfare in Independent Africa*, p. 30.
71. Mampilly, *Rebel Rulers*, pp. 68–73.
72. Staniland, *Networks of Rebellion*, p. 33.
73. Schlichte, "With the State Against the State?" p. 256.
74. Korpi, "Power Resources Approach vs. Action and Conflict."
75. Staniland, *Networks of Rebellion*, pp. 20–23.
76. Day and Reno, "In Harm's Way."
77. Leites and Wolf Jr., *Rebellion and Authority.*
78. Kalyvas, *The Logic of Violence in Civil War.*
79. Maynard, *Healing Communities in Conflict*, chap. 5.
80. Schlichte, "With the State Against the State?" p. 261.
81. Korpi, "Power Resources Approach," p. 38.
82. Pierson, *Politics in Time*, pp. 33–37.
83. Balcells and Kalyvas, "Did Marxism Make a Difference?"
84. Korpi, "Power Resources Approach," p. 38.
85. Baumeister, Bratslavsky, Finkenauer, and Vohs, "Bad Is Stronger than Good."
86. Petersen, *Understanding Ethnic Violence*, p. 37.
87. Snyder, *From Voting to Violence*; Figueiredo Jr. and Weingast, "The Rationality of Fear."
88. Mahoney, "Path Dependence in Historical Sociology."
89. Doom and Vlassenroot, "Kony's Message: A New Koine?" pp. 20–21; for more on Kony's rural background, see Green, *The Wizard of the Nile.*
90. Clapham, *Africa and the International System*, p. 59.
91. Migdal, ed., *State in Society*; Boone, *Political Topographies of the African State*; Gibson, "Boundary Control."
92. Reno, *Corruption and State Politics in Sierra Leone.*

93. "War in the North," *Africa Confidential*, 24 May 1996; Schomerus, "The Lord's Resistance Army in Sudan," pp. 24–28.

94. "NRA Captures Kony Weapons," *New Vision*, 26 July 1994.

95. "Kony Gets Better Weapons," *Sunday Vision*, 20 March 1994.

96. "Why Has NRA Failed to Finish Off Kony," *Monitor*, 12 May 1995.

97. Interviews with ex-LRA fighters, Gulu, January 2008; "Kony Returns to Sudan," *Monitor*, 26 August 2003.

98. "Sudan Invasion Documents Seized," *New Vision*, 13 December 1995.

99. "Kony to Abduct 10,000," *Sunday Vision*, 21 July 1996; "Sudan Cuts Aid to Kony," *New Vision*, 20 November 1996; "Short-Lived Peace," *New Vision*, 21 February 1996; "Kony Ordered to Capture Town," *Crusader*, 19 March 1998; "LRA Fights to Beat Sudan's Ultimatum," *Sunday Monitor*, 2 August 1998.

100. "Kony Under House Arrest," *New Vision*, 17 April 1999.

101. "We've Got 4bn Worth from Kony," *New Vision*, 18 August 2002.

102. "Report on Kony War," *New Vision*, 1 January 2006.

103. The Enough Project, *Kony to LRA;* Agger and Hutson, *Kony's Ivory.*

104. Collier, *Economic Causes of Civil Conflict.*

105. Terry, *Condemned to Repeat?*; Stedman and Tanner, "Refugees as Resources in War."

106. Brown, *The International Dimensions of Internal Conflict*, p. 580.

107. Byman, Chalk, Hoffman, Rosenau, and Brannan, *Trends in Outside Support for Insurgency Movements.*

108. Collier and Hoeffler "Greed and Grievance in Civil War"; Berdal and Malone, "Greed and Grievance."

109. Staniland, "Organizing Insurgency."

110. Byman, Chalk, Hoffman, Rosenau, and Brannan, *Trends in Outside Support*, pp. xiv-xv.

111. Weinstein, *Inside Rebellion,* p. 10.

112. Day, "Bush Path to Self-Destruction."

113. Biddle, *Military Power*; Millet and Murray, *Military Effectiveness*; Brooks and Stanley, eds., *Creating Military Power*; Rosen, *Societies and Military Power.*

114. Kalyvas and Balcells, "International System and Technologies of Rebellion."

115. Clapham, *Private Patronage and Public Power*, p. 12.

116. Schlichte, "With the State Against the State?" p. 254.

3

Multiple Fates:
Rebel Groups in Uganda

Caution is not cowardice; even the ants march armed.
—Ugandan proverb

Rebellion in Uganda, particularly since the victory of Yoweri Museveni's National Resistance Army (NRA), reflects the history of political fragmentation and multiple reversals in Uganda's political status hierarchies since independence in 1962. Even under colonial rule, Uganda's range of ethnic and regional groupings took on rigid political identities, some of which ascended to political dominance while others languished at the margins of state authority. Upon independence, Milton Obote became Uganda's head of state and consolidated political networks made up largely of his own northern Langi tribe and also the Acholi ethnic groups, which had previously dominated the British colonial security forces. Their status was upended in 1970 when Idi Amin overthrew Obote, subsequently killed off most senior northern officers, and elevated his own West Nile tribesmen to key positions in the Ugandan government. By 1980, Obote had again reversed this pattern and ended Amin's rule with the help of the Tanzanian army, only to be himself overthrown in a coup d'état in 1985 by two Acholi men, Tito and Bazilio Okello, after struggling to eliminate the NRA's rebellion.[1] In 1986, the NRA pushed out the Okellos' military junta, marking a renewed ascendance of southern elites at the expense of northern elites.

Although the NRA's 1986 victory ended years of political upheaval, its subsequent transformation of Ugandan state politics initiated a new phase of protracted conflict that aggravated its fragmented nature and further fractured the country's political establishment. Some elements of this establishment joined the new regime. Other groupings fled to the bush and reorganized as a range of rebellions. The tenuousness of the NRA's consolidation of authority also created space for the formation of rebel groups that had never walked the corridors of state power. In other words, the years of civil war and state decline that followed the NRA victory seemed to establish rebellion as the main language of politics for both insiders and outsiders.

Later on, in January 2000, the Ugandan government's Amnesty Act embodied the NRA's approach of "pacification through reconciliation." The act provided blanket amnesty to all Ugandans who had engaged in armed rebellion against the state since 1986. Fighters from a range of groups could now renounce rebellion in return for forgiveness, leave the bush, and go home. From another perspective, amnesty was either already built into separate peace agreements between the Ugandan government and a given rebellion or was intended to strip individual fighters away from those rebel groups not offered an agreement collectively. Either way, by January 2009, a total of 22,995 fighters from *twenty-nine* different rebel groups had trickled out of the bush into regional reception centers established throughout the country.[2]

Not one of these groups seized power. Instead, they experienced a range of fates. There is a strong temptation to draw a straight line between the fates of Uganda's rebels and the more traditionally defined drivers of conflict and its outcomes. For instance, the NRA, plus the multiple groups that emerged after 1986 to fight it, all claimed some form of political grievance against the Ugandan government, despite varying in ethnic, regional, or religious composition. All of these groups operated from rural or peripheral patches of rugged terrain.[3] Nearly all of them preyed upon ordinary Ugandans in one way or another. Some received sponsorship from the Sudanese government that granted access to resources and sanctuary.[4] Indeed, the broader literature on civil war and rebellion generally associates variations of these factors with conflict onset, duration, and termination.

But a closer theoretical and empirical look illuminates a different perspective on how these conflicts ended. The fact that no single rebel challenger replaced the NRA does not necessarily mean incumbent victory occurred in all cases. Rather, each rebellion that emerged since 1986 came from different segments of Uganda's fragmented political society, reflecting variations in their political embeddedness. In responding to these rebellions during the same period, the Ugandan government and by extension the army, the Uganda People's Defence Forces (UPDF) treated each rebellion quite differently, which shaped multiple fates.[5]

The story of Uganda's rebellions is not just about a single conflict dyad or conflict outcome. Rather, the groups investigated here represent the entire inventory of possible fates offered in this book, including outliers (see Table 3.1). On its own, the NRA is an important case of victory domination. But it also sets the scene for Uganda's myriad rebellions since 1986, each of which fought the NRA within a compact geographical area and the same relative time span. These dimensions of Uganda's multiple conflicts provide one of Africa's most compelling contexts to conduct controlled comparisons of rebels and to examine the diversity of their corresponding fates. In addition, Uganda is a suitable laboratory to test and rule out the salience of resources on the fates of rebels. Although the technology of rebellion is a clean indicator of rebel capacity, it remains a limited predictor of rebel fates. Above all, Uganda's rebellions reflect different degrees of political embeddedness that correspond to their place in political society.

To tackle the question of Ugandan rebel fates, I divide their complex stories into three comparative frames. The first considers the victory domination of the NRA as a historical bookend for analyzing the many rebellions after 1986. It then considers those cases that experienced the fate of victory incorporation. The Uganda People's Democratic Army and the Uganda People's Army fought brief yet intense insurgencies until signing peace accords and incorporating into the Ugandan government. The second frame compares two rebellions from Uganda's West Nile region, which both emerged from Idi Amin's fallen regime but experienced divergent fates: The West Nile Bank Front (WNBF) met defeat disintegration, whereas a related but separate

Table 3.1 The Fates of Uganda's Rebels

Rebellion	Political Embeddedness	Technology of Rebellion	Fate
NRA	High/Medium	Asymmetrical	Victory domination
UPDA	High	Asymmetrical	Victory incorporation
UPA	High	Asymmetrical	Victory incorporation
WNBF	Medium	Asymmetrical	Defeat disintegration
UNRF II	High	Asymmetrical	Victory incorporation
NALU	Low	Asymmetrical	Defeat elimination
UMLA	Low	Asymmetrical	Defeat elimination
NDA	Low	Asymmetrical	Defeat elimination
ADF	Low	Asymmetrical	Disintegration/persistence

group, the Uganda National Rescue Front II (UNRF II) met victory incorporation. The West Nile cases illustrate how time can matter to political embeddedness, as well as the nature of the regime in which rebel leaders were embedded.

I also examine three groups that experienced defeat elimination: the National Army for the Liberation of Uganda (NALU), the Uganda Muslim Liberation Army (UMLA), and the National Democratic Army (NDA). This comparative frame also considers the fate of the Allied Democratic Front (ADF), which was an amalgam of NALU, UMLA, and the NDA. I consider this an outlier case that does not neatly correspond to this book's framework. Although the ADF was considered to have disintegrated in the Ugandan context, the rebellion has since reemerged as a key actor in eastern DRC's ongoing conflicts. The ADF case raises questions about rebel demise and resurgence, and the role of ungoverned territory and transnational, armed actors.

Variants of Victory

Victory Domination: The National Resistance Army (NRA)

In the African context, the NRA of Uganda is a flagship case of rebel victory by domination. What explains this fate? A deep look shows that NRA leader Museveni was simultaneously a political insider and an outsider, helming a rebellion that was incompletely embedded politically but nevertheless highly cohesive. After five years of fighting an asymmetrical guerrilla war, the NRA captured the Ugandan state despite regime change in Kampala that prompted a shift in counterinsurgency strategies from elimination to control.

The NRA's relationship to Uganda's prewar politics says much about its corresponding fate, but not in ways that are clear by looking at state institutions at the time of the rebellion's founding. The organizational nucleus of what would become the NRA was formed in the world of political exile, far afield of Ugandan state politics. As early as the late 1960s, Museveni led the University Students' African Revolutionary Front at Dar es Salaam University, where he began to nourish his politics with revolutionary ideology. Soon his study group established contacts with Frelimo rebels, traveling to its liberated zones in Mozambique. Not only were these firsthand experiences in observing rebellion formative,[6] they also provided a site for Museveni's own scholarly research on Franz Fanon, violence, and revolution.[7] After completing his studies, he returned to Uganda and served a brief stint as a "researcher" in President Obote's office.[8] Following Amin's seizure of state power, by virtue of his association with the political establishment, Museveni found himself among many political exiles living in Tanzania.

There he helped form the anti-Amin Front for National Salvation (FRONASA).[9] Threadbare and resource scarce, FRONASA spent most of the 1970s stumbling between Tanzania and Uganda, clandestinely moving weapons, trying to establish guerrilla bases, and preparing for a fight that never quite materialized. The first "invasion" of September 1972, Museveni writes, "was in reality an encounter between two groups of fools: Amin's group on the one hand, and ours on the other."[10]

Things began to turn around from 1976 to 1978 when Museveni and twenty-eight fellow Ugandan revolutionaries returned to Mozambique to undergo training in the Frelimo liberated zone of Montepuez. This experience prepared key FRONASA cadres for the critical juncture of Amin's invasion of Tanzania in 1978, which provided the pretext for a full conventional counterattack by a coalition of anti-Amin forces. Heavily undergirded by the Tanzania People's Defence Force (TPDF), Museveni's FRONASA fought alongside the smaller pro-Obote force of Kikosi Maalum, pushing the Ugandan army into retreat until the coalition sent Amin into exile on 11 April 1979. Together they replaced his regime with a rickety partnership of Ugandan exile politicians called the Uganda National Liberation Front (UNLF).[11] Along the way, FRONASA swelled to 9,000 fighters whom Museveni had recruited from Uganda's southwestern region.

In the brief period that followed, Museveni navigated the various power struggles among factions of the national army, serving briefly as minister of defense, minister of regional cooperation, and vice chair of Uganda's Military Council. Yet political and ethnic schisms in the military—now called the Uganda National Liberation Army—saw Uganda burn quickly through two lackluster presidents, Yusuf Lule and Godfrey Binaisa.[12] A key obstacle to regime consolidation, Omara-Otunno notes, was that although the military was disorganized, no single political faction could dominate the government without its backing.[13] As it happened, Museveni's chief political rival, Paulo Muwanga, briefly became a military ruler until elections of December 1980 reinstalled Milton Obote as Uganda's head of state. These elections were widely perceived as rigged, and Museveni's failed electoral bid as leader of the newly minted Uganda Patriotic Movement (UPM) prompted his return to the bush to fight.

By these measures, Museveni can be considered a political insider whose embeddedness and status reversal could theoretically provide the foundation for the NRA. But although the group included several such insiders, the core of its organization, and the crucial link between Museveni and "the most useful military cadres in the whole struggle,"[14] was largely constructed outside the country during exile, consolidated in the early days of the NRA.

The precursor to the NRA was the People's Resistance Army (PRA), and it was only a small clutch of thirty-five FRONASA cadres whom Museveni knew personally during their time in exile. For their first operation on 6 February 1981, a paltry twenty-seven rebels attacked the Kabamba Military Training Wing in order to acquire weapons. The maneuver was only marginally successful and was followed by another lackluster string of hit-and-run raids in the Luwero Triangle, which were carried out during a six-month period of Museveni's absence and under the weaker leadership of Sam Magara.[15] After Museveni returned from abroad, he deliberately suspended operations[16] to critically reassess the organizational foundations of the PRA. By late 1981, after a "period of concealment,"[17] the PRA had officially changed its moniker to the NRA and emerged with a commitment to a "protracted people's war"— a guerrilla insurgency that would anchor itself within a highly central- ized inner core and a decentralized network of civilian support based in the Luwero Triangle.

The Army Council and High Command occupied the top of the NRA hierarchy, under which stood an array of zonal forces in charge of recruitment and supply, with mobile forces responsible for capturing weapons from the army when possible. A range of subcommittees and administrative units supported this structure,[18] and the group's Ten- Point Program outlined NRA ideology based on Leninist principles of democratic centralism.[19]

With the leadership-cadre linkage well established, the NRA began to take on several types of recruits. The first came from a reservoir established during Museveni's brief tenure in the Ministry of Defence. There he had tried to stack the army with former FRONASA fighters and new recruits from his ethnic base in the southwest, which initially composed around two-thirds of the UNLA.[20] But following the elec- tions, the ultimate integration of FRONASA fighters into the new national army dragged out and was patchy and incomplete. As a result, many fighters, now feeling marginalized, decamped to join Museveni's new rebellion.[21] At this early juncture, the NRA also attracted groups of professionals and students from Makerere University in Kampala.[22]

Yet the most significant part of the NRA's organizational structure was its incorporation of the civilian population as a source of recruits and as a basis for its guerrilla war economy. Although Museveni had received a small cache of arms from Libya, the NRA was quite resource scarce and had to rely on a clandestine political network of civilian supporters in the Luwero Triangle. The NRA's distinct civilian orientation predated its insurgency, having been acquired in Mozambique. Yet as the NRA grew, its leadership faced a number of cleavages that threatened organizational cohesion. There were clear professional, class, and intellectual schisms within the group. But the largest was the hierarchical distance between its primarily Banyankole cadres and the NRA's social base in the Luwero Triangle, which was a heterogeneous mix of Bagandan peasants and other ethnicities.[23]

The NRA therefore required a mechanism to reinforce the populist ideology of "comradeship" that undergirded the rebellion.[24] The subsequent creation of the Resistance Council (RC) system integrated communities directly into the NRA's broader structure.[25] Although the RC was largely designed to supply the NRA with economic support, it also reinforced the NRA's organizational cohesion. The RC system essentially replaced sectarian traditional authorities[26] with political commissars (PCs), who were responsible for local power arrangements, disseminating "political education" to civilians, and above all, recruiting fighters. PCs became the lynchpins between RCs and the NRA's fighting units. Suitable recruits were sent to the Nkrumah Training Unit and subsequently distributed into fighting units based on merit and experience instead of ethnicity.[27] Most important, all NRA members were equally expected to submit to the explicitly nonsectarian Code of Conduct,[28] which defined responsibilities and relationships to one another and to civilians.[29]

With this organizational endowment, the NRA created RC-run "safe zones" within large swaths of the Luwero Triangle, but it faced a hostile Obote regime that allowed no space for negotiations. This fundamental political gulf between Obote and Museveni was largely a residue of their shaky anti-Amin coalition that never quite coalesced without TPDF guidance.[30] It is likely that Obote, viewing himself as the rightful heir of regime authority, considered Museveni to be no more than an irritant outsider. Thus, in pursuit of the NRA's elimination, the UNLA army launched the counterinsurgency campaign Operation Bonanza in June 1982.[31] The rebels were largely able to outmaneuver this first effort, but the UNLA regrouped and launched its second assault, the Grand Offensive, in January 1983, which sent three-fourths of the total UNLA fighting force to encircle the NRA in the Luwero Triangle.[32]

With only 4,000 of its own troops, the NRA was stopped in its tracks and forced to relocate north to the arid Singo and Ngoma Plains. During this period, the NRA created the Resettlement Commission to shepherd thousands of civilian refugees from Luwero for fear they would be slaughtered.[33] Stranded in a sparsely populated territory, by 1984 the NRA's defeat by elimination looked imminent, and the NRA was forced to subordinate its linkages to civilians in favor of military priorities, turning inward for another significant restructuring. A successful string of bank robberies in the Hoima region provided a much-needed cash influx to reinvest in the organization.[34] By 1985, the rebellion had resumed its military advantage, stabbing westward and establishing new liberated zones. There the NRA resumed previous patterns of RC-based rebel-civilian relations, which increased the number of fighters to 10,000.

A final critical juncture in the NRA's path to victory domination occurred on 27 July 1985, when the Obote regime was overthrown in a relatively bloodless coup in the capital, Kampala. Tensions within the UNLA had in fact begun in December 1983, when the army's chief of staff, the well-respected Oyite Ojok was killed in a helicopter crash.[35] The aftermath was the factionalization of the army along ethnic lines, particularly between Acholi fighters and Ojok's replacement, Smith Opon Acak, a Langi like Obote.[36] The ensuing power struggles culminated in a coup and the seizure of the government by two Acholi military officers, Bazilio and Tito Okello. To be sure, the ensuing destabilization in Kampala enabled the NRA to expand its territorial control throughout parts of Uganda. But the Okellos responded to this expansion by enlisting the help of several rebellions that were NRA rivals. The junta incorporated these rebel groups into the newly established Military Council[37] with the intention of having them join the fight against the NRA.[38]

Nevertheless, a surprise shift in regime strategy occurred, and a small space for accommodation opened within the ruling junta in an attempt to form a government of national unity.[39] One possible reason for this shift from elimination to control is that the NRA now held much of Uganda's productive coffee-producing territory. This control deprived the state of revenue and effectively cut off western Uganda from neighbors that depended on its road network, which put further pressure on the Okellos to do business with Museveni.[40] Moreover, the NRA was successful in creating regional and international political networks, conferring a degree of legitimacy on the rebellion that the junta did not bother cultivating.[41]

Peace talks commenced in August 1985, chaired by President Moi of Kenya.[42] Even though the Okello delegation was ill prepared for negotiations, four months of talks still produced the Nairobi Agreement on 17 December of that year. The settlement laid out a power-sharing agreement between the government and all recognized armed groups, a plan to restructure the army, a timetable for elections, and other key provisions.[43] The weak accord, largely negotiated in bad faith against the backdrop of ongoing civil war, got little traction and was never fully implemented. Museveni, intransigent and mistrustful of the Okellos, refused to take up his former post as vice chair of the Military Council. Meanwhile, fighters from all government factions continued to conduct poorly coordinated counterinsurgency operations that targeted civilians. This ongoing territorial destabilization provided cover for the NRA to continue its expansion against a weakened army and divided Military Council.[44] By January 1986, rather than using rebellion to negotiate into the prevailing political establishment, the NRA was able to leverage negotiations to march to Kampala and achieve the fate of victory domination, the mechanics of which have been well documented.[45]

To recap the NRA's path to victory domination, recall that the rebellion began with an intact set of prewar political networks reinforced by a deliberate investment in a cohesive organization. As Amaza points out, "The NRA could have become a loose, non-cohesive organization comprised of factions."[46] Instead, Museveni maintained and replicated the RC system in territories under NRA control as the war unfolded.[47] Facing a regime strategy of elimination for most of the war, there were few paths to victory other than domination, a path the NRA still pursued despite the small opening provided by the Nairobi Agreement. Rather than serving as a true possibility for incorporation, the accord merely provided the NRA with a chance to execute a tactical feint to quickly overwhelm government forces and capture the state.

Victory Incorporation:
The Uganda People's Democratic Army (UPDA)

When the NRA marched into Kampala in January 1986, the UNLA junta was so heavily fragmented that separate groups controlled different parts of the city. Many UNLA members surrendered or defected to the incoming NRA victors. But its two dominant factions, allied initially to resist Obote's second regime and then redirected against the NRA, fled the city.[48] The first of these factions was composed of Acholi soldiers who followed Bazilio Okello, key coup-maker from 1985 and head of the UNLA's Tenth Brigade. The second faction, under the command of Gad Wilson Toko, was a brew of disenfranchised Amin-era elites and

members of two anti-Obote rebellions from Amin's West Nile region—
the Uganda National Rescue Front (UNRF) and the Former Uganda
National Army (FUNA). As these factions moved north, the NRA gave
chase, capturing the northern town of Gulu by March and driving the
remaining ex-UNLA into southern Sudan.[49] Despite initial cooperation
between these factions, any chance for future teamwork broke down following a rapprochement between traditional West Nile leaders, and the
NRA convinced Toko to withdraw from the alliance. The Acholi remnants of the ex-UNLA—3,000 of them—became the core of the Uganda
People's Democratic Army (UPDA). The former national army, now
rebranded a rebellion, launched its first attack upon the northern town of
Pece on 20 August 1986, in a bid to regain control of the state.[50]

The UPDA was a politically embedded rebellion—essentially a
reconstituted government military force driven by the reversal of its
members' status and organized along the contours of previous regime
politics. Its organizational structure mirrored that of the UNLA, with
Bazilio Okello at the helm of leadership, which was then surrounded by
key ex-UNLA strongmen. Dozens of ex-UNLA rank and file were promoted to serve as junior officers, positioned to preside over a fighter tier
augmented by Acholi youth recruited from the northern Ugandan countryside, making the UPDA become 4,000–5,000 strong. Meanwhile, former prime minister Eric Otema Allimadi led the rebellion's political
wing in exile, the Uganda People's Democratic Movement (UPDM).

Although UPDA's organizational core of leaders and cadres had a
high initial level of cohesion, the group nevertheless faced a number of
setbacks, some of which were related to the technology of warfare. By
some measures, the UPDA should have had the capacity to fight a more
conventional war, as it had already amassed a relatively large quantity
of weapons. One year earlier, while he was still in Kampala and presid-
ing over his six-month junta, Bazilio Okello had transported 400 tons of
arms and ammunition from UNLA armories in Kampala to his own
rainy-day stockpiles in Gulu and Kitgum.[51] These shipments included a
substantial delivery from a Belgian arms company, Fabrique Nationale,
that ironically was shifted north one month prior to the NRA victory in
Kampala.[52] Yet, many of these weapons turned out to be defective—
some were leftover guns from the 1974 Arab-Israeli war and arrived
with mismatched Soviet bullets.[53]

Complicating resource problems further was the group's brief
refuge-seeking layover in southern Sudan. There the UNLA cadres fled
with what they could carry after having been hit hard by the NRA and
driven from Gulu.[54] At first, Sudan's government tolerated the ousted

UNLA in light of suspicions that the new NRA regime had links with the Sudan People's Liberation Army. The regime in Khartoum initially used UNLA fighters to fight southern Sudan's rebels.[55] And at one stage, the UNLA even intercepted a shipment of arms from Ethiopia destined for the SPLA.[56] Sudan also provided the main organizational conduits between ex-UNLA fighters and a few Amin-era ex-Uganda Army (UA) soldiers, a combination that formed the UPDA's initial core.[57] In any event, a southern Sudanese official had soon disarmed, subsequently rearmed, and by 1987, had expelled the Ugandan rebels from Sudanese territory.[58] In the meantime, the UPDM was unsuccessful in securing resources for its armed wing.[59]

Thus, although the UPDA's military foundations conferred organizational cohesion upon the group, these advantages were insufficient to overcome capacity shortfalls required to meet the NRA on equal footing, even as the new regime struggled to transition from a rebellion to a state army. Attempting to fight a more conventional war against the NRA, but with limited capacity, the UPDA experienced a series of battlefield losses. The most significant of these occurred in Corner Kilak in early 1987, where the NRA killed upward of 700 rebels and seized over 1,000 weapons.[60] Such thrashings cost the UPDA dearly in resources as the NRA also sheared away key senior cadres who were replaced with younger and less experienced junior officers, a maneuver that weakened the bonds of cohesion forged between the group's initial leaders and cadres.

Another factor that hurt the UPDA was the decision to use political outsiders in an attempt to shore up its fighter tier, particularly through the mobilization and recruitment of rural Acholi youth. By late 1986, the spirit medium Alice Auma Lakwena formed the Holy Spirit Mobile Forces (HSMF) as a battalion within the UPDA. Lakwena gained a following by attracting fighters with a promise of salvation through ritual purification and military victory, and she even had a few initial battlefield successes in the northern districts of Apac and Lira. Yet in battle, she adopted unorthodox practices, the most notable of which included commanding her fighters to smear shea butter oil on their bodies for protection and encouraging them to throw stones at enemy soldiers, believing they would explode like hand grenades. Soon such ineffective tactics led to heavy battlefield losses and put her at odds with UPDA senior commanders.[61] Within a year, her group broke off, siphoning 2,000 fighters from the mainstream UPDA.[62]

In addition to Lakwena, the rise of Joseph Kony within UPDA ranks further disrupted the group's cohesion, as he also began to attract fighters to his own unit through appeals to Acholi spiritual beliefs and identity. When key UNLA strongman Major Opia was killed in 1987, Kony assumed command of his Black Battalion and asserted himself as the primary spiritual leader within the UPDA. Like Lakwena, his reliance on unconventional means for military organization led to poor battlefield outcomes, which were met by skepticism and hostility by many within the UPDA senior leaders. When they called for his arrest, he escaped with 800 fighters, and the ensuing pursuit expended significant UPDA ammunition.[63]

By mid-1987, the UPDA had endured major losses and was facing defeat by elimination.[64] More military stumbles further drained scarce resources and removed key insider cadres who were replaced with outsiders—Lakwena and Kony—who in turn peeled off junior officers and hundreds of young, fresh recruits to form their own groups. Thousands more defected following a general amnesty offered by the regime in Kampala,[65] as the UPDA struggled to keep up pressure against an assertive NRA in the northern districts of Gulu and Kitgum. Soon, the NRA intercepted radio messages between UPDA commanders, who betrayed their desperation in the bush by discussing their supply shortages and their inability to sustain NRA-inflicted losses. Lieutenant Colonel Terensio Okulu of the UPDA delivered a message that the rebellion was ready to talk.[66]

So began the UPDA's path to victory by incorporation. Seeking to control but not entirely eliminate the group, the NRA was eager to end the costly war and was willing to bring members of the former army into the new regime. Acholi elder Tiberio Okeny Atwoma initiated talks by conducting a 145-day assessment that convinced the NRA leadership to pursue negotiations. By late 1987, Salim Saleh, who was Museveni's brother and chief of combat and operations, began clandestine contact with UPDA commanders through civilian intermediaries. Four months of confidence building among military commanders soon bore fruit. Formal talks began on 17 March 1988 at the Acholi Inn in Gulu, with the NRA team led by Salim Saleh and the UPDA team led by Bazilio Okello. Further rounds of talks culminated in the Pece Peace Accord of 3 June 1988. The political settlement established a cease-fire, granted cash allowances and amnesty to up to 10,000 fighters, absorbed many of them into the NRA with their military rank intact, and promised long-term political reform.[67] Newly integrated rebels, now soldiers, joined the army's campaigns against those scatterings of the Lakwena and Kony groups that still remained in the bush. In the meantime, the UPDM, which was excluded from the Pece talks, eventually reached its own, separate accord in 1990 with the NRA that allowed their senior members to return to Uganda.

What explains the UPDA's victory through incorporation? At several key junctures, the NRA could have eliminated the rebellion militarily. But the group had emerged as part of a historical contest for political ascendancy between northern and southern elites. The UPDA's political embeddedness produced its organizational core, and because this included key insiders—members of the UNLA junta—the group possessed a good degree of cohesion and a strong sense of its own status within Ugandan political society. Once it ran out of bullets on the battlefield, the UPDA was nevertheless well positioned to do business with the NRA, which pursued a strategy of accommodation with a known quantity in order to draw elites into an emergent patronage network as a less costly, nonviolent strategy of political control. These dynamics allowed the UPDA to achieve victory through incorporation against the backdrop of asymmetrical irregular warfare.

Victory Incorporation: The Uganda People's Army (UPA)

The roots of the Uganda People's Army, and the key predictor of its fate of victory incorporation, lay in the east-central Teso region's historical relationship to state authority. Long a stronghold of Milton Obote's Uganda People's Congress (UPC) political party, Teso had enjoyed the relative benefits of being within the orbit of regime patronage. What made this relationship distinct is how successive Ugandan governments managed the region's chronic experience with cattle raiding, which experienced several dramatic shifts in tandem with the country's changing regimes.

In the immediate aftermath of Idi Amin's fall in 1979, cattle raiders from the northeastern region of Karamoja took advantage of the generalized disorder to loot the Moroto barracks armory and turn its weapons against neighboring Teso in a rash of cattle rustling.[68] Once Obote was reinstalled as Uganda's head of state in the early 1980s, he responded to insecurity in Teso by initiating the creation of a local self-defense militia. In addition, Obote brought the Teso region and its people even closer to his regime by actively recruiting Iteso men into what became his own "Special Forces," a British-trained personal guard and paramilitary organization that he deployed against the NRA rebellion. Yet when Obote was again overthrown in 1985, the Okello junta disbanded the Special Forces. Without a link to the incumbent regime, members of the now-abandoned Teso militias began colluding with the Karamojong in fresh cattle raids. After the NRA's victory in 1986, things changed again as the new regime deployed battalions into Teso, which brought a mixture of both protection and predation. The key shift here occurred when NRA troops were redeployed to suppress the UPDA and the HSMF, leaving the entire Teso region vulnerable to renewed cattle raiding.[69] Taken together, these factors—the purge of the Special Forces, the neglect of the region, the lack of protection from cattle thieves—galvanized the status grievances of those who would form the UPA.

Understanding the UPA's path to victory incorporation also requires a look at its organizational structure, which had two components. The first component was its political wing, the Uganda People's Front (UPF), which was spearheaded by a small clutch of disenfranchised elites from the Obote regime who had languished in exile in the 1980s. These included Peter Otai, former deputy minister of defense; Ateker Ejalu, former managing director of Uganda Railways Corporation; David Anyoti, minister of information and broadcasting; and Colonel William Amaria, deputy minister of internal affairs. These political apparatchiks, though politically embedded on an individual basis, had few connections to one another. Scattered among Kenya, Zambia, and the United Kingdom, they brought little to UPA's organization and often hobbled its message with contradictory public statements. True to prediction, their collective goal was to claim stewardship over the UPA's ground operations in order to gain leverage in renegotiating to establish new positions in the NRA regime. Yet seldom did they ever present a coordinated effort with forces on the ground, a shortcoming that was further hamstrung by Otai's tendency to move in and out of the UPA and other, smaller armed groups such as the Ninth of October Army (NOA).

The second component of the UPA's organization consisted of the ex–Special Forces that led its ground operations, which had an intact endowment of leaders and cadres alike, drawn from shared experiences of working within the security apparatus of Obote's regime. Followers consisted of Iteso ex-militia, rural youth, and even some criminals who used the cover of rebellion to engage in their own cattle rustling.[70] The UPA's leader was the unfortunately named Hitler Eregu, who had been the deputy commander of the Special Forces.

The UPA had been created initially to protect Teso cattle from ongoing raids from neighboring Karamoja. But once government soldiers began engaging the rebels in direct military confrontations, the group began using symbolic strikes to garner support from broader Teso society.[71] Grasping the UPA's historical contours and its linkage to the previous political establishment, Museveni offered the entire group amnesty and sent a team of Iteso ministers to convince them to abandon war.[72] But the July 1989 Kumi crisis, during which untethered government soldiers burned civilians alive in a railcar, reignited the rebellion in earnest.[73]

The UPA reorganized geographically into different brigades—Central, Solar, Saba Saba, Ostrich, and ASK. Political commissars Max Omeda and Charles Eswau mobilized local fighters and coordinated UPA operations in the bush. Yet this structure soon began to unravel. As the NRA's ongoing strategy of control through amnesty gradually peeled off UPA commanders, those who remained in the bush became increasingly localized and predatory, which undercut popular support for the rebellion overall. In addition, political infighting splintered the UPA ground forces further as UPF rivals attempted to co-opt and play commanders off one another.

From the standpoint of its parity with the Ugandan military, the UPA conflict can be considered asymmetrical. Indeed, resource scarcity recurrently plagued the rebellion. Much of its initial supply came from the capture of arms and ammunition from the NRA, which became insufficient as the war intensified. Eregu traveled to Zambia to find support from the exiled Obote, but he was rebuffed and sent away with only $200 in travel money. He then spent an entire year in Nairobi with no contact with his ground forces, during which time the UPA hemorrhaged such commanders as Jesus Ojirot of the Ostrich Brigade.[74] Meanwhile, resources promised by the UPF never materialized, and even Otai's reputation as a "checkbook liberator" bore no fruit.[75] The schoolyard rivalry between Adjallo and Omaria split the UPF irreconcilably, casting the UPA's ground operators adrift from their political operatives.[76]

At one stage a small supply of military hardware and funding was made available by the UPA's "external coordinator," Musa Francis Ecweru. High-level officials in Nairobi had provided him with small sums of cash to purchase arms and ammunition from shady NRA units in Teso and Jinja, but this pipeline turned out to be unreliable. Ecweru's most successful deal involved the acquisition of 500,000 rounds of ammunition from the Kenyan government, but Ugandan authorities intercepted the shipments before they were even delivered. Overall, these sporadic resource trickles were insufficient to sustain ground operations.

Before long, both the UPA's military wing and its opportunistic political exiles began responding to government overtures, opening a path to victory accommodation. By 1990, the Presidential Commission for Teso engaged the UPA in peace negotiations that included amnesty, a presidential pardon, local security guarantees, formal inquiries into the root causes of the rebellion, and economic aid.[77] The amnesty provisions immediately brought in hundreds of fighters.[78] Top figures such as Ecweru slotted easily into political appointments.[79] Without key cadres on the ground, what remained of the UPA's organization fragmented into four small groups.[80] Some fighters, including Eregu, joined other rebellions.[81] Eregu ultimately left Uganda in May 1992 and was killed later that year in Kenya.[82] Residual violence persisted in the Teso region, but it had much more to do with local score settling than with organized rebellion, and many fighters continued to surrender.[83]

In sum, the case of the UPA is similar to that of the UPDA as the rebellion contained both disenfranchised political elites and members of the Ugandan state's security apparatus, which provided a modicum of operational cohesion and a path to incorporation into the NRA regime. Although the group's two factions often worked at cross-purposes, its operational core survived pressures to fragment because of distinct endowments transplanted from the Special Forces, augmented by a state-established militia. Facing a strategically superior military adversary, the UPA's political embeddedness nevertheless prompted the incumbent NRA to extend to the group the opportunity for a political settlement that absorbed the bulk of the rebellion and stabilized the region.[84]

Divergent Rebel Fates in West Nile

Consider the historical institutional position of Uganda's West Nile. A visit shows a region that is arguably more culturally and economically linked to the Democratic Republic of Congo and Sudan and quite peripheral to Ugandan politics.[85] It is also the former home region of Idi Amin. As ruler of Uganda in the 1970s, Amin expanded access to state privilege for people from the West Nile, who had historically been on the periphery of the country's political and military hierarchy and who had systematically been excluded from educational opportunities.[86] With Amin in power, the Ugandan military now became the primary mode of advancement for West Nile men. Mazrui describes this ascension as a "military ethnocracy," consisting of a "lumpen militariat"— semiorganized and semiliterate soldiers who claimed a share of power and influence in an otherwise privileged meritocracy of the educated.[87] The military, however, also became the central organ of government and the primary instrument of Amin's personal authority. His Special Research Bureau and Public Safety Unit was the coercive apparatus that towered over all aspects of Ugandan politics. It violently purged rivals, both real and perceived, particularly targeting Obote loyalists, which upended Acholi and Langi domination of the armed forces.

Omara-Otunnu observed that throughout the 1970s, Amin's "promotion and liquidation of officers on the basis of language and ethnic affiliation gave the army hierarchy a distinctive ethnic composition."[88] By 1977, the number of commissioned officers in the army leaped from 300 to 855. By 1978, 68 percent of these officers came from West Nile.[89] Amin's retinue consisted almost exclusively of his Sudanic-speaking Muslim kinsmen such as the Lugbara. His own Kakwa group composed more than half of West Nile recruits and was the largest of any group of soldiers in Uganda, which also included non-Ugandan Kakwa from Sudan and Zaire.[90] The elevation of Muslim Kakwa officials such as Amin's chief of staff, Colonel Mustafa Adrisi, narrowed his regime's patronage at the expense of other West Nilers.[91] Following Amin's dramatic expulsion of Asians from Uganda, economic spoils were divided largely among his co-ethnics, as the West Nile region itself saw little development. As non-Kakwa watched Amin become more and more dysfunctional and paranoid, their resentment began to coalesce around a West Nile opposition within an increasingly weakening regime.[92]

As discussed earlier, Uganda's 1978–1979 war with Tanzania led to Amin's overthrow and the reinstallation of Milton Obote. The Tanzanian army pacified the West Nile region with little violence against civilians, and northern Acholi and Langi soon repopulated the national army, now called the Uganda National Liberation Army. This reconstituted force exacted reprisals on any and all West Nile soldiers and civilians, culminating in the Ombachi Massacre of 1981.[93] As a result of such violence, nearly half the West Nile population became refugees in southern Sudan and eastern Zaire. During this time, many former soldiers became impoverished and dependent on international aid and sporadic handouts from the Sudanese government.[94] Within the austere environment of refugee camps, two fresh rebellions emerged from the ruins of Amin's former army to fight the UNLA: the Former Uganda National Army and the Uganda National Rescue Front. Although their status hierarchy grievances against northern military and political elites were well established, ethnic and religious divisions that had festered during the Amin regime now manifested as violent cleavages between the two rebel groups. For the first half of the 1980s, FUNA and the UNRF squared off against one another nearly as often as they fought their shared adversary, the UNLA.[95]

Facing heavy military pressure, the two groups continued to factionalize along ethnic lines.[96] FUNA—led by Amin strongman Isaac

Lamongo and composed of ethnic Kakwa and Madi—dissolved into Sudan and Congo. The UNRF, composed of ethnic Aringa and led by Moses Ali and Amin Onzi, met a different fate. While the NRA was still beginning its bush war in 1981, Ali met with Museveni in Tripoli, where they both reached a power-sharing agreement in anticipation of an NRA victory. This accord was in fact honored in 1986, and since the NRA has been in power, Ali has been granted successive cabinet and prime ministerial posts.[97]

But there were to be downstream consequences of the FUNA-UNLA schism and Ali's choice to align with Museveni. By 1986, the ascendancy of the NRA regime soon consolidated two sets of West Nile ex-officials: those who languished in Sudan and those who regained access to state institutions in Kampala. These divergent groups eventually coalesced around the two rebellions of the 1990s, the West Nile Bank Front and the Uganda National Rescue Front II.

This pair of cases presents a compelling comparison that challenges the central claim of this book—that political embeddedness necessarily confers organizational cohesion and status. These cases suggest that time and regime change can shape the positionality of a rebellion within political society and its status vis-à-vis new incumbents. They also raise important questions about the effect of external actors on the organizational autonomy of rebel groups (discussed in Chapter 6). Yet, upon examination, the respective political embeddedness of both the WNBF and the UNRF II is still salient in the sense that the organizational anatomy of each group closely followed the contours of regime politics of Idi Amin. As these politics were largely fragmented and contentious, they created organizational dynamics that carried over to the formation of new rebellions in West Nile, and subsequently shaped their corresponding fates.

The West Nile Bank Front (WNBF)

Understanding the fate of the WNBF begins by examining its historical institutional origins, particularly in that its organization was a plain reflection of the Amin regime of the 1970s. Recall that although the UNRF had entered into an agreement with the NRA that incorporated it into the new regime, remnants of the disintegrated FUNA had scattered into southern Sudan and had more or less vanished. Every now and then during the late 1980s, ex-FUNA fighters would skirmish with the UPDA and other groups, even occasionally joining them. The men of Amin's former army weathered several more years in southern Sudan, impoverished and aging, until they found a new leader. Former Amin official

Juma Oris had held the posts of minister of lands, information, and then foreign affairs until Amin removed him in 1978.[98] Following his ouster, Oris spent several years living in southern Sudan. Working as an itinerant mercenary for the Sudanese military, he became alienated from those in Amin's immediate retinue, and from Ugandan politics more generally. But by the early 1990s, the Sudanese regime in Khartoum was facing its own set of challenges from the SPLA and sought additional muscle to counter its operations. Members of the Sudanese military made a calculation that Ugandan rebels (which included the UNRF II, the ADF, and the LRA) would serve as suitable proxies that could both fight the SPLA and destabilize Uganda. Thus, they gathered those former junior officers from Amin's army adrift in southern Sudan and placed Oris at their organizational center. By 1993, the WNBF was born, based in the Sudanese towns of Morobo, Kaya, and Dudulabe.

Oris was the WNBF's titular leader, but he shared command with the group's main political commissar, Zubairi Atamvaku, who had been a former Constituent Assembly delegate from Arua District and who resigned in protest over the NRA allowing the SPLA to operate in West Nile District.[99] Surrounding the two men were cadres also from Amin-era politics. Lieutenant Colonel Abdallatif Tiyoa, the WNBF's deputy commander, was trained in Pakistan and served under Amin as brigade commander in Mbale, only to be imprisoned for seven years after the regime's fall. Released by Okello, he worked as a petty trader in Sudan and joined Oris in the hope of being reinstated as an officer in Uganda's military.[100] Joining him was Lieutenant Colonel Samuel Athocon,[101] who had served as the chief engineer for the Uganda Air Force under Amin, and then as the managing director of the *Uganda Times*. Disillusioned by the NRA, he did several stints in the UPDA, the HSMF, and the NOA before helping form the stillborn National Democratic Front (NDF) with other ex-Amin officers to expel Museveni.[102] To expand its ranks of fighters, the WNBF recruited hundreds of disenfranchised, unemployed youth from West Nile District. Unskilled and uneducated as a result of years spent as refugees, many were lured by the promise of $300 each.[103]

These former insiders, however, did not confer the expected level of cohesion upon the group that one might associate with having institutional proximity to Ugandan politics. Aside from their shared experience in Amin's regime and as ex-army refugees, there is little evidence that Oris or his cadres shared a political network before or even during their period of rebellion. Oris himself was not particularly popular with cadres or the rank and file. He seemed to have no close personal relationships and clashed often with his commanders. Tiyoa complained of "poor administration," and Athocon argued that Oris saw the WNBF as his "property."[104] Atamvaku was not a military man, but he demonstrated organizational savvy that won him popularity with new fighters but contempt from the older soldiers.[105] He observed that 80 percent of recruits received only two to three weeks of training and were given unwarranted promotions as officers without any previous experience, presumably to shore up Oris's low popularity.[106]

Despite these organizational obstacles, up to 2,500 WNBF fighters were ready to fight by late 1994. In mid-1995, they launched attacks into Arua and Koboko Districts across the Kaya River from the Sudanese border.[107] WNBF operations initially focused on laying land mines and obtaining food and recruits, but their indiscriminate shelling of villages from across the border created massive population displacement.[108]

Meanwhile, the group's stated goals were never clear, oscillating between reinstating Idi Amin to power (despite his clear noninvolvement)[109] and carving out an autonomous West Nile state.[110] Even the rebellion's name, the "West Nile Bank Front" was not by the group's own design, but a branding bestowed by a Ugandan journalist covering their operations.[111] Its originally intended name—the Uganda Army–West Nile Front (UA–WNF)—reflected the main objective of many of its senior members to rejoin the state military because, according to them, the UA was never "officially" disbanded.[112]

The WNBF's rickety organizational foundation was further damaged by the group's resource acquisition strategies, as it received support from Sudan only in exchange for fighting the SPLA.[113] WNBF fighters wore Sudanese uniforms, carried their weapons, and bore material with Arabic inscription.[114] At first, this support provided the WNBF with the capacity to launch hit-and-run attacks into the West Nile from the Sudanese garrison towns of Kaya and Oraba-Miju.[115] In addition, the group was often able to avoid detection by receiving supplies through eastern Zaire.[116] Soon Oris resembled less of a former Ugandan political insider than a middleman for the Khartoum regime, which already had experience in exploiting him.

As mentioned above, the WNBF was one of several Ugandan rebellions that Khartoum supported—but they often competed for this patronage.[117] At times Sudanese officers intervened in the WNBF hierarchy, shuffling its fighters into other groups while some units were disassembled and recombined regularly. For instance, after washing up in Sudanese garrison towns, former fighters from the National Army for the Liberation of Uganda (NALU is discussed later in this chapter) were teamed up with the WNBF.[118] Elsewhere, some 200 UMLA fighters formed the ballast of the WNBF's Tenth "Niran" Battalion, while the UMLA's "Bantu" elements were eventually added to the ADF in eastern Zaire (also see below).[119] By May 1995, the WNBF and LRA were actively pooling resources, even planning and executing operations together. At one point, cooperating with Kony's LRA became one of Sudan's conditions for supporting the WNBF.[120] In one bizarre instance of collaborating with the Zairean authorities, WNBF fighters were sent to help the Zairean army control market towns.[121]

Eventually, tensions mounted between Oris and Khartoum over conflicting strategic priorities and chronic nonpayment of fighters, and by mid-August 1995, Oris was jailed in Juba.[122] His recalcitrance ultimately resulted in his handlers' replacing him. They selected Atamvaku, who became the WNBF's main interlocutor with the Sudanese army[123] and eventually the chief coordinator of all anti-Museveni groups based in southern Sudan.[124] Not unexpectedly, leadership disputes between Oris and Atamvaku broke out, prompting a Sudanese commander to take complete operational command of the WNBF.[125]

The contingent nature of the asymmetrical battlefield soon stressed the WNBF's already divided internal structure. Oris, a member of the Alur group, elevated Amin's Kakwa tribesmen within the rebel hierarchy while ethnic Aringa were systematically denied senior posts and passed over for promotion. The same rifts that had emerged within Amin's army of the 1970s, and again resurfaced between FUNA and the UNRF, persisted between members of the WNBF—Kakwa versus Aringa, Muslim versus non-Muslim. Following the contours of these ethnic and religious cleavages, disagreements flared over the rebellion's purpose. Ethnic Kakwa fighters joined out of loyalty to Amin—many were lured into the WNBF with the promise of his restoration and were dismayed to find he was not involved.[126] Urban Muslim youths collectively called "Tabliqs," which I describe more fully later in the chapter, fought for Islam. The Aringa were motivated by a sense of betrayal. Others wished to see the "foreigner" Museveni ousted.[127]

In terms of the playing field, fighting an asymmetrical conflict against the Ugandan army posed a number of challenges for the WNBF, and the group's chronic thirst for resources exposed it to a range of threats. Despite Sudanese military hardware, fighters remained unpaid and with little food and medicine, requiring nonmilitary incursions into West Nile for basic supplies, and they were compelled to use human runners for lack of proper communications equipment.[128] And like many groups under pressure, the WNBF hemorrhaged fighters regularly.[129] Although there were no formal overtures to offer the WNBF any sort of peace accord, a blanket amnesty for its fighters provided opportunities to join the UPDF, often with maintaining rank.[130] As a result, between mid-1996 and early 1997, the WNBF shed upward of 1,000 fighters through surrenders alone.[131] In a last-ditch attempt to control the border area against incursions by the emergent Banyamulenge rebels of Zaire, Sudanese officers tried to retrain fresh recruits but were unsuccessful in finding any willing fighters.[132]

Meanwhile, the theoretical presumption of former insiders being able to slot into Uganda's political establishment did not materialize for the WNBF. Aside from allowing some fighters to keep their rank as they integrated into the UPDF, in dealing with its leaders, Museveni did not consider their status within Ugandan politics. Instead, the regime in Kampala pursued the WNBF's elimination, deploying the UPDF along-side regional allies—the anti-Mobutu Banyamulenge in Zaire, and the SPLA in Sudan.[133] Any hope of the WNBF rallying the grass roots to their cause was met with hostility, as the war-fatigued traditional authorities of West Nile never discouraged the Ugandan government's approach.[134] In fact, civilian militias from the West Nile region requested arms from the UPDF to help fight the rebels.[135]

In light of its eroded political embeddedness and resource acquisition problems, the WNBF's path to defeat by disintegration did not take long. By March 1997, the SPLA's advance toward Yei in southern Sudan overran an already unraveling WNBF. A carefully laid seven-mile ambush killed up to 2,000 rebels of all Ugandan stripes, including Sudanese and Zairian soldiers. The SPLA also captured the lion's share of what remained of the WNBF's high command and severely wounded Oris.[136] As fighters scattered into Sudan and Zaire, the SPLA and Banya-mulenge seized them and handed them over to the UPDF for treason tri-als.[137] Others surrendered without charge in the months that followed.

In sum, the WNBF's fragmented organizational endowment under-mined its cohesion and ability to fight collectively. Most interesting here is the temporal distance of its leadership from Ugandan state poli-tics, which suggests that as time passes or as regimes change, the bene-fits of political embeddedness diminish. In this case, the historical role of Oris and other WNBF senior commanders in Amin-era politics never guaranteed their entry into the new political establishment, save for those who surrendered without a formal settlement. Instead, the internal divisions of the WNBF, combined with Oris's opportunistic resource strategies, further exposed the group to military threats in the wider sub-region, undermining the rebellion's cohesion even more, until it effec-tively met defeat by disintegration in early 1997.[138]

The Uganda National Rescue Front II (UNRF II)

The UNRF II ("Rescue II") has often been erroneously cast as a splinter faction of the WNBF.[139] Though it arose independently of the WNBF, Rescue II was nevertheless akin to the other West Nile rebellions in that it also reflected Amin-era politics, particularly the schisms within the Amin regime that manifested as open conflict between the Kakwa-dominated FUNA and the Aringa-based UNRF. Unlike the WNBF, however, Rescue II was able to overcome these internal divisions and marshal its historical proximity to regime authority to achieve victory via incorporation.

Recall that in 1981, the UNRF's Moses Ali had entered into an agreement with Museveni with the aim to share in the NRA's post-victory political dispensation.[140] Shorn up by a renewed accord in July 1986, the Joint Military Integration Committee incorporated members of both the NRA and the UNRF, making UNRF leader Moses Ali the deputy prime minister; cadre lieutenant general Amin Onzi became deputy minister of works; and cadre major general John Onah became ambassador to Egypt. In addition, the NRA integrated a battalion of UNRF fighters and decamped the remaining ex-rebels for resettlement at home in the West Nile region.[141] Thus, the NRA effectively appeared to have accommodated a significant group of West Nile elites early in the formation of its regime.

However, the incorporation of the UNRF into the NRA's new regime soon began to break down, as ex-rebels found their access to the political establishment blocked. Many ex-UNRF fighters who had been integrated into the national army discovered they were not allowed to keep their ranks as part of the agreement, and some were even demoted.[142] Many others did not receive the resettlement packages that they were promised. Moses Ali, now comfortably ensconced in a cabinet post, was given 250 million USH (then about $250,000) to distribute to his fighters. Instead, he generously helped himself to these funds.[143] Finally in 1989, the NRA's promise of elections after four years was extended an additional five, which played into a broader perception that the agreement between the UNRF and the NRA was not being honored.[144] As a result, many ex-rebels began to agitate and instigate.

Museveni believed that Ali was behind the West Nilers' protests and had him arrested. He then put in motion a campaign to systematically harass former UNRF members. Many were arrested and detained without trial, in some cases killed extra-judicially. Meanwhile, in the West Nile region, general discontent persisted as the promise of development, political equality, and inclusion was far from being met. Hardship was particularly acute among those who remained in southern Sudan. For this population, ongoing attacks by the SPLA created additional animosity, particularly because of the SPLA's alliance with the NRA.[145]

These factors drove a knot of ex-UNRF, along with a fresh group of ethnic Aringa recruits, to Zaire, where they slowly began to organize. But the inchoate rebellion merely languished there until 1997, when civil war in Zaire pushed the group into southern Sudan, and there it took on the UNRF II name. At its core was ex-UNRF fighter Ali Bamuze, who had also served in the King's African Rifles and the UA. Joining this core were former members of Bamuze's UNRF battalion, which still carried memories of having received particularly harsh treatment by the NRA as they came out of the bush in 1986. Bamuze himself had witnessed the execution of his own battalion commander at the hands of the NRA.

In establishing his cadres, Bamuze invited a number of Aringa functionaries from Uganda's professional classes who had managed to remain embedded within state institutions since 1979. During this time, many Amin-era elites who had survived the NRA were now being targeted by the regime financially, and they sought redress.[146]

Gathered in southern Sudan, Rescue II produced a written charter and an organizational structure that divided the rebellion into military and political wings, the latter having twelve members and a much more dominant role in decisionmaking. With Bamuze as titular leader, under him hierarchically sat the force commander deputy, and beneath him, a division commander oversaw four geographically based brigade commanders who each led roughly 500–600 fighters. Political commissars were attached to each level of military organization. At its peak, the group was 3,000 strong. Each week, Rescue II held what was known as the *baraza*, a meeting to discuss issues, strategies, and roles. Its explicit mandate was to use the rebellion to negotiate back into the state on better terms for themselves and for West Nile as a whole. It appeared that Rescue II had come into rebellion with substantial organizational endowments acquired from and developed within the very same state institutions it now sought to fight.

Like other Ugandan rebellions, Rescue II fought an asymmetrical irregular conflict and was not at parity with the UPDF. Nevertheless, the group's start-up costs were met in part by accessing stockpiled weapons. Most important, Bamuze reengaged Moses Ali's previous ties to an extensive pan-Islamic support network that included Pakistan, Libya, and the Palestinian Liberation Organization (PLO).[147] Entrepreneurial political commissars soon expanded this network to include Saudi Arabia, Turkey, and even the United States and United Kingdom to collect hard currency that was used locally to purchase essential items such as food.[148]

To round out its resource network in a way that made sense geographically, by 1997 Rescue II joined the array of Khartoum-backed rebellions that were already operating out of southern Sudan.[149] Similar to other pan-Islamic linkages, the key connection here was Khartoum regime ideologue Hassan al-Turabi, who had come to wield sizable influence in Sudanese politics, with an additional ambition to make a large regional footprint for political Islam. At this juncture, al-Turabi sought a viable substitute for the WNBF, which had already visibly begun its disintegration. Interestingly, the leadership of the WNBF and Rescue II met on numerous occasions. Yet they never found a way to work together, due to long-standing divisions held over from the Amin period, as WNBF leader Atamvaku refused to work with any ethnic Aringa. In any case, Bamuze was promoted to major general by the Sudanese army, and he participated in meetings in Juba together with the LRA's Joseph Kony and other Ugandan rebels to plan Juba's defense against the SPLA.[150] Rescue II, fulfilling its obligations to its sponsor, fought alongside the Sudanese army against the SPLA, losing up to sixty-five fighters in one battle.

Throughout the 1997–1998 period, Rescue II recruited up to 1,000 Muslim youths for training in Juba.[151] The group launched a series of sporadic attacks into Aringa County from Kajo Keji and Rojo in southern Sudan and set numerous ambushes against the UPDF.[152] Even though such attacks destabilized the region, several factors began to shift that set the group on a path to rapprochement with Kampala. First, recruitment pressures from Khartoum compelled the rebellion to engage in increasingly predatory behavior as it launched raids against civilian targets in Aringa County for supplies and fighters. Given the collective resistance that had developed among West Nile traditional authorities to any armed insurgency, the Ugandan government realized it could capitalize on community-initiated persuasion to bring the rebellion into dialogue.[153] By late 1998, contacts between the UPDF and UNRF II began via the Aringa-Obongi Peace Initiative Committee (AROPIC), whose leaders acted as mediators.

By 1999, Rescue II's resource linkages to Sudan were upended as Sudanese president Omar al Bashir imprisoned al-Turabi, and the rebellion's sanctuary in southern Sudan became increasingly tenuous. Moreover, Sudan was now drawing increased international attention on account of the embassy bombings in East Africa carried out by al-Qaeda. Demonstrated linkages between Khartoum and Osama bin Laden compelled Bamuze to back away from Sudanese sponsorship, particularly to avoid any entanglements in the Bashir-Turabi rift.[154] Finally, the 1999 Nairobi agreement between Uganda and Sudan temporarily suspended Khartoum's overt support for any of Uganda's rebel groups.

Under these circumstances, with a severely undercut resource base acting as a push factor and AROPIC's community-based overture a pull factor, a series of confidence-building measures began with a small group of political commissars quietly housed in the Ministry of Internal Affairs.[155] Negotiations unfolded slowly over two years, after which Bamuze began to test the sincerity of the Ugandan government by releasing combatants into UPDF custody, and they were received in good faith and unharmed.[156] This was the first in a series of surrenders that eventually left only 400 fighters divided into three battalions based in Rojo.[157] Soon, the rebellion formally sued for peace. Face-to-face meetings with Museveni produced the broad contours of a peace agreement.[158] The two sides agreed to a cease-fire on 15 June 2002, which paved the way for formal talks that the UNRF II attended with a detailed agenda.[159]

The Peace Agreement Between the Government of Republic of Uganda and the Uganda National Rescue Front II was signed on 22 December 2002 in the West Nile town of Yumbe, which soon after became its own administrative district.[160] The agreement's articles provided for formal cessation of hostilities; the dissolution, demobilization, reintegration, and resettlement of combatants; and the integration of rebel officers into the UPDF. It also contained broad provisions that committed more development initiatives for the West Nile. Bamuze was named a general in the UPDF, where he oversaw ex-combatants' affairs until his death in 2015.[161]

To recap: The political embeddedness of the UNRF II's leaders and cadres was well established in advance of its rebellion, which conferred upon it sufficient levels of internal cohesion and ties to regime politics. Well into its conflict with the Ugandan government, the group experienced an interruption in its resource base rooted in regional geopolitical shifts, and soon its trajectory unfolded in a way that increased its likelihood of victory incorporation. Although they are differently tempered by time and regime change, the two divergent cases of rebellion in West Nile illustrate varying configurations of political embeddedness that correspond fairly well to the predictions made by the framework presented in this study. Although both were Sudan's proxies, Rescue II differs starkly from the WNBF in that its members had been part of a pre-existing mode of political accommodation. Rescue II thus maintained a sort of continuity of political embeddedness that its members had cultivated in spite of their grievances against Museveni. In contrast, the WNBF was one regime removed from domestic state politics, with its amalgam of former Amin officials unable to shepherd a rebellion toward any variant of victory.

Outsiders and Outliers

Uganda has also had its share of outsider rebellions that have experienced variants of defeat. This section examines in detail the bizarre case of the Allied Democratic Front (ADF), which was initially a composite of three smaller, shorter-lived rebellions that preceded it but then metastasized into what is now a transnational phenomenon that defies a precise characterization in line with this study's theoretical framework. By this measure, until 2007 the ADF very much resembled a classic outsider rebellion. Based in the Democratic Republic of Congo and supported by the Sudanese government, the ADF violently flailed around the borderlands of Uganda and DRC until it disintegrated following a bush war against a regime unwilling to extend any form of political accommodation. Yet after a lull in operations, the ADF became a significant player in the more complicated conflict environment of eastern DRC. What makes the ADF an outlier now is that its resurgence may mark a shift to a different kind of armed group entirely, one that is simultaneously embedded in a social base and transnational in nature, able to persist far outside the purview of state institutions. In what follows, I trace the development of the ADF through three phases. First, I examine three groups that were eliminated by the Ugandan army—the National Democratic Army (NDA), the Uganda Muslim Liberation Army (UMLA), and the National Army for the Liberation of Uganda (NALU). I then look at the ADF's formation and its operations throughout the late 1990s until it fled Uganda and disintegrated in eastern DRC. Finally, I consider the ADF's resurgence as a contemporary Congolese phenomenon.

The National Democratic Army (NDA)

The NDA was one of Uganda's lesser-known rebellions of the 1990s, emerging from the Mpigi and Mukono regions of the country. The group comprised a small crop of disparate, low-ranking NRA deserters disgruntled from their experiences during the NRA's bush war.[162] The NDA was also tangentially associated with a broader movement that sought greater political decentralization in Uganda but did not get much traction.[163] Indeed, the group's rhetoric reflected these strands and played into local political rivalries,[164] although its primary goal was to negotiate higher ranks in the army.

At the center of the NDA was an outsider named Herbert Kikomeko Ssedyabanne, also known by his nom de guerre, Itongwa.[165] He had deserted the NRA in November 1994 after a checkered history in the Army General Headquarters.[166] Known as a good fighter, he was nevertheless a politically illiterate, marijuana-smoking loner, whose lack of formal education limited his advancement within the NRA. He soon turned to the urban "Bwaise crowd" gang culture after several stints in military prison, and this was the foundation upon which he built the NDA.[167] Itongwa was able to recruit a small following of 400–700 men, many of whom were similarly disenfranchised NRA fighters who had few linkages to one another before joining Itongwa in the training camps he had set up deep in Luwero.

The NDA began low-level operations in February 1995 by attacking police stations, with the perpetrators wearing NRA uniforms.[168] To recruit more fighters, the NDA conducted a series of prison breaks. But rather than raise its profile as a legitimate rebellion, such moves cast the group as criminals, a characterization that deepened as fighters raided villages to acquire basic resources.[169]

Giving the NDA no quarter, Museveni pursued a strategy of elimination and called for Itongwa's death.[170] His criminal label hardened with the murder of Masaka police boss Eris Karakire, which put a 5 million USH bounty (about $5,000) on Itongwa's head.[171] The tipping point, however, was the kidnapping of the Minister of Health, James Makumbi, in April 1995.[172] Although Makumbi was eventually freed, Museveni rejected Itongwa's request for a settlement[173] and stepped up efforts to eliminate the entire NDA.[174]

So began the NDA's rapid path to defeat elimination. In a last-ditch effort to survive, Itongwa clumsily joined forces with another small group, the Federal Democratic Movement (FEDEMO), which slightly bolstered numbers and added a veneer of authority to his blustery public resolve.[175] But the ad hoc alliance between Itongwa and FEDEMO leader Mpiso quickly broke down over leadership issues.[176] Meanwhile, Itongwa's top deputies, when not on the run or in hiding, were found and abruptly killed or captured, or they surrendered. Seeing the proverbial writing on the wall, the NDA's second in command, Lieutenant Kikanya, turned himself in as the group's remaining fighters scattered.[177] Of the group's fifteen founding members, only Itongwa remained in the NDA, hiding in the Kampala suburbs, then fleeing to

Kenya until his arrest in early 1996.[178] Following a protracted extradition wrangle, he was repatriated and imprisoned.[179]

In sum, as briefly shown above, the NDA was a politically nonembedded rebellion that fought an asymmetrical irregular war against the NRA regime. The group's associated lack of organizational cohesion and its low status vis-à-vis the regime in Kampala, accelerated by chronic resource constraints, led to the rebellion's rapid defeat by elimination.

The Uganda Muslim Liberation Army (UMLA)

Another unfamiliar rebellion that emerged in 1995 was the Uganda Muslim Liberation Army.[180] Known by several names, such as the Hoima or Buseruka rebels, the label that best captured their place within Ugandan political society was the pejorative "Tabliqs." This referred to the Tabliq Youth Movement, a group of radicalized urban Muslims that claimed to represent Uganda's disparate Muslim population, which had occupied a disadvantaged position within Uganda since the colonial period.[181]

The UMLA's main grievance was based upon its historical claim that the NRA had killed a number of Muslims during its bush campaign against the government in the early 1980s.[182] The group also claimed that the NRA had later imprisoned several Tabliqs who clashed with their chief political rival, the Uganda Muslim Supreme Council, over control of a Kampala mosque.[183] Among those imprisoned was Jamil Mukulu, who would play a pivotal role in the formation of the ADF once he was released in 1993.

It is clear that the UMLA held no firm linkages to Ugandan politics, but there are conflicting accounts regarding its initial leadership. One disputed view holds that after serving two years, an imprisoned Tabliq named Sheikh Sulaiman Kakeeto established a base near the west-central town of Hoima with Sudanese support, yet little is known about how this external linkage was established.[184] Another version claims that in 1992, three young Tabliqs—Abbey Lubinga, Ibrahim Kisaalita, and Abdul Karim Seruwagi—set up a base camp in Hoima. This fledgling rebellion, apparently called the Liberation Tigers of Uganda, struggled for several years to get off the ground, hampered by resource scarcity and by Seruwagi's arrest.[185] The story holds that at one point, two sympathetic NRA deserters, Captain Ali Kyamanywa and Captain Ali Faisal, joined the Tabliqs in Hoima, supplying a few weapons and some uniforms. Either way, the UMLA seemed to be an amalgam of random discontented outsiders, and it remained inactive until February 1995, when 100 rebels launched a highly publicized raid of the Buseruka police station.[186] Strangely, the group's operation coincided with an unrelated attack on the palace of a local notable, King Iguru. Likely a local political dispute, the unidentified attackers left a note in Arabic saying they would "come again."[187]

In pursuit of the group's elimination, the Ugandan government's military response was swift and decisive. Surprise attacks on the UMLA base in Kayera, about twenty-seven miles from Hoima, killed as many as ninety-two rebels over several days.[188] Interestingly, French and Kinyarwanda-speaking fighters were found among those captured, which suggests that recruitment into the UMLA extended outside of Uganda, adding to the disparate nature of the group.[189] Most of those captured, however, were Tabliqs who carried pamphlets written in Arabic,[190] hinting that the UMLA may have had preliminary connections to Sudan, which had during that period begun setting up rear bases for Ugandan rebels on Zairean soil.[191] By this stage, however, these connections were tenuous at best and did not yet translate into hard support.

As I have explained here, the UMLA's underdeveloped organization of outsiders, its low political status, and its resource constraints meant it could not withstand the UPDF's rigorous pursuit. Like the NDA, the UMLA's lack of political embeddedness meant weak organizational bonds between leaders and cadres and no opportunity for accommodation with the NRA regime. Against the backdrop of a quick asymmetrical war, the group was defeated and eliminated.

The National Army for the Liberation of Uganda (NALU)

Understanding the National Army for the Liberation of Uganda requires a brief overview of its deeper historical roots. In the 1950s, western Uganda experienced the Ruwenzururu rebellion, a revolt of the Tooro kingdom's ethnic Bakonjo and Baamba against the British colonial administration.[192] Even after Uganda's independence, the group continued to reject the central government in Kampala. The Ruwenzururu sought to establish its own kingdom, one that would erase colonial boundaries and effectively merge Uganda's ethnic Bakonjo and Congo's ethnic Bananda.[193] In 1982, the rebellion ended when the movement's political leader, Charles Wisely Iremangoma, surrendered to Obote's government and paved the way for a political settlement.[194] The chief broker of this accord was a man named Amon Bazira, who came from the Rwenzori region and served as Obote's deputy minister of land, mineral and water resources.[195] However, following Obote's ouster in 1985, Bazira jumped bail on a murder charge and fled to Zaire, where he attempted to re-galvanize rebellion in the region by tapping into unresolved regional grievances.[196]

Although Bazira had some political background as an insider, he was unable to marshal forward any identifiable cadres from Uganda's political establishment, even though the Okellos' coup in 1985 ejected many fellow elites. At the same time, he faced problems recruiting people from his own home region, as the Rwenzururu kingdom had supported the NRA's bush war and was sympathetic to Museveni's new regime. Instead, Bazira turned to a former Rwenzururu commander, Richard Kinyamusitu, and a small crop of disenfranchised veterans who had been sidelined in the 1982 negotiations,[197] or not sufficiently compensated by the NRA.[198] The inchoate group was also able to attract Zairian Mai Mai fighters from the border town of Kasindi and a small group of veterans from Zaire's Simba rebellion of 1964.[199]

Based in the Zairean towns of Beni and Lubero, NALU launched its rebellion in August 1989, abducting officials, burning villages, and killing over 100 people.[200] In response to NALU operations, the NRA pursued the group's elimination in earnest, hunting them in the border region between Uganda and Zaire.[201] Above all, Museveni refused to grant Bazira amnesty, even though he was a former state official.[202]

From the outset, NALU suffered from cohesion problems associated with its meager prewar organizational endowments, and schisms appeared almost immediately.[203] Those loyal to Kinyamusitu broke away from the mainstream faction allied to Bazira, who had begun to recruit hired muscle in the absence of any preexisting political network of potential cadres.[204] Infighting escalated and NALU started shedding fighters,[205] and soon two experienced commanders defected to the NRA.[206] In a strange reversal, at one point a handful of stray government soldiers joined NALU but then rapidly absconded once they discovered the group had scarce resources and such a shambolic high command.[207]

The arrival of veteran commander Christopher Ngaimoko gave a short boost to rebel operations,[208] but it also gave way to more infighting that led to his death in Zaire.[209] Ongoing military pressure eliminated other commanders and forced surrenders until at one point, NALU possessed more weapons than fighters.[210] Even with this surplus, fighters continued to desert in response to poor living conditions and the ongoing hardships of fighting against a merciless foe.

In terms of NALU's resource base, early support, or at least initial promises of assistance, came from Presidents Mobutu of Zaire and Moi of Kenya.[211] At times Zairean military and Cameroonian Special Forces were spotted among NALU's ranks.[212] Yet it is unclear how much external support actually materialized. As a result, Bazira was in a constant search for resources and was soon forced into a series of shady deals with a set of new actors.[213] He became involved in the trafficking of counterfeit currency and was a middleman between the governor of Zaire's gold-rich Katanga Province and a group of Kenyan politicians.[214]

NALU met its defeat once Bazira's overreach exposed him to unanticipated threats. In August 1993, he was found dead fifty miles outside Nairobi.[215] It remains unclear whether his death was the result of an NRA sting operation or the fallout of an unpleasant meeting with the pro-Obote Ninth of October Army.[216] Either way, NALU was now leaderless and fragmented, resource-scarce and stranded in the bush. Already factionalized, the rebellion rapidly folded under ongoing UPDF pressure, and its paltry remnants retreated into Zaire.[217]

NALU represents somewhat of an outlier in the sense that Bazira failed to transform his role as a former political insider into the power resources needed for organizational cohesion. He also failed to project the political status required to reenter Ugandan politics. In fact, it remains unclear why Museveni refused to do business with Bazira, which is particularly interesting, given the history of the Rwenzori region and the previous accommodations made to the Ruwenzururu, especially considering Bazira was the chief broker. NALU's story becomes even more compelling when folded into the case of the ADF, to which I now turn.

The Allied Democratic Front (ADF)

Since 1995, there have essentially been two Allied Democratic Fronts: one Ugandan, the other Congolese. Each ADF iteration has shared an organizational anatomy of political outsiders, with both groups unable to marshal rebellion toward penetrating the prevailing institutional order of either Uganda or DRC. In addition, both versions of the ADF converge geographically, having occupied the porous and lightly governed border region between the two countries, thus sharing a regional genealogy of rebellion that runs from the colonial era, through the Ruwenzururu and NALU, to the present.

Where they diverge, however, raises fresh questions about some of the core assumptions that predict the fates of rebels. To be sure, the story of the first iteration of the ADF follows the contours of the argument here—that it was an amalgam of anti-Museveni groups that disintegrated as the ADF fought a highly unsympathetic regime that consistently pursued a strategy of elimination against it. The second iteration, however, serves as somewhat of an outlier that is only partially captured by a theory of political embeddedness. Although the first ADF met defeat via disintegration in 2001, it was not *fully* vanquished, limping away and reconstituting itself as a new borderland entity in the years that followed. This outcome—*rebel resurrection*—sits outside the range of fates considered in this book's framework but is nevertheless an important one to consider. On the other hand, key elements of continuity between the two ADFs, particularly its leadership and ongoing recruitment networks, suggest *persistence* as an alternative conceptualization of the ADF's overall trajectory. This matter of rebel persistence is discussed in more detail in Chapter 6.

Either way, the ADF's current incarnation can be considered an outlier because it remains far outside the conception of political embeddedness articulated here. To be sure, as I will show, the new ADF's positionality vis-à-vis state politics may very well still explain its shortage of opportunities to bargain and settle with both Ugandan and Congolese governments. Yet the group has taken on fundamental transnational character, perhaps possessing an alternative mode of embeddedness within the socioeconomic milieu of a lightly governed border region rather than within the context of state institutions and regime politics.

To begin to understand the ADF, it is important to examine its organizational foundations located within the stories of the previous three rebellions considered in this section. The modal fate of the NDA, UMLA, and NALU was defeat by elimination, yet some of their surviving fighters nevertheless went on to constitute the core of the Allied Democratic Front. The ADF emerged at the confluence of these defeated remnants and the overarching regional security alliance of Sudan and Zaire against Uganda.[218] Understanding the organizational roots of the ADF and the nature of its formation does much to explain its subsequent trajectory. This begins with a brief examination of the surviving members of the NDA, UMLA, and NALU, those not killed or captured by the UPDF as their rebellions were eliminated.

As these dispossessed fighters washed up in the borderlands of Sudan and Zaire, many came into contact with the Sudanese Army Security Service.[219] Consider first ex-NALU fighters. Following Bazira's death, they spent months attempting to regroup under Amos Kambere, a former Obote member of parliament for the Rwenzori region, who had resettled in Canada.[220] Yet even under new leadership, NALU forces remained broken and derelict in eastern Zaire. By 1995, NALU's official surrender had signaled the formal end of the rebellion.[221] Some fighters joined the Interhamwe in Zaire,[222] while others made their way to Sudan and joined the WNBF, which had already been receiving support from Sudan.[223] At this juncture, a key ex-NALU commander, Ngaimoko, came into contact with survivors of the UMLA who had reached Zaire following the group's defeat, among them the Tabliq commander Yusuf Kabanda.[224] Around the same time, Jamil Mukulu began to reassert leadership over the remaining Tabliqs and resumed recruitment of militarized Muslims to bring them closer to the resource orbit of Khartoum.[225] Finally, it is important to note that shortly before the NDA's elimination, Itongwa had approached NALU to seek an alliance. He attended an organizational meeting in Kasindi, Zaire, and thus made contact with a wider external network.[226] Although Itongwa's subsequent arrest would deprive him of a role in any future cooperation, these connections with NALU opened a path for many of his fighters after the NDA's defeat.

This amalgam of fighters fit neatly into anti-Museveni recruitment and resource networks that had been steadily developing in the wider region. Although the Zairean government did not have the where-withal to support a new rebellion, it could provide territorial sanctuary so long as the Sudanese government provided resources for fighting. In joining together former NALU, UMLA, and NDA fighters, along with the pliable scraps from the WNBF and other anti-Museveni groups, the incumbent regimes in Zaire and Sudan now had a fresh proxy with several advantages. The ability to operate out of eastern Zaire opened up a new southwestern front against Uganda. Also, many ex-NALU fighters had knowledge of the region's difficult and mountainous ter-rain and were able to reestablish former bush camps. In addition, ex-UMLA fighters had developed key pan-Islamic linkages to Sudanese backers who had begun to cultivate ties with the Tabliq Youth Move-ment. And ex-NDA fighters added some extra muscle.[227] Finally, a radical group of London-based Bagandan neomonarchists, the Allied Democratic Movement, provided some political support and the basis for the new rebellion's name.[228]

There is little doubt that any ADF operations would not have been possible without the active involvement of outside interests. In 1995, the group incubated its organization in Zaire, with Khartoum providing the lion's share of training, coordination, and resources.[229] Observers made numerous sightings of "Arab" trainers in their main operational base in the town of Beni.[230] In addition, the ADF established a rear base in Mobutu's hometown of Gbadolite, where it received deliveries of weapons and supplies. Also in Gbadolite, the Zairean army allowed ADF fighters to join in the mining of gold and other minerals.[231] Building off the criminal enterprises cultivated by Bazira during the NALU rebellion, Zairean officers also colluded in the trafficking of stolen vehicles and counterfeit currency to help finance ADF operations.[232] Foreign fighters occasionally fought alongside the ADF during their operations. For instance, in June 1997, fighters from the Zairean army, WNBF, Interhamwe, and a Burundian rebel group [233] reinforced the ADF's brief occupation of the town of Bundibugyo in order to acquire supplies.[234]

On 13 November 1996, the ADF launched its first operations in the Kasese region, attacking from the border towns of Mpondure and Karambi. A typical operation would involve a targeted raid, followed by heavy losses of rebel fighters, and a subsequent retreat into the mountainous borderlands. Yet taken together, ongoing ADF attacks in the late 1990s killed up to 1,000 civilians and displaced upward of 175,000.[235] By mid-1998, the ADF was at its zenith, conducting coordinated bomb attacks at two popular restaurants in Kampala[236] and launching a brutal attack on the Kichwamba National Technical Institute, in which it killed up to fifty people and abducted at least 100 more.[237]

As the ADF developed, however, it became clear that it had no discernible agenda, was a confusing jumble of leadership, and was fond of issuing competing claims from different parts of its membership. Scattered factions broadcast a range of vague demands through the press. For instance, the group's Tabliq column claimed to fight for Islamic rule in Uganda.[238] Some statements demanded the removal of Museveni from power because he was a "Rwandan Tutsi," while others called for the restoration of multiparty politics or released nebulous calls for a "friendly atmosphere of brotherhood with all our neighbors."[239] Attacks became less and less coordinated and increasingly targeted civilians,[240] with competing NALU, Tabliq, and NDA factions each claiming responsibility for them.[241]

The ADF thus faced serious problems of organization and leadership. The demand for independent recognition indicated a low level of cohesion within the ADF, and outright infighting between the Bakonjo NALU faction and the "original" ADF Tabliqs drove a harder wedge between the rebellion's disparate elements.[242] Above all, the ADF leadership was uncertain. The vicissitudes of battlefield failures unearthed a confusing array of characters, with no single leader, no tangible ranks assigned to fighters, or any discernible hierarchy.[243] Although some commanders such as Ngaimoko, Kabanda, and Kisokeranio were identifiable as members of previous rebellions, their names went unrecognized in the broader context of Ugandan politics, even as they each claimed the mantle of ADF leadership.[244]

The ADF's disconnected organizational endowment was a good predictor of its patchy operations in southwestern Uganda. It also illuminated the group's collective distance from Ugandan politics and the correspondingly low threat it posed to the regime in Kampala. To be sure, the ADF's NALU elements suggested a diluted association with the region's history and politics. Yet for many people living in southwestern Uganda, the group was largely viewed as an alien force with few local social connections, let alone any linkages to a broader political establishment.[245]

Above all, the ADF's politically disembedded organizational foundation meant it faced few prospects for negotiation. As a consequence, Museveni pursued a heavy-handed operation to eliminate the group.[246] Although the Ugandan government required no justification for this strategy, once Jamil Mukulu emerged as the ADF's titular leader in 1996, it exposed the rebellion to accusations of having transnational linkages to al-Qaeda. And once the ADF appeared on the US Terrorist Exclusion List after 9/11,[247] this foreclosed all possibilities for any accommodation with the rebellion. Instead, Uganda's army consistently targeted and killed ADF commanders and seized their weapons.[248] During the late 1990s, pitched battles between the UPDF and the ADF kept the group confined to the border regions.[249] Ultimately, Operation Mountain Sweep in 1999 drove the ADF into Congo, where it effectively disintegrated over the course of several years.[250] Even so, during these years sporadic ADF activity was occasionally detected, but not enough to constitute a legitimate threat to the Ugandan state, and the rebellion was declared defeated in 2007.[251]

The ADF Reborn

To repeat, the ADF has not operated within Uganda's borders since 2007. Instead, it has since become a Congolese phenomenon, albeit with some ongoing apolitical Ugandan ties. Often described as a "lost" rebellion, the ADF has demonstrated a remarkable ability to adapt to the borderlands between Uganda and the DRC and to cope with the military operations of the Congolese armed forces and UN peacekeepers. Its organizational structure has integrated into the socioeconomic milieu of the Rwenzori region, giving the insurgency a distinct resilience and a transborder identity that does not slot into any discrete measure of political embeddedness. Although it lost external state sponsorship long ago, the group maintains recruitment and resource linkages through Uganda and across the wider East African subregion. It has been deemed a "foreign" armed group by the UN Group of Experts on the Democratic

Republic of the Congo. For these reasons, ADF is still considered an outsider rebellion within the context of this study's framework.

To begin, an examination of the ADF's activities since leaving Uganda is in order. In the aftermath of Operation Mountain Sweep, the ADF was all but a spent force, and by 2001, its remaining 200 fighters had limped into the DRC. It was during this period that the fragments of the rebellion began a lengthy process of recombining and reorganizing. The key move was to gradually diffuse itself into the socioeconomic fabric of Congo's mountainous borderlands, enabled to a large extent by individuals' historical linkages to NALU, and the ADF's intimate knowledge of its former bases in the region.[252]

During this period as the group began to rebuild, it became one of many dangerous players operating in various and shifting combinations as part of a high-stakes regional conflict.[253] By 2005, the ADF had become formally recognized as a security threat in eastern Congo, particularly following the failure of the Uganda Amnesty Commission to demobilize (its mostly Congolese) ADF fighters through its office in Beni. And though individual fighters were always able to receive amnesty from the Ugandan government, there were no opportunities for any ADF leaders to enter Uganda's political establishment via bargaining and negotiation. Instead, alongside the tepid offer of amnesty always stood the modal response of seeking to eliminate any ADF fighter who crossed into Ugandan territory.

The Armed Forces of the Democratic Republic of Congo (FARDC) and the UN peacekeeping operation in Congo (MONUSCO) have conducted a series of joint military operations to eliminate a resurgent ADF. Launched in December 2005, Operation North Night Final was mildly successful, upending ADF camps, killing at least ninety fighters, and driving the remaining rebels deeper into the bush.[254] Those ADF fighters able to cross into Uganda were repulsed or killed by the UPDF until permanently blocked in 2007. Although the ADF pushed for negotiations with MONUSCO[255] and the Ugandan government[256] during this period, nothing beyond the surrender of several fighters materialized.

After lying low for some time, by 2010 an emboldened ADF launched fresh attacks, sometimes directly against MONUSCO and FARDC deployments. Such affronts prompted a pair of anti-ADF operations—Rwenzori and Radi Strike. Neither was particularly effective in eliminating the group, instead generating upward of 100,000 internally displaced in DRC's North Kivu Province. In the years that followed, the ADF again regrouped and grew in number to around 2,500 fighters, who appeared better trained, better equipped, and bolder than before. In January 2014, FARDC launched Operation Sukola directly at the ADF's stronghold of Beni, which scattered fighters and significantly weakened the group but did not entirely vanquish it.

From these accounts emerges a discernible pattern in the dynamics of the second iteration of the ADF and the way it fits into the region's broader conflict. The first part of the pattern is the ADF's ongoing operations that most often involve violence against civilians. These events prompt FARDC and MONUSCO counteroperations that are more or less successful in upending the ADF's main bush camps and in eliminating chunks of its fighters. These moves are then followed by the rebellion miraculously regrouping and resuming its activities. The ADF then exacts reprisals against civilians thought to have collaborated with FARDC and MONUSCO, thus reactivating the pattern.

What has made the ADF so resilient? To be sure, it has maintained the ability to operate in borderlands where there is little penetration of state institutions. Here the group has enjoyed high levels of local integration into a "borderland identity"[257] and has also taken on a distinct regional mobility. Together these factors have facilitated recruitment of fighters and the acquisition of resources through commercial and ideological networks that have remained remarkably intact.

Organizationally, the ADF has maintained a simple but flexible structure, able to break apart and reconstitute itself against the vicissitudes of regional insecurity and military pressure. Historically, it has always been a highly secretive group tightly centralized around the "supreme command" of Jamil Mukulu, who has controlled the ADF's strategic direction and its financial networks since the 1990s. Having up to twenty-seven aliases and multiple passports, Mukulu has been able to travel among ADF bases, regional capitals, and elsewhere in search of resources.[258] Around Mukulu are a range of Ugandan and Congolese cadres with a variety of roles. For instance, David Lukwago (aka Hook, Ashraf, Rashid) has acted as the group's operational commander, with ADF intelligence falling under a man named Benjamin Kisonkorey. Much of the group's recruitment has been through abducting young potential fighters in DRC. Yet the ADF has also maintained regional conscription networks, particularly those that extend to Muslim communities in eastern Uganda, and they promise new recruits employment and education in return for joining the rebellion.[259] The one key factor shared by ADF commanders, cadres, and fighters alike is that they all possess unknown names and unrecognizable faces within the context of Ugandan and Congolese politics.

Since being cut loose from Sudan in the late 1990s, the ADF has developed a diverse strategy of resource acquisition. The first set of strategies has connected Mukulu to his fighters on the ground via extensive global networks. According to UN reports, Mukulu and other members of the Ugandan diaspora based in the United Kingdom and Kenya have sent the ADF multiple cash influxes from Western Union—100 such transfers in 2010 alone.[260] In addition, observers have suggested that the ADF has leveraged its Islamic identity to cultivate linkages to like-minded transnational actors. For instance, different sets of foreign military instructors, specifically Pakistani and Moroccan, that specialize in urban warfare and terrorist tactics have been sighted in ADF training bases.[261] However, efforts to link the ADF with other Islamic armed groups in Africa, namely, Somalia's Al Shabab, which implicate the group in the bomb attacks that took place in Kampala in 2010, remain unsubstantiated.[262]

Most important, the ADF's integration into the region's multiple commercial economies has allowed the group to be self-sustaining and self-financing. In addition to tapping into local food production,[263] ADF strongmen have come to control a number of illicit cross-border markets in gold, timber, and coffee, all of which generate revenue for the rebellion. For instance, seizure of the ADF's own meticulous records showed shipments of timber from Beni to Nairobi.[264] Such control extends to the region's everyday economy, including transport networks and even the levying of a $300 tax on anyone who simply wishes to use a chain saw.[265] The ADF thus resembles an organized crime syndicate more than a rebellion, in that much of its violence against civilians is conducted to enforce contracts, recover debts, and settle disputes in an environment where there are few active state institutions. As the International Crisis Group has pointed out, the political economy of the ADF "is profitable [and] therefore [a] lasting threat."[266]

At the time of this writing, the ADF is in the process of entering another cycle of demise through disintegration. Following Mukulu's arrest in Tanzania in April 2015, ongoing military pressure in eastern DRC has continued to disrupt training camps in order to scatter ADF fighters and has substantially weakened the group. In the past, fighters always tended to regroup in the Beni area, but now there is no centralized leadership. Consequently, the ADF has fragmented along lines of individual commanders, who are formally naming their factions and are taking on ideological and national contours.[267] The processes that led to disintegration of the first iteration of the ADF are again at play with the second, and any chance of achieving a victory via incorporation into either Congolese or Ugandan politics remains very much out of reach for the outsider-based rebellion.

Conclusion

Uganda provides an excellent context for examining the diversity of rebel groups and their corresponding fates. Each of Uganda's rebellions that have been explored in this chapter shared characteristics that might have predicted similar fates. Each fought within a relatively compact geographic space within the first two decades of NRA rule. Controlled comparisons of these cases have provided a high degree of variation between insider-heavy rebels and outsider-heavy rebels.

What do the nine cases presented here tell us about the fates of rebels? First, motives and means are insufficient explanations. Each rebellion sought to either overthrow incumbents or fight themselves into a bargaining position with them, and they experienced a range of fates. And where resource scarcity would have predicted a defeat for the NRA, it did not; not a single one of those rebellions with external support met any variant of victory. Instead, on balance, though not always producing a seamless explanation, political embeddedness is a more reliable predicter of the fates of Uganda's myriad rebel groups than other factors.

Indeed, a more fine-grained look at the grievances of each rebellion shows that those licking their wounds from a loss of status within Uganda's political establishment were most likely to go on to victory accommodation. These groups—the UPDA, the UPA, and the UNRF II—had essentially already met the start-up costs of their insurgencies before they even began, having developed relationships between rebel leaders and cadres, and cultivating political networks that were historically linked to state institutions, which opened a path to a regime strategy of control. In contrast, the NDA, UMLA, and NALU had few prewar organizational endowments that could be marshaled toward any fate beyond defeat elimination, as the Ugandan government had no interest in the alternative. And although NALU's leader, Amon Bazira, was an Obote-era elite, his rebellion was not a prewar organizational construct—he instead attempted to appropriate the remnants of the defunct Ruwenzururu movement for his own political aims.

The WNBF is a compelling case in that although it contained a number of state elites from the Amin era, it suggests that political embeddedness can diminish, and cohesion can atrophy over time. In addition, the group's factionalized organizational endowment reflected the politics of Idi Amin's regime, which was deeply divided along ethnic, religious, and regional lines. As disparate commanders competed with one another over control of the rebellion and access to resources, the WNBF met defeat by disintegration.

Some additional questions remain. First, the ADF case presents the dual challenge of explaining its defeat disintegration and its resurgence years later. In its early incarnation of the 1990s, the group had no discernible organization and no clear political links to Ugandan politics. There was therefore no clear path to accommodation through a political settlement, and the ADF was unable to withstand the Ugandan government's explicit strategy of elimination, which eventually led to its disintegration as the group was pushed from the country and drawn into a more complex regional conflict in the DRC. Yet there are several parts to the ADF's story not adequately captured by the framework of this study. Although declared defunct in 2007 by the Ugandan army, the ADF enjoyed a resurgence and became a key player in eastern DRC's wars. This suggests two possible outcomes not addressed here—either *persistence* or *resurgence*, both of which imply that the ADF never really died. In addition, that both incarnations of the ADF included remnants of NDA, UMLA, and NALU also raises questions about the extent to which these groups were truly eliminated.

Second, it is clear that hard resources did not play an outsized role in the fates of Uganda's rebels. But even though resources per se might not have shaped the military trajectories of each insurgency, an additional look at the regional politics *behind* those resources may reveal an additional factor that shapes the organization and behavior of insurgents more generally. Uganda's chronically untidy relationship with its Sudanese and Congolese neighbors predates the NRA regime. In the 1960s, Uganda was a conduit for Israeli military support to the Anya-Nya rebellion, and in 1975, Idi Amin claimed a large swath of southern Sudan. Even Obote's attempts at "good neighborliness" in the 1980s were met with Sudan's provision of sanctuary to ex-officials from the Amin regime.[268]

Regional politics since 1986 ushered in a new phase of tit-for-tat proxy warfare, with Uganda supporting insurgencies in Sudan and eastern DRC, and Sudan and DRC supporting insurgencies in Uganda in turn. As the WNBF, UNRF II, and ADF cases show, their sponsors played a larger role than simply providing resources. Here were outside regimes that were instrumental in shaping the organizational configuration and strategic direction of Ugandan rebellions. These dynamics raise questions about the autonomy of such groups. They also may change the calculus of incumbent regimes weighing whether to do business with rebellions that are directed by hostile neighbors. In other words, how the political imperatives behind resource provision, and the associated regional geopolitics, contribute to rebel fates is a topic for further inquiry.

Finally, an obvious question raised by this chapter is why on earth has Uganda experienced so many insurgencies, particularly since 1986? Although the answer is not the focus of this book, it may nevertheless be rooted in the NRA's postvictory political dispensation, which has key implications for postwar political stability more generally. An additional question is then, what modes of political order follow victory domination? In the Ugandan case, the NRA's transformation from a rebellion to a ruling regime has been more or less successful, if measured by its three decades of staying power since its rare victory. But at the same time, at least in a pure Weberian sense, it took two decades for the regime to deal with Uganda's range of armed challengers and to achieve a full monopoly of control over the country. A final question is then whether the factors that explain the fates of rebels can explain full, incomplete, or failed postvictory regime consolidation. I return to this set of questions raised above in more detail in Chapter 6.

Notes

1. Kasozi, *Social Origins of Violence in Uganda, 1964–1985.*
2. Government of Uganda Amnesty Commission, *Reconciliation in Action*, p. 14.
3. Fearon and Laitin, "Ethnicity, Insurgency, and Civil Wars."
4. Prunier, "Rebel Movements and Proxy Warfare."
5. Day and Reno, "In Harm's Way."
6. Museveni, *Sowing the Mustard Seed*, pp. 28–31.
7. Museveni, "Fanon's Theory on Violence."
8. Ngoga, "Uganda," p. 94.
9. Museveni, *Sowing the Mustard Seed*, pp. 54–55.
10. Ibid., p. 63.
11. Ibid., pp. 106–113.
12. Lule's presidency lasted a short sixty-eight days.
13. Omara-Otunnu, *Politics and the Military in Uganda, 1890–1985*, p. 148.
14. Ibid., p. 92.
15. Weinstein, *Inside Rebellion*, pp. 142–143.
16. Ngoga, "Uganda," p. 95.
17. Amaza, *Museveni's Long March*, p. 34.
18. These were the External, Finance and Supplies, Political and Diplomatic, and Publicity and Propaganda Subcommittees.
19. Ngoga, "Uganda," p. 96.
20. Omara-Otunnu, *Politics and the Military in Uganda*, p. 150.
21. Museveni, *Sowing the Mustard Seed*, p. 117.
22. Ngoga, "Uganda," pp. 98–100.
23. Kasfir, "Guerrillas and Civilian Participation," p. 282.
24. Weinstein, *Inside Rebellion*, p. 142.
25. Ngoga, "Uganda," p. 96; Weinstein, *Inside Rebellion*, p. 176; Amaza, *Museveni's Long March*, pp. 44–46.
26. Kasfir, "Guerrillas and Civilian Participation," pp. 281, 286.

27. Ngoga, "Uganda," p. 99.
28. Weinstein, *Inside Rebellion*, pp. 140–145; Kasfir, "Guerrillas and Civilian Participation," p. 276; Ngoga, "Uganda," p. 102.
29. Ngoga, "Uganda," p. 102.
30. The one attempt at "negotiations" occurred in October 1984, where NRA officials were instead killed by soldiers upon arrival in the Kampala suburbs. See Amaza, *Museveni's Long March*, p. 104.
31. Ngoga, "Uganda," p. 103.
32. Weinstein, *Inside Rebellion*, p. 266.
33. Kasfir, "Guerrillas and Civilian Participation," p. 288.
34. Kutesa, *Uganda's Revolution, 1979–1986*, p. 269.
35. Ngoga, "Uganda," p. 103.
36. Omara-Otunnu, *Politics and the Military in Uganda,* pp. 160, 163.
37. Ibid., p. 166.
38. These included the Former Uganda National Army (FUNA), the Uganda National Rescue Front (UNRF), the Uganda Freedom Movement (UFM), and the Federal Democratic Movement of Uganda (FEDEMU).
39. Omara-Otunnu, *Politics and the Military in Uganda*, p. 166.
40. Amaza, *Museveni's Long March*, p. 109.
41. Omara-Otunnu, *Politics and the Military in Uganda,* p. 168.
42. Amaza, *Museveni's Long March*, p. 105.
43. Omara-Otunnu, *Politics and the Military in Uganda,* pp. 186–203.
44. Amaza, *Museveni's Long March*, pp. 107–111.
45. Kainerugaba, *Battles of Ugandan Resistance*, pp. 155–182; Museveni, *Sowing the Mustard Seed*, pp. 172–176; Kutesa, *Uganda's Revolution 1979–1986*, pp. 237–249; Amaza, *Museveni's Long March*, pp. 111–113.
46. Amaza, *Museveni's Long March*, p. 31.
47. Kasfir, "Guerrillas and Civilian Participation," p. 290.
48. "Uganda: In Extremis," *Africa Confidential*, 11 December 1985; Amaza, *Museveni's Long March*, p. 110.
49. "Uganda: Mission Completed," *Africa Confidential*, 12 March 1986.
50. Doom and Vlassenroot, "Kony's Message," pp. 14–15.
51. "Uganda: The Final Thrust," *Africa Confidential*, 26 February 1986.
52. "Uganda: By Storm," *Africa Confidential*, 29 January 1986.
53. "Uganda: The Final Thrust," *Africa Confidential*, 26 February 1986.
54. "Bazilio Withdraws Heavy Weaponry Towards Sudan," *Focus*, 7 March 1986.
55. Woodward, "Uganda and Southern Sudan, 1986–1989," p. 180.
56. "Bazilio, Sudanese Rebel Forces Clash," *Focus*, 27 June 1986.
57. "Uganda: Northern Troubles," *Africa Confidential*, 3 September 1986.
58. "Bazilio Expelled from Sudan," *Focus*, 6 January 1987; interview with General Pecos Kutesa, Kampala, August 2011.
59. Lucima, *Protracted Conflict, Elusive Peace*, p. 22.
60. "Uganda: False Messiah," *Africa Confidential*, 4 February 1987.
61. "A Fish Monger Who Became Rebel Leader," *New Vision*, 22 December 1999.
62. "Uganda: Top Rebels," *Africa Confidential*, 18 February 1987.
63. Interview with former UPDA fighter, Kampala, July 2011.
64. "UPDA High Command Destroyed," *Focus*, 13 October 1987.
65. "Uganda: Military Solution," *Africa Confidential*, 8 July 1987; "Rebels Continue to Surrender," *Focus*, 6 October 1987.
66. "Uganda: War Report," *Africa Confidential*, 13 May 1987.

67. Behrend, *Alice Lakwena and the Holy Spirits*, p. 173; Lucima, *Protracted Conflict, Elusive Peace*, pp. 29–31.

68. Epelu-Opio, *Teso War, 1986–1992*, p. 38.

69. Ibid., pp. 40–46.

70. Ibid., p. 48.

71. "Soroti Ambush Kills Eight," *New Vision*, 12 May 1989; "UPA Rebels Attack Lira," *New Vision*, 31 May 1989.

72. Interview with Justin Epelu-Opio, former chairman of the Commission for Teso, July 2011.

73. "NRA Captures UPA Documents, Weapons," *New Vision*, 5 January 1990; "Misery Blamed on Rebels," *New Vision*, 8 March 1990; "UPA Rebels Attack Atiriri," *New Vision*, 1 March 1990.

74. "Jesus Ojirot Shot Dead," *New Vision*, 22 April 1989.

75. "Iteso Love Museveni," *Monitor*, 22 April 1994.

76. Interview with Epelu-Opio, July 2011.

77. Epelu-Opio, *Teso War*, pp. 18–35.

78. "Rebel Surrenders Soar in Soroti," *New Vision*, 26 April 1990; "70 Rebels Killed in Soroti," *New Vision*, 28 June 1990; "UPA Rebel Surrenders," *New Vision*, 8 May 1992.

79. Epelu-Opio, *Teso War*, p. 50.

80. "UPA Splits Up," *New Vision*, 14 November 1992.

81. "Soldiers Join Anti-NRM Groups," *Monitor*, 29 June 1993.

82. "Eregu Reported Killed in Kenya," *New Vision*, 29 October 1993.

83. Interview with Epelu-Opio, July 2011; "Kumi Rebels Strike," *New Vision*, 19 July 1993; "UPA Rebels Killed," *New Vision*, 26 October 1993; "UPA Rebels Surrender," *New Vision*, 3 November 1993; "UPA Thugs Kill 3 in Kumi," *New Vision*, 13 October 1993.

84. "Teso: Guns Fall Silent, Returns to Peace," *New Vision*, 19 September 1993.

85. Leopold, *Inside West Nile*.

86. Omara-Otunnu, *Politics and the Military in Uganda*, pp. 125, 130.

87. Mazrui, *Soldiers and Kinsmen in Uganda*, p. 127.

88. Omara-Otunnu, *Politics and the Military in Uganda*, p. 133.

89. Ibid., pp. 134–135.

90. Mazrui, *Soldiers and Kinsmen in Uganda*, p. 49.

91. Ibid., p. 129.

92. Interview with former UNRF II commander, July 2011.

93. Uganda National Rescue Front II, *Agenda for Peace Talks with the Government of the Republic of Uganda*, p. 3.

94. Gersony, *The Anguish of Northern Uganda*, p. 82.

95. Rwehururu, *Cross to the Gun*.

96. Refugee Law Project, "Negotiating Peace," pp. 6–7; "UNRF—Brigadier Moses Ai Given Minister of Tourism and Wildlife," *Focus*, 29 August 1986.

97. Refugee Law Project, "Negotiating Peace," pp. 5–10; Rwehururu, *Cross to the Gun*, pp. 156–173.

98. "Who Is Behind the West Nile Rebellion?" *Sunday Vision*, 17 September 1995.

99. "CAD Drops SPLA Claim," *New Vision*, 1 December 1994.

100. "Oris's Deputy Appeals to Museveni for Clemency," *New Vision*, 9 April 1997.

101. Athocon is Alur for "dead person who is still seen alive."

102. "Why Fighting Must Rage On," *Sunday Vision*, 6 April 1997.

103. "Rebels Recruit in West Nile," *Sunday Vision*, 28 May 1995; "Arua Getting Insecure," *New Vision*, 21 June 1995; "Why West Nile Youth Join Rebels," *Crusader*, 28 June 1996; Refugee Law Project, "Negotiating Peace," p. 14.

104. "Why Fighting Must Rage On," *Sunday Vision*, 6 April 1997.

105. Interview with Ugandan journalist, July 2010.

106. "Rebels Promoted," *New Vision*, 19 January 1996; "Oris Deputy Appeals to Museveni for Clemency," *New Vision*, 8 April 1997.

107. "2,500 Col. Juma Oris Men to Attack Uganda-Bigombe," *Monitor*, 18 November 1994.

108. "Oris Rebels Shell Koboko," *New Vision*, 13 February 1996.

109. "Rebels Want Idi Amin President," *New Vision*, 29 May 1995.

110. "Oris Rebels Want West Nile State," *New Vision*, 10 June 1995; "West Nile Rebels Head for Arua," *Sunday Vision*, 21 April 1996.

111. Interview with *New Vision* journalist, July 2011.

112. "Why Fighting Must Rage On," *Sunday Vision*, 6 April 1997.

113. "Oris Rebel Officer Reveals Sudan Role," *New Vision*, 3 May 1996; "West Nile Sold Off—Oris Rebels," *New Vision*, 12 February 1996.

114. "Col. Oris Rebels Invade Uganda," *New Vision*, 10 April 1996; "Oris Rebels Shelled," *New Vision*, 5 October 1996.

115. "Thousands Flee Sudan Border as Tension Mounts," *Sunday Vision*, 20 August 1995; "WNBF Rebels Change Location," *New Vision*, 15 September 1995.

116. "SPLA Battles over Oris HQ," *New Vision*, 30 December 1995; Prunier, *From Genocide to Continental War*, p. 86.

117. "Army Helicopters Attack Oris Rebels," *New Vision*, 23 September 1996.

118. "NALU, Oris to Unite," *New Vision*, 11 September 1995.

119. Interview with Ugandan journalist, July 2010.

120. "Oris, Kony Merge," *New Vision*, 10 July 1995; "Eight Kony, WNBF Rebel Soldiers Defect," *New Vision*, 16 August 1995; "Kony, Oris Plan Assault," *New Vision*, 26 August 1996.

121. "W. Nile Rebels Fight in Zaire," *Sunday Vision*, 2 February 1997.

122. "Oris 'Held' in Sudan," *New Vision*, 18 October 1995.

123. "Former CAD Named New Rebel Leader," *New Vision*, 12 January 1996.

124. "Atamvaku Is Now Rebel Link," *New Vision*, 2 December 1996.

125. "Oris Rebels Desert Camps After Shelling," *New Vision*, 18 April 1996.

126. "Former Rebels Want Moses Ali's Neck," *Crusader*, 15 October 1996.

127. "Oris Men: Tribal Split," *New Vision*, 28 August 1996.

128. "Koboko Deserted," *New Vision*, 15 January 1996; "Ex-Oris Officer Appeals on Killing," *New Vision*, 29 August 1996; "Civilians Capture WNBF Commander," *Monitor*, 7 January 1997.

129. "Oris Rebels Defect," *Sunday Vision*, 4 August 1996; "More Oris Men Give In," *New Vision*, 6 August 1996.

130. "Museveni to Recruit Oris Rebels," *New Vision*, 15 October 1996; "UPDF Absorbs 500 Rebels as 70 Get Abducted," *Monitor*, 6 November 1996; "517 Oris Rebels to Join UPDF," *New Vision,* 8 November 1996.

131. "160 Oris Rebels Surrender in Arua," *New Vision*, 17 April 1996; "Oris Men Surrender," *New Vision*, 7 February 1997.

132. "Sudan Officers Retrain with Oris Men at Omgbokoro," *New Vision*, 25 February 1997.

133. "SPLA Battles over Oris HQ," *New Vision*, 30 December 1995; "SPLA Pound Oris Rebels," *Sunday Vision*, 4 February 1996; "Banyamulenge Eject Oris," *New Vision*, 3 March 1997.

134. Confidential interview with son of Arua elder, January 2008.

135. "Arua Residents Get Guns," *New Vision*, 18 October 1996; "Villagers to Fight Oris Rebels," *New Vision*, 4 December 1996; "Civilians Capture WNBF Commander," *Monitor*, 7 January 1997.

136. "2,000 Killed in Bloody Ambush," *New Vision*, 17 March 1997; Prunier, *From Genocide to Continental War*, p. 133.

137. "Zaire Rebels Hand Over Oris Rebels," *New Vision*, 26 March 2 1997; "SPLA Captures Oris Top Chiefs," *Sunday Vision*, 6 April 1997.

138. "Oris War Over, Says Commander," *New Vision*, 2 June 1997; Refugee Law Project, "Negotiating Peace," pp. 19–20.

139. Day, "The Fates of Rebels."

140. Ali is credited with having introduced Museveni to Gaddafi during this period.

141. Uganda National Rescue Front II, *Agenda for Peace Talks*, pp. 5–6.

142. Refugee Law Project, "Negotiating Peace," p. 11.

143. "Oris Rebels Blame Ali," *New Vision*, 4 September 1996; "Moses Ali Denies Chewing Rebel Money," *Crusader*, 17 October 1996.

144. "Museveni's Dishonesty Caused War, Says Former Rebel," *Crusader*, 17 October 1996.

145. Interview with Ugandan journalist, June 2011.

146. Interview with former UNRF II commander, Kampala, August 2011.

147. Ibid., July 2011.

148. Ibid.

149. "Oris, Kony Forces Form United Front," *New Vision*, 5 April 1997.

150. "Aringa Ex-Rebels Speak Out," *New Vision*, 26 August 1997; "RDC Warns of LRA, UNRF II Rebel Attack," *Crusader*, 21 August 1997; "Arua Youth Recruited to Sudan," *New Vision*, 24 July 1997.

151. "Rescue Front Men Attack from Sudan," *New Vision*, 7 August 1997.

152. "West Nile Rebel Group Splits," *New Vision*, 19 June 1996; Uganda National Rescue Front II, "Agenda for Peace Talks," pp. 7–8.

153. Refugee Law Project, "Negotiating Peace," pp. 20–25.

154. Ibid., p. 24.

155. Interview with former UNRF II commander, Kampala, July 2011.

156. Refugee Law Project, "Negotiating Peace," p. 24.

157. "119 UNRF Rebels Give Selves Up," *Monitor,* 1 January 1999; "39 UNRF II Rebels Surrender," *New Vision*, 26 November 1999.

158. "Bamuze Sends 40 to Meet Museveni," *Monitor*, 17 August 2000.

159. Uganda National Rescue Front II, "Agenda for Peace Talks," pp. 13–24.

160. "The Peace Agreement Between the Government of the Republic of Uganda and the Uganda National Rescue Front II," December 24, 2002.

161. "Gen. Ali Bamuze Passes On," *New Vision*, 5 October 2015; "Gen. Bamuze Collapses at J&M Airport Road Hotel, Dies," *Monitor*, 4 October 2015.

162. "Mpigi People 'Return to the Bush to Fight NRM'?" *Weekly Topic*, 19 July 1989.

163. Interview, Center for Basic Research, June 2011; "Buwambo: CGR Warns Baganda," *New Vision*, 16 February 1995; "Otafiire Blames Buwambo Raid on Federo Die-Hards," *New Vision*, 20 February 1995; "Katikkiro Disowns Attackers," *New Vision*, 25 February 1995.

164. "Mpigi RCs Accused of Recruiting Rebels," *New Vision*, 5 December 1994; "Mpigi CGR Names Rebels," *Monitor*, 16 December 1994; "There're Rebel Camps in Mpigi, CGR Says Again," *New Vision*, 17 December 1994.

165. "Itongwa Warned," *New Vision*, 18 February 1995; "Itongwa Meets Press in Bush," *New Vision*, 24 March 1995.

166. "Buwambo: NRA Deploys Soldiers," *New Vision*, 14 February 1995.

167. "Who Is Maj. Itongwa the 'Federo Rebel Leader'?" *Sunday Vision*, 5 March 1995.

168. "Gangsters Raid Buwambo Police," *New Vision*, 11 February 1995; "'Buwambo Thugs Are Robbers,'" *New Vision*, 13 February 1995.

169. "Families Flee After Mpigi 'Rebel' Attack," *Monitor*, 13 February 1995; "Masaka Thugs Attack Village," *Sunday Vision*, 12 March 1995.

170. "Itongwa Will Be Killed—Museveni," *Monitor*, 31 March 1995.

171. "Who Killed Masaka Officer?" *Sunday Vision*, 26 February 1995.

172. "Dr. Makumbi Goes Missing," *Sunday Vision*, 2 April 1995; "Rebels Sighted Before Dr. Makumbi Vanished," *Monitor*, 3 April 1995; "Dr. Makumbi Held by Itongwa Rebels," *Monitor*, 5 April 1995; "We Have Makumbi, Rebel Group Claims," *New Vision*, 5 April 1995.

173. "Makumbi Free," *New Vision*, 6 April 1995; "Itongwa Sets Conditions for Talks with NRM," *Monitor,* 23 June 1995.

174. "Compromise with Itongwa Ruled Out," *New Vision*, 19 June 1995.

175. "Mpiso Joins Itongwa," *New Vision*, 4 April 1995; "Itongwa Swears to Keep Fighting," *New Vision*, 5 May 1995.

176. "Rebels Threaten Full-Scale War," *Monitor*, 5 April 1995.

177. "Itongwa's Deputies Netted in Luwero," *New Vision*, 13 April 1995; "Itongwa Alone," *New Vision*, 22 May 1995; "Itongwa Soldier Netted," *Sunday Vision*, 18 June 1995; "'Itongwa Rebels' Nabbed in Lira," *Monitor*, 2–4 August 1995.

178. "Itongwa Hiding in City Suburbs," *New Vision*, 3 June 1995; "Itongwa Flees to Kenya," *New Vision*, 1 December 1995; "Itongwa Captured," *Monitor*, 2 February 1996.

179. "Itongwa Brought Back to Kampala," *New Vision*, 3 February 1996.

180. The UMLA is referred to elsewhere as the Uganda Freedom Fighters Movement (UFFM).

181. Kayunga, "Islamic Fundamentalism in Uganda," p. 71.

182. Prunier, *From Genocide to Continental War*, p. 84.

183. Titeca and Vlassenroot, "Rebels Without Borders in the Rwenzori Borderland?" p. 158.

184. International Crisis Group, *Eastern Congo: The ADF-NALU's Lost Rebellion.*

185. "Hoima Rebels' Activities Began as Video Shows," *Sunday Vision*, 5 March 1995; "Hoima Rebels Began in 1992," *Sunday Vision*, 5 March 1995.

186. "Hoima Rebel Leaders Named," *Monitor*, 1 March 1995.

187. "Thugs Attack Hoima Police," *New Vision*, 23 February 1995.

188. "Police Arrest Hoima Rebels," *New Vision*, 24 February 1995; "NRA Kills 63 Hoima Rebels," *Monitor*, 27 February 1995; "Rebel Toll Rises to 92," *New Vision*, 28 February 1995; "NRA Ambushes Rebels at Kaseeta," *New Vision*, 1 March 1995.

189. "Who Attacked Hoima Police?" *Monitor*, 24 February 1995.

190. "NRA Kills 63 Rebels in Hoima," *New Vision*, 27 February 1995.

191. "Hoima Rebel Leaders Named," *Monitor*, 1 March 1995.

192. Prunier, *From Genocide to Continental War*, p. 82.

193. Doornbos, "Understanding the Rwenzururu Movement."

194. "Kasese Insecurity: A Historical View," *New Vision*, 21 September 1992; also see Syahuka-Muhindo, "The Rwenzururu Movement and the Democratic Struggle," and Bamusede Bwambale, *The Faces of the Rwenzururu Movement.*

195. Others claim Bazira was head of Obote's intelligence service.

196. Scorgie, "Peripheral Pariah or Regional Rebel?" p. 84.

197. "Ex-Minister Sets Up Rebel Group in W. Uganda," *Guide,* 28 June 1989.

198. Titeca and Vlassenroot, "Rebels Without Borders?" p. 157.

199. International Crisis Group, *Eastern Congo,* p. 3.

200. "Five Killed in Kasese Attack," *New Vision,* 18 August 1989; "Shooting Breaks Out in Kasese," *Guide,* 23 August 1989; "Rwenzururu Rebels Abduct Officials," *New Vision,* 23 August 1989; "Rebels Kill Nine on Oct. 9th," *New Vision,* 12 October 1989; "Rebels Plan Offensive on Fort Portal," *Independent Observer,* 24 August 1989; "Kasese Rebels Burn Offices," *New Vision,* 16 January 1990.

201. "Kasese Rebel Camp Destroyed by NRA," *New Vision,* 29 December 1989; "NRA Pursues Kasese Rebels," *New Vision,* 25 January 1990.

202. "Bazira Can't Get Amnesty," *New Vision,* 13 May 1993.

203. "Rwenzururu Splits," *New Vision,* 20 June 1989; "Kasese Rebels Split by Row," *New Vision,* 4 November 1989.

204. "Kasese Rebels Surrender," *New Vision,* 4 December 1990; "Rwenzururu Rebels Surrender to DA," *New Vision,* 11 January 1992.

205. "Kasese Rebels Surrender," *New Vision,* 4 December 1990.

206. "Rwenzururu Rebels Surrender to DA," *New Vision,* 11 January 1992.

207. "Kasese Rebels Weakened," *New Vision,* 8 April 1991.

208. "NALU Rebels Regroup," *New Vision,* June 1992; "NALU Rebels Abduct 14 People," *New Vision,* 9 July 9 1992; "NALU Rebels Strike," *New Vision,* 24 July 1992; "Kasese Insecurity Worsened in July," *New Vision,* 11 August 1992.

209. "NALU Rebel Killed," *New Vision,* 27 October 1992; "Rebels Surrender," *New Vision,* 4 December 1992.

210. "Ex-NALU Rebel Implicates Bazira," *New Vision,* 15 March 1993.

211. Prunier, *From Genocide to Continental War,* p. 83.

212. "Rebels Killed in Shootout," *New Vision,* 3 September 1992.

213. "NALU Rebel in Rwanda Talks," *Sunday Vision,* 4 July 1993.

214. "Obote Implicated in Bazira Murder," *Monitor,* 17 September 1993.

215. "Amon Bazira Killed in Nairobi," *Monitor,* 20 August 1993.

216. "Did NRM Kill Bazira?" *Monitor,* 24 August 1993.

217. "NALU Troops Panic," *New Vision,* 13 September 1993.

218. "Why Does Zaire, Sudan Team Up Against Uganda?" *New Vision,* 4 December 1996.

219. Prunier, *From Genocide to Continental War,* p. 86; "100 Tabliqs Join Juma Oris Rebels?" *The Crusader,* 6 August 1996; "600 Tabliqs Join Oris Men," *New Vision,* 28 August 1996.

220. "NALU Rebels Regroup," *New Vision,* 30 September 1993; "NALU Picks Boss," *New Vision,* 19 November 1993.

221. "20 Rebels Killed in Bundibugyo," *New Vision,* 17 March 1995; "Kasese Calms Down as NALU Gives Up," *New Vision,* 1 August 1995.

222. "NALU Linked to Interhamwe," *New Vision,* 24 April 1996.

223. "NALU, Juma Oris to Unite," *New Vision,* 11 September 1995.

224. "'NRA Had No Special Orders to Kill,'" *Sunday Vision,* 5 March 1995.

225. "Rebel Recruiter Held," *New Vision,* 14 March 1995.

226. "'Itongwa' Visited Us—NALU Defectors," *New Vision,* 19 June 1995; "Itongwa Linked to Kasese Invasion," *New Vision,* 10 December 1996.

227. "Why Has the Insurgency Gone On for This Long?" *New Vision,* 17 June 1998.

228. Prunier, *From Genocide to Continental War,* pp. 85–87.

229. "Why the UPDF Has Not Wiped Out the ADF," New Vision, 6 October 1998; "Mobutu, Bashir Gave ADF Guns," *New Vision,* 10 September 2001.

230. Hovil and Werker, "Portrait of a Failed Rebellion"; African Rights, *Avoiding an Impasse*; "Kasese Attack Planned in Sudan," *New Vision*, 19 November 1996; "Arabs Seen Among Kasese ADF Rebels," *Crusader*, 28 December 1996; "Arabs Training Kasese Rebels, Says Escapee," *New Vision*, 31 December 1996.

231. "Mobutu Gave ADF Gold Mines—Benz," *New Vision*, 19 September 2001.

232. "ADF Rebels Blamed for Fake Currency Supply," *New Vision*, 24 February 1998.

233. "Zaire Soldiers Join Rebel ADF," *New Vision*, 28 March 1997; "Rebels Capture Bundibugyo Town," *Crusader*, 17 June 1997.

234. "Rebels Occupy Bundibugyo," *Monitor*, 17 June 1997; "Bundibugyo Town Overrun by Rebels," *New Vision*, 17 June 1997.

235. African Rights, *Avoiding an Impasse,* p. 1.

236. "City Bombs Rock Speke, Nile Grill," *Sunday Monitor*, 5 April 1998; "ADF Bombed Speke, Nile," *Crusader*, 7 April 1998.

237. "Massacre! ADF Burns 50 Students to Death in Kichwamba," *New Vision*, 9 June 1998; "The Day the Terror Struck in Kichwamaba," *New Vision*, 15 June 1998.

238. "UPDF Pounds Zairean Town to the Ground," *New Vision*, 20 November 1996: "Kasese Rebel Leader Former Mulokole," *Crusader*, 26 November 1996.

239. "Is Museveni Loosing [*sic*] Popularity?" *People*, 27 November 1996.

240. "The 1997 Cancer in Uganda," *New Vision*, 7 January 1998.

241. "Uganda: Museveni's Backyard," *Africa Confidential*, 1 August 1997; "Heaven Help Kasese," *New Vision*, 18 January 1997; "ADF, Itongwa Claim City Bombs," *Crusader*, 2 August 1997; "NALU Claims K'la Blasts, Warns Envoys," *Monitor*, 27 August 1997; "NALU Claim Bwindi Raid," *Monitor*, 13 March 1999.

242. "ADF Factions Clash," *New Vision*, 11 January 1999; "ADF Rebels Execute 20," *New Vision*, 19 February 1999.

243. "ADF Command: Who Is Who," *New Vision*, 5 October 1998.

244. "Top ADF Rebel Loses Leg," *New Vision*, 8 July 1997.

245. "The ADF: Rebels Without a Cause," *Monitor*, 10 December 1999.

246. "Using Hammer on Western Rebels, but Small Stick on Kony and Co.," *Monitor*, 21 November 1996; "Army Commander Rushes to Battlefront," *Monitor*, 17 November 1996.

247. "'Osama's Man,'" *Sunday Monitor*, 28 October 2001.

248. "50 Invaders Killed in Kasese Fighting," *New Vision*, 5 December 1996; "Kasese Rebels Circulate Document," *New Vision*, 16 December 1996; "Kasese ADF Rebel Leader Feared Dead," *Crusader,* 24 December 1996; "Gov't, Rebels Fight On for Bundibugyo," *Monitor*, 19 June 1997; "200 Rebels Killed, Bundibugyo Retaken," *New Vision*, 20 June 1997.

249. "Containing the Storm," *Sunday Vision*, 24 November 1996; "UPDF Pursues Rebels into Zaire," *New Vision*, 30 November 1996.

250. International Crisis Group, *Eastern Congo,* p. 5.

251. Day, "The Fates of Rebels," p. 447.

252. "500 Rebels Run to Kasese," *Crusader,* 10 December 1996; "Kasese War Escalates as Rebels Vow to Stay," *Crusader*, 5 December 1996; "Rebels Plan Guerrilla War," *New Vision*, 7 December 1996

253. Clark, *The African Stakes of the Congo War;* Kevin C. Dunn, *Imagining the Congo.*

254. Titeca and Vlassenroot, "Rebels Without Borders?" p. 160; International Crisis Group, *Eastern Congo,* p. 6.

255. International Crisis Group, *Eastern Congo,* p. 7.

256. Titeca and Vlassenroot, "Rebels Without Borders?" p. 161.

257. Scorgie, "Peripheral Pariah or Regional Rebel?" p. 83.

258. United Nations Security Council Report no. 738, annex 7, 2 December 2011, p. 181.

259. Ibid.; United Nations Security Council Report no. 433, 19 July 2013; United Nations Security Council Report No. 42, 23 January 2014; interviews with Uganda Amnesty Commission, August 2011.

260. United Nations Security Council Report no. 42, annex 11, 23 January 2014, p. 121.

261. United Nations Security Council Interim Report no. 596, paragraph 111, 29 November 2010, p. 31.

262. When Jamil Mukulu's son was arrested in Nairobi in November 2011, reports surfaced that he was bailed out by Al Shabab. United Nations Security Council Report No. 843, 15 November 2012.

263. Titeca and Vlassenroot, "Rebels Without Borders?" p. 163.

264. United Nations Security Council Report no. 738, annex 10, p. 184.

265. International Crisis Group, *Eastern Congo,* p. 11.

266. Ibid., p. 10.

267. United Nations Security Council Report no. 466, 23 May 2016.

268. Ofcansky, "Warfare and Instability Along the Sudan-Uganda Border."

4

The Fates of Insiders: Rebel Groups in Sudan and Côte d'Ivoire

My friend, we survived! I do not know . . .
—Major General Obuto Mamur Mete,
SPLA

On 9 July 2011, the Republic of South Sudan became Africa's fifty-fourth independent state, arising from the 2005 Comprehensive Peace Agreement (CPA) that ended a twenty-two-year civil war between the Sudan People's Liberation Army (SPLA) and the incumbent regime in Khartoum. In the weeks that followed the seemingly auspicious day of independence, the congested new capital of Juba was blanketed in celebratory radio and television loops, bright banners and billboards. Official statements announced the South's final liberation from a long history of oppression and enslavement at the hands of the northern Sudanese "enemy." Old-guard rebels took up top positions in new ministries and governorships, while the SPLA transitioned into a national army, its upper ranks drawn from the rebellion's innermost circles. George Clooney made an obligatory cameo appearance to bolster his Sudan-oriented activism. Conversations with many former SPLA commanders and leaders revealed that most of them were convinced that independence was the proper and inevitable outcome of their struggle, and a testament to the SPLA's capacity and resolve to achieve victory. Independence was a reward for years of rebellion and the hardship it entailed.[1]

The Sudan People's Liberation Army (SPLA)

For most southern Sudanese, the historical memory of their relationship to Khartoum-centered state institutions was long based on subordinate

101

political status associated with the subjugation, exploitation, and humiliation of non-Muslims. The *longue durée* of this story has been treated in great detail elsewhere.[2] And I do not attempt to explain the birth of South Sudan here. Instead, I seek to explain the incorporation of the SPLA into the Sudanese government through the 2005 CPA, a political settlement that only established conditions for independence—a fate that SPLA leaders did not always anticipate during their rebellion against successive incumbent regimes in Khartoum. Although most depictions of Sudan's civil war are cast along a distinct north-south cleavage, the SPLA's path to victory by incorporation followed the contours of political networks that developed over decades of Sudanese state politics, which often incorporated southern elites before the SPLA rebelled. In what follows, this section tells the story of the SPLA's fate by first situating the southern rebellion within the historical institutional context of the period directly following independence, which led to Sudan's first civil war. It then examines the aftermath of this first conflict and how it created permissive conditions for the SPLA to emerge. The rest of the section shows how the SPLA's political embeddedness led down the path to the CPA, against the backdrop of shifts in the technology of rebellion.

Sudan's First Civil War

Consider first the institutional foundations of the colonial state in Sudan. Although that system privileged northern elites and worked via existing precolonial political arrangements based in Khartoum, the British colonial administration's distinct Southern Policy nevertheless incorporated an educated class of southerners into colonial state institutions. It also created the Equatoria Corps, a battalion of Christian, English-speaking Sudanese based in southern Sudan.[3]

Through those policies, the colonial period created a crop of southern Sudanese political and military elites who developed their own set of political aspirations. In the waning days of British colonial rule, southern elites had made some modest gains in populating the country's Legislative Assembly. But by the mid-1950s, the politics of Sudan's independence erected a range of obstacles that blocked their collective goals. During this period, the northern-dominated political establishment had few incentives to form any coalitions with their southern counterparts. Northern elites shut down the constitutional process of national integration that would otherwise have considered southern wishes for federalism, which would have granted southern Sudan political autonomy from Khartoum.[4]

Instead, Khartoum implemented the distinct policy of "Sudanization"—essentially Arabization and Islamization—that populated all southern civil administrative and military posts with appointees from the north, widening the political gulf between northerner and southerner. In garrison towns throughout the south, mutual suspicion and personal tensions flared between southern troops and the "Arab soldiers" who now commanded them. On 18 August 1955, disputes boiled over into a full-blown mutiny at the garrison in Torit, which led to chronic insecurity in the region. Ex-mutineers fled to the bush and continued to launch sporadic attacks, which only justified the collective punishment by Khartoum-backed soldiers against all southerners.[5] Things deteriorated further after a 1958 coup in Khartoum brought General Aboud's military regime to power, which pursued even more aggressive Sudanization policies that created waves of refugees and radicalized southern politics.[6] With their movements restricted and political parties banned, those southern elites still operating within mainstream Sudanese politics became convinced that the small political gains they had achieved were now at risk, and they found themselves as unwarranted outsiders in independent Sudan's political order.

By the early 1960s, two key sets of southern actors joined forces to form the southern Sudan's first rebellion, the Anya-Nya.[7] The first were southern political elites who, operating mostly in exile, formed the Sudan African National Union (SANU) and sought political, economic, and military support abroad. Although overarching regional norms explicitly discouraged overt assistance to any secession movement in Africa, governments in Uganda, Congo, and Ethiopia nevertheless provided "subtle yet essential" assistance by providing travel allowances and territory for the southern politicians to organize and recruit.[8] Despite factionalization and some financial troubles, this group established a broad network of southern intellectuals and exiles committed to both armed resistance and self-determination in southern Sudan.[9]

The second set of actors were army defectors and ex-mutineers who had been freshly released from their prison sentences for the Torit mutiny. On the ground, both political and military leaders tried to shepherd the Anya-Nya, which started as a loose affiliation of regional groups with separate command structures, the core of which was composed of southern military cadres.[10] At the onset, these resource-scarce rebels fought an asymmetrical guerrilla war against the Sudanese army largely with traditional weapons,[11] while occasionally acquiring modern armaments through raids, supplemented by a supply of equipment they intercepted from the neighboring Simba rebellion in Congo.[12]

At this juncture, the Anya-Nya faced the triple problem of resource scarcity, internal military divisions, and disagreements between the political elites who operated via remote control. But by the late 1960s, such issues were finally solved by the elevation of Joseph Lagu as the group's leader. An army defector, he successfully consolidated both the political and the military wings to create the South Sudan Liberation Movement (SSLM). Lagu's links to the Israeli Defense Forces infused the group with arms seized from Arab armies during the Six Day War,[13] which empowered him to reorganize the SSLM command structure and streamline its political wing.

These tightening links between southern exiles and fighters on the ground enlarged the broader southern political coalition, thus increasing the threat posed by southern Sudan to the regime in Khartoum, whose brutal counterinsurgency methods alienated southerners and fed grassroots support for the rebels.[14] Regime politics thus began shifting toward the accommodation of southern elites in the hopes of ending the costly conflict. By 1964, a new caretaker government in Khartoum legalized political parties and allowed southerners in Khartoum to form the Southern Front (SF) led by Abel Alier and Clement Mboro, who became the minister of the interior. At the Round Table Conference in 1964, both SF and SANU lobbied for the south's self-determination while continuing to clandestinely support southern rebels, as parliaments repeatedly dissolved and reformed into weak and shifting coalitions.

On 25 May 1969, a key change in Sudanese regime politics occurred when army colonel Gaafar Nimeiry staged a successful coup d'état. Although he had the backing of a small group of military men calling themselves the "Free Officers," his ideological mix of Arab nationalism and socialism was insufficient to assemble an effective political coalition of northern political parties. Instead, Nimeiry sought to bolster his weak position by allying with Alier, who had ongoing links to southern exiles. With this development, the broader southern political and military movement was now ripe for accommodation by the relatively unstable regime in Khartoum. This new effort to co-opt formerly embedded southern leaders into fresh ruling elite networks paved the way for a victory by incorporation by the southern rebels. With key southern political players now installed within new political dispensation in Khartoum, the correspondingly ascendant SSLM was able to fight Nimeiry's regime into a bargaining position by 1972.[15]

The Rise and Fall of Southern Sudanese Politics

The 1972 Addis Ababa Agreement ended the first Sudanese civil war and further embedded southern elites into Sudan's civil and military institutions. The new Permanent Constitution codified the accord, which also carved out the autonomous Southern Regional Government (SRG) that gained rudimentary economic powers, and allowed for the creation of the elected Regional Assembly. As the accord was implemented, Lagu oversaw the absorption of SSLM fighters into a combined People's Armed Forces (PAF), and Alier was made president of the south's High Executive Council (HEC), as well as minister of southern affairs, and the Sudan's second vice president. The personal relationships among Nimeiry, Alier, and Lagu undergirded much of the accommodation,[16] but nonetheless, the new political dispensation granted by the Addis Ababa Agreement soon began to unravel along several dimensions.

First, the prospect of combining northern and southern fighting units into a broad-based national army over the period of five years proved problematic.[17] Within the new PAF, northerners remained deployed in strategic southern garrisons, which grated on their southern counterparts, who were recommissioned at lower-than-expected ranks and given shoddy, used equipment.[18] Many senior fighters were forcibly retired, purged, or transferred out of the south entirely.[19]

Second, grinding poverty and the persistent problem of stalled economic development in the south aggravated unresolved southern grievances. The SRG's limited fiduciary powers, already poorly defined, were systematically subordinated to Khartoum's economic priorities of oil exploration, mechanized farming and migrant labor, and the digging of the Jonglei canal in the south.[20] In addition, efforts to put ex-fighters to work in the stagnant southern economy exceeded the SRG's small budget, and southern politicians were now beholden to paltry cash transfers from Khartoum, for which they had to beg regularly.[21]

Above all, Khartoum's gradual manipulation of the Addis Ababa Agreement blocked the full reintegration of southern elites into state institutions, and they remained merely extensions of a one-party presidential system with Nimeiry at its center.[22] This essentially thwarted the expectations of these elites—keeping at arm's length their aspirations to be equal partners in a new political dispensation, and renewing and stoking southern status hierarchy grievances in the process. Nimeiry intervened regularly in southern politics as the SRG's political portfolio shrank and as the HEC was ultimately dissolved. In addition, Nimeiry became adept at exploiting cleavages among southern elites,[23] making promises to those moderates who toed Khartoum's line[24] while outright imprisoning those who spoke out against his regime. As the members of the Legislative Assembly routinely pushed back against legislation that would further harm southern Sudan economically or politically, their votes were met with a presidential veto or simply ignored.

By 1977, Nimeiry's political need to maintain southern members of his ruling coalition faded as he reconciled with his main rival political parties in the north, the Umma and the Democratic Unionist Party (DUP).[25] This new ruling coalition brought in hard-liners committed to abrogating the Addis Ababa Agreement and dismantling the SRG. In a few years' time, the Regional Government Act of 1980 was enacted, splitting northern Sudan into five regions and shifting the freshly created oil-rich Unity State to the north. It also split the SRG into three new administrative areas—Upper Nile, Equatoria, and Bahr el Ghazal. Deploying the rhetoric of local political participation, Khartoum stripped away local powers from southern officials, shrank ministerial portfolios, and neutered the Regional Assembly. Nimeiry also purged national politics of southern parties,[26] sending their remaining officials jockeying for increasingly scarce resources and regional assets.[27]

Key allies of Nimeiry's new ruling coalition in Khartoum were the Islamist hard-liners who pushed for and passed the September Laws of 1983, which institutionalized sharia law for the entire country, including southern Sudan. These moves added to the region's sharply worsening political fortunes the additional sting of ideological and religious marginalization, which was enough to finally convince most southern elites that the prospect of politically coexisting with their northern counterparts within state institutions was an illusion. Badal notes that at this point, "from a single political entity the South had been reduced to a mere geographical expression."[28]

In sum, although the Addis Ababa Agreement provided a path to victory incorporation for the SSLM, and by extension offered the prospect of southern Sudan's broader political accommodation, its ultimate failure resulted from fundamental shifts in Nimeiry's regime opposition strategies that no longer required southern support vis-à-vis his northern rivals. The moves that followed signaled the final dislodging of southern elites from Sudanese political institutions that they had only nominally occupied over the course of the agreement's steady erosion. The aspirations of these elites to penetrate and occupy Sudan's mainstream political establishment, on any terms, were thwarted. Former insiders, after having spent years cultivating political roles, now found themselves *unwarrantedly* cast as outsiders to mainstream Sudanese politics. But the decline of southern Sudanese politics did not occur in a vacuum of resistance. As the 1970s unfolded, southern dissidents got busy organizing and pushing back, particularly those threatened by the inequitable rearrangements of the PAF in the south. Soon widespread arrests of agitating southern politicians were accompanied by massive defections from the army and police.[29] From the melee emerged a new coalition of southern elites and military commanders, who joined with remnants of the Anya-Nya. The September Laws were enough to alienate most southerners and render them open to the prospect of renewed rebellion.[30] By 1983, these growing forces pushed the SPLA to emerge as the new rebel challenger in Sudan.

Embedded Rebels

The previous discussion is important because it shows how the main actors of the southern rebellion were not necessarily separate and distinct from the evolution of Sudan's political networks since independence. As will become clearer in this section, the SPLA emerged from the wreckage of southern Sudanese politics. Yet as a result, it also came into rebellion with the organizational endowments associated with political embeddedness that had developed by fits and starts over several contentious decades of the country's shifting coalition politics. When the SPLA came on the scene, its organizational anatomy was made up of several moving parts that converged upon broad-based "national force" that, at least in the early years of the rebellion, displayed a modal pattern of cohesion that overcame numerous pressures.

Anchoring the rebellion was Colonel John Garang de Mabior, who had entered the Sudanese military as an ex-Anya-Nya in 1972. In this capacity, he had gone on to receive US military training at Fort Benning and earned a PhD in agricultural economics from Iowa State University. In the initial stage of the rebellion, while he was embedded in Sudan's politico-military establishment as head of both the Military Staff College in Omdurman and military production and research,[31] Garang quietly cultivated a network of underground dissidents within the military. These included southern battalion commanders Kuanyin Kerubino and William Nyuon, and military intelligence officers Salva Kiir and Thon Arok Thon. Together, these five men comprised the initial core of the SPLA, which headed up its organizational structure largely modeled on the Sudanese army.[32] In July 1983, Kerubino sparked a mutiny in the garrison towns of Bor, Pibor, and Pochalla, which Nyuon soon joined in

the town of Ayod.[33] Naively sent to Bor by Khartoum to quell the upris-
ing, Garang simply joined Kerubino, setting off a wider exodus of entire
battalions of southern troops and their commanders from Sudan's
national army into the SPLA's ranks.[34]

As the SPLA increasingly took and held territory in the south, its
Political Military High Command (PMHC) became the organizational
lynchpin of an ethnically diverse rebellion that was compelled to take
on emerging governance roles.[35] Slotting into this structure were educated southerners who had previously occupied positions within state
institutions, particularly in universities, technical and vocational col-
leges, and other government training institutions.[36] The SPLA found
that such actors, totaling into the hundreds, were useful rebel adminis-
trators, as they were already experienced bureaucrats who had acquired
authority and had learned organizational principles well before 1983.
Many became key advisers to Garang or political commissars within the
SPLA's rudimentary civil administration. Other key professionals such
as doctors and judges carried out these same roles within the rebellion.[37]
Thousands of boys, who faced school closures across southern Sudan,
followed their former headmasters to join the rebellion. At the lower
end of the SPLA's hierarchy were scores of rural youth who joined
largely out of self-defense.

The SPLA differed from the Anya-Nya and the SSLM in two key
ways. First, its predecessors had separate military and political wings,
but the SPLA merged them into the singular PMHC. Second, and most
important, Garang eschewed the separatist agenda of the previous southern rebellions. Instead, as outlined in the 1983 SPLA Manifesto, Garang
explicitly promoted a unified, democratic "New Sudan" that integrated
all of the country's diverse groups under a single political entity.[38] Following that principle, the SPLA proposed that Sudan should be governed
through a new process of elite accommodation that both integrated and
transformed the country's divided political networks into a more egali-
tarian, democratic whole. And although southern political elites had long
maintained secession as their primary goal, their newly formed United
Sudan African Parties (USAP) threw their lot in with the SPLA.

The SPLA and the Technology of Rebellion

The lion's share of Sudan's civil war was arguably characterized by symmetrical, irregular warfare, although these dynamics changed after the
country became an oil exporter after 1999. Yet overall, during the course
of conflict, the limited capacities and fluctuating fortunes of the

Sudanese Armed Forces (SAF) and the SPLA converged into a long-term stalemate that extended the life of Sudan's civil war. Territorial control over parts of Sudan—Africa's largest country at the time—largely followed the predictions of symmetrical, irregular war, with loosely identifiable lines separating north and south. Huge swaths of southern Sudan came to fall under the SPLA where it established a rudimentary state, although the southern regional capital of Juba remained a small island of state control throughout the war as a government garrison town.[39]

During the early years of the war, the SAF's southern campaigns were full of demoralized troops and insufficient logistical support, and the SAF often faltered in the face of a more cohesive and determined SPLA.[40] Unable to field a large army across such vast distances, a modal pattern of counterinsurgency strategies carried out by successive regimes in Khartoum involved the use of proxy militias. Khartoum motivated its proxies with promises of future political and economic rewards or provided divisive narratives that convinced militiamen of the need for retribution against certain ethnic groups in the south, particularly the populous Dinka. This strategy was often supplemented with the aerial bombardment of civilians, clumsy affairs in which bombs were literally rolled out of the back of aging Antinov aircraft.[41] Yet from 1999 onward, Sudan's oil revenues significantly increased the capacity of the SAF, which never gave up its use of proxies.[42] Gradually, the war took on a more asymmetrical pattern, although by this time the SAF had become more concerned with the clearing and securing of territory for oil exploration and drilling than with engaging rebels on the battlefield as the main security-related priority.[43]

As to the SPLA, its organizational core adapted to the conditions of its broader resource environment. Arguably the most important were the rebellion's foreign alliances, and the SPLA could not have weathered the 1980s without a robust resource network with Ethiopia at the center.[44] With heavy backing from the Derg regime in Addis Ababa, the SPLA received weapons, training, and most important, a territorial rear base. Ethiopian advisers strengthened the SPLA's political commissars and military command, helping Garang consolidate his leadership role over potential rivals.[45] In return, the SPLA helped fight anti-Derg rebels.[46]

In 1991, the fall of the Derg regime was followed by the SPLA's ejection from Ethiopian soil, a move that cast the group adrift from its chief sponsor. Although this stalled the SPLA for almost three years and reversed many of its military gains, the group nevertheless adapted to alternative resource networks.[47] Resource linkages with Zimbabwe channeled surplus weapons and equipment from rebellions in southern

Africa, notably the South West African People's Organization (SWAPO) and the African National Congress (ANC).[48] Even Zairean president Mobuto gave Garang a tour of Goma's military training facilities.[49]

Yet key to the SPLA rebounding was the 1989 military cooperation agreement with Ugandan president Museveni, which provided equipment, training, travel documents, and free passage through Uganda.[50] Moreover, Kenya's border town of Lokichoggio became an essential way station for the SPLA,[51] with Nairobi as the key diplomatic conduit to international donors. The SPLA therefore benefited from a humanitarian war economy from the UN's Kenya-based Operation Lifeline Sudan (OLS), a massive cross-border relief operation that invariably became a large resource for the SPLA through the distribution of humanitarian aid, by explicitly building the capacity of SPLA civil and political institutions[52] and conferring a degree of external legitimacy by creating "humanitarian wings" for each faction.[53]

Regime Strategies

On the surface, the dominant pattern of Khartoum's strategy for dealing with the SPLA was eliminating the rebellion via military means, which led to counterinsurgency campaigns that were particularly harsh toward the south's civilian populations. Khartoum deliberately engineered famine in southern Sudan as a way to undermine the SPLA's guerrilla war economy.[54] Yet alongside military operations, Khartoum also pursued a subtler strategy of co-optation that occasionally sought to accommodate southern political elites and key ethnic constituencies.

With a weak army and the impetus to control vast geographical distances, by far the most common strategy was to exploit sectarian divisions in southern Sudan to create and use proxy forces against the SPLA, as mentioned above.[55] Under the umbrella of the People's Defense Forces (PDF), Khartoum amassed a sizable militia of indoctrinated youth to carry out operations against any opposition the regime identified. Among these forces were the Arabic-speaking Baggara militias of Sudan's Kordofan region, also known as the Muraheleen, which played a large role in helping create famine conditions among the Dinka populations of Bahr el Ghazal in the late 1980s and 1990s.[56] And as described in Chapter 3, Khartoum also armed and trained a range of Uganda groups to fight the SPLA.

Most important, however, was Khartoum's co-optation of ethnic Nuer political and tribal leaders, and the manipulation of southern ethnic divisions to weaken the SPLA and mire the rebellion in internecine conflict. This strategy began with former Anya-Nya leaders Gai Tut and Akwot Atem, who in the 1980s had fallen out with Garang's leadership and were subsequently pushed out of the SPLA by the rebellion's Ethiopian patrons.[57] This new faction set up a separate "Anya-Nya 2" command with a renewed division between military and political wings, and most important, established a politburo in Khartoum. With support from the Sudanese government, the faction systematically hindered SPLA operations in the Upper Nile region, disrupted supply lines to Bahr el Ghazal, and worked to secure oil fields for the government.[58] This approach of using southern rebel factions against the SPLA reflected a pernicious dualism, in which Khartoum pursued a broader "peace from within strategy" that co-opted SPLA rivals with promises of future political accommodation within Sudan's political establishment.

Khartoum also exploited well-developed anti-SPLA sentiments that had developed in other regions of southern Sudan, particularly Equatoria. After all, the regional capital of Juba had been the administrative seat of the SRG, and Equatorians had been the ballast of the Anya-Nya, viewing themselves as the natural heirs to and leaders of southern Sudanese political identity. It was no surprise that many harbored suspicions of the SPLA, an ethnic "Dinka army," which often behaved appallingly toward ordinary Equatorians as it expanded its territorial control throughout the south.[59] Indeed, many civilians resisted the SPLA's arrival in Equatoria in 1985,[60] and those who did join the rebellion remained subordinate to Dinka officers, which exacerbated exploitable tensions.[61] Khartoum responded by funneling arms to ethnic Toposa and Mundari militias, as well as Murle groups as far afield from Equatoria as Pibor in the Jonglei region.[62]

The nadir of Khartoum's co-optation strategy, however, was the creation of the umbrella United Democratic Salvation Front (UDSF) and its armed wing, the South Sudan Defense Force (SSDF), which recruited Garang's chief rival, Riek Machar, against the SPLA. Khartoum's instrumentalization of Machar and a range of Nuer militias became a persistent pattern for much of the civil war, which developed distinctly ethnic contours that also led to intra-Nuer conflict.[63]

Yet Machar's UDSF amounted to little more than shadow administration for Khartoum in southern Sudan, and it had no authentic authority with ordinary southern Sudanese. Instead, its real power lay with the harder-edged SSDF, especially the militia commander Paulino Matiep, who commanded an inchoate amalgam of Nuer fighters.[64] Although it increasingly factionalized along clan lines, Matiep remained a regional strongman and a veto player in relations with Khartoum and in inter-Nuer politics. Machar's attempt to revamp these factions into the South Sudan Independence Army (SSIA) ultimately drove out other strongmen who had defected from the SPLA—Lam Akol, Kerubino, and Nyuon—each of whom had formed his own anti-SPLA factions also supported by the Sudanese government.[65] Such purges stripped Machar of support for his authority as well as his organizational capacity. This left what remained of his group beholden to Machar's whimsical, ad hoc decisions, which could not manage the growth of competitive local power bases. His resource dependency on Khartoum left no room for him to maneuver its ongoing series of vague promises to "determine the aspirations" of southern Sudan that were dangled in front of him. Indeed, by collaborating with Khartoum and instigating intra-southern violence, his legitimacy among southern fighters plummeted and motivated many of them to rejoin Garang's mainstream SPLA rebellion.[66]

Truncated Accommodation

As Khartoum pursued a patchy military strategy against the SPLA through its weak military and its proxies, there were several frayed threads of accommodation that ran through the war as well. During the early years of the war, Khartoum continued to rule southern Sudan through military appointees while keeping the role of southern politicians on the margins.[67] In these same years, prospects for political accommodation with the SPLA were dim. Although, by fits and starts, some political actors in Khartoum occasionally extended political overtures alongside the regime's dominant strategy of seeking to eliminate the SPLA. Indeed, in line with previous patterns of fair-weather alliances between northern and southern elites, some elites in Khartoum sometimes viewed Garang as a potential coalition partner. The Koka Dam Declaration of 1986, for instance, brought together the SPLA and a group of northern and southern political parties, providing a list of general principles for moving forward that became the basis of future talks.[68] Yet such rare, optimistic signs of any progress collapsed in the face of intransigence on all sides.[69]

Garang was particularly wary of moves toward consolidating Sudan as an Islamic state, and he refused several invitations to Khartoum to thrash out an accord. In fact, he rejected any overtures toward a political settlement that did not provide for a constitutional convention for all Sudanese political parties.[70] On this basis, when the head of the Sudanese National Security Service, Omar el Tayeb, went to Addis

Ababa to strike a deal with the SPLA, he was sent packing.[71] Complicating matters further were the cycles of regime change in Khartoum,
which moved the players on the board and changed their associated
political interests in doing business with the SPLA. After Nimeiry's
1985 departure, talks between his replacement, Sadiq al-Mahdi, and
Garang yielded nothing. And the 1989 coup regime of Omar al Bashir
led to the dominance of Islamist hard-liners in the National Islamic
Front government that froze talks indefinitely.[72]

Into the 1990s, regional and international actors began to drive
peacemaking efforts in Sudan. In 1992 and 1993, Nigerian president
Ibrahim Babangida led failed peace talks in Abuja, Nigeria's capital.[73]
Still more significant was the parallel effort by the regional Intergovern-
mental Authority on Development (IGAD), which sought to address the
destabilization the Sudanese civil war was unleashing upon the group's
other members—Ethiopia, Eritrea, Kenya, and Uganda. In March 1994,
IGAD established the Standing Committee on Peace in Sudan, and in
the years that followed, Nairobi became an unofficial political headquarters for southern factions and the epicenter for an ongoing cycle of
negotiations aimed at rapprochement between north and south.

Publicly, Garang remained committed to a unified secular Sudan.
IGAD's Declaration of Principles (DoP) articulated language that mirrored this overarching goal and also included a right to southern self-
determination through a referendum.[74] In response, the Sudanese government entrenched its view for a unified Sudan—under Islamic law.
Khartoum also continued its cynical "peace from within" strategy
through Machar and other southerners by signing a series of parallel
agreements that contained only ambiguous language about southern
self-determination, which only eroded Machar's position. Recall that
Machar's standing among southern Sudanese was far from stellar. After
a brief period leading the ineffective and highly factionalized Sudan
Popular Defence Forces (SPDF), in 2000 Machar left the Sudanese government[75] and, hat in hand, returned to the SPLA fold to begin his own
rapprochement with Garang.[76]

The Path to Victory by Incorporation

Consider first the SPLA's ability to maintain organizational cohesion in
the face of multiple pressures over the course of the war. The first step
toward achieving this was Garang's savvy, centralized control over the
SPLA's military endowments and nonmilitary elements, which arguably
was enabled with Ethiopian support.[77] During the 1980s, this mode of

organization helped score a number of operational successes, which eventually led to dividing territory into distinct zonal forces.[78] Strategic control over such a far-flung command area was uneven, and local commanders maintained a degree of autonomy. Garang was often disconnected from the day-to-day operations in such a wide area of operations, preferring to move among Addis Ababa, Boma HQ, and various international capitals in the pursuit of political support. Given geography and logistics, the Political Military High Command rarely even met in its entirety, providing few opportunities to address fundamental questions about the grand strategies. But the SPLA held together remarkably well, and Garang enjoyed a great deal of legitimacy as a rebel leader.

Yet Garang also maintained a distinct authoritarian style, which agitated some members of the PMHC. In 1991, with the fall of the Derg, the loss of the SPLA's chief backer was not simply a loss of essential resources. It brought to the fore internal power struggles that were now freed from the restraining influence of Ethiopian advisers, precipitating a large-scale crisis of fragmentation within the rebellion.

Riek Machar, a Nuer, and Lam Akol, a Shilluk, created and led what became known as the SPLA-Nasir faction. Both were engineers educated in the United Kingdom and represented the less embedded but educated, peripherally institutionalized class of SPLA cadres. As such, they did not bring into the rebellion sizable organizational endowments derived from previous association with Sudan's prewar political establishment. But they had followings in their own right, and in the 1980s, they rose within the ranks of the SPLA and assumed zonal commands in the Upper Nile, a long-neglected theater that saw its Nuer fighters pulled away to operations in Equatoria. Occupying nonvoting, marginal roles with the PMHC, they grew tired of Garang's intolerance of dissent and began plotting for his removal with the help of remaining Nuer fighters in both Upper Nile and Gambela. The Nasir Declaration and the document "Why Garang Must Go Now" convincingly laid out the reasons for the split: Garang's authoritarianism, the SPLA's pattern of human rights abuses and widespread use of child soldiers, and the abandonment of separatism in favor of unity.

Although the remainder of the PMHC remained intact under Garang, the mass exit of Nuer fighters punched a giant hole in the SPLA's organization, and subsequent defections of Kerubino, Nyuon, and Arok Thon opened up fresh internecine battlefronts.[79] What began as a leadership dispute between Garang and Machar morphed into a brutal ethnic conflict between Dinka and Nuer in the Upper Nile and Jonglei regions.[80]

Surviving such crippling factionalization required Garang to expand the rebellion's political scale and scope. In line with this goal, the SPLA held its first National Convention in April 1994,[81] whose "New Sudan" approach reinvigorated the group's organizational capacity and tightened its political control over southern Sudan by developing a civil administration and promoting broader connections to local authority structures. Although the SPLA spent much of the 1990s mired in interfactional warfare, the efforts to establish rudimentary governance structures in southern Sudan stood in stark contrast to Machar's role as a proxy for Khartoum.

Now consider Garang's durable persona within Sudanese political society, and his mastery of Sudan's domestic political networks. Indeed, he had always portrayed the SPLA as a broad national movement and had actively courted disenfranchised leaders of northern opposition parties throughout the conflict.[82] By the 1990s, the SPLA joined an expanded network of Sudanese opposition called the National Democratic Alliance (NDA),[83] made up of traditional northern opposition groups[84] and military elites disenfranchised by the 1989 coup in Khartoum, a group calling itself the Legitimate Command of Armed Forces. This coalition of northern and southern elites represented the majority of Sudanese and conferred a new degree of legitimacy upon Garang as a political leader.[85]

The Asmara Declaration of 1995 elevated Garang to the role of the NDA's joint military commander.[86] Following this, Eritrea began hosting military training bases for the NDA's armed members, the SPLA and the Sudanese Armed Forces (SAF). This opened a new eastern front in the broader civil war as the SPLA extended control into new regions such as the Blue Nile and Nuba Mountains.[87] Meanwhile, Garang maneuvered his NDA allies to accept IGAD's DoP in the Asmara Declaration. This expanded set of actors, now aligned with the SPLA's priorities,[88] collectively increased the threat to the regime in Khartoum and most certainly got the attention of regime elites. The SAF continued parallel military operations, and the SPLA's foothold in a broader political alliance facilitated moves toward accommodation.

The story of the SPLA's victory by incorporation had long included external actors. But by 2002, international interest in ending the long civil war had become almost fetishized by a number of actors, namely, the "troika" of the United States, the United Kingdom, and Norway that helped rejuvenate the IGAD peace process and exerted pressure on Sudanese government leaders and Garang to reengage a peaceful path to conflict resolution. Despite some false starts and efforts to link

negotiations to "benchmarks,"[89] efforts resulted in the Machakos proto-
col, which confirmed the basic contours of a potential agreement.[90]
Intensive and contentious negotiations unfolded over the following
months and years against the backdrop of ongoing warfare in Sudan as
both sides maneuvered for more leverage in the negotiation.[91]

Ultimately, the process set the scene for the Comprehensive Peace
Agreement in 2005.[92] Although it did not deliver all key demands,[93] the
accord established the Interim National Constitution (INC) and through
a "grand bargain" addressed the key issue of self-determination through
a referendum after a six-year period, in exchange for the continuation of
sharia law in the north.[94] In addition, the accord established power and
wealth sharing between north and south under the Government of
National Unity (GNU) that gave Garang the vice presidency. The war
was now over, with the SPLA having negotiated itself into Sudanese
politics on terms favorable enough to establish a future referendum on
its eventual independence.

In sum, the civil war between the Sudanese government and the
SPLA has perennially been miscast as a binary narrative "between the
Muslim North and largely Christian and animist South." Yet this is an
oversimplification of a protracted affair with many moving parts and
multiple, overlapping, often contradictory sets of interests. To be sure,
the focus on the SPLA here has necessarily sidestepped some explanatory factors that might have contributed to the 2005 CPA that put an
end to Africa's longest conflict. That said, the goal of this section has
been to show the historical institutional linkages between the SPLA
and the *longue durée* of Sudanese politics. It has illuminated the
nature of the SPLA's political embeddedness, which conferred upon it
organizational cohesion and the positionality within political society
to eventually penetrate Sudan's political establishment and achieve a
victory via incorporation.

The Forces Nouvelles

In recent years, Côte d'Ivoire has begun an uneven but steady recovery
from its civil war, moving toward something that better resembles the
political stability and economic prosperity it once enjoyed during the
decades following its independence. Indeed, heralded as the "Ivorian
miracle," the country was once considered a model for African development, as a strong single-party system under founding president Félix
Houphouët-Boigny harnessed the wealth generated by plantation agri-

culture and high commodity prices, particularly for cocoa, of which the country remains the world's largest producer.

Although the current situation in Côte d'Ivoire may be trending positive, it is nevertheless still emerging from not one, but two interconnected civil wars that unfolded over a decade. Each reflected a trend of decline that began under Houphouët-Boigny but accelerated after his death in 1993. Characterized by economic decay, spiraling unemployment, growing poverty, and the rise of political and communal violence, Ivorian politics passed through a contentious period of instability marked by flawed elections, coups, and ultimately civil war and rebellion. Most important, during this period successive leaders seized upon the concept of Ivoirité—"Ivorian-ness"—as the basis for citizenship. Initially used as a blunt instrument to exclude Alassane Ouattara, the country's current president, from national politics in the 1990s, Ivoirité soon transformed into a discrete policy and therefore a more fundamental source of political exclusion, identity conflict, and intercommunal violence that invariably affected most ordinary Ivorians.

The Forces Nouvelles rebellion emerged as a flashpoint for these dynamics. It was also a composite of several groups, represented by military and political elites from different segments of Ivorian political society who had significant linkages to state institutions. At its core was the Mouvement Patriotique de Côte d'Ivoire (MPCI), which was largely composed of disenfranchised Ivorian soldiers from the northern part of the country. Launching its first attacks from Burkina Faso in September 2002, the group was also a response to the narrowing of citizenship criteria to exclude many northerners from Ivorian state politics. The MPCI soon merged with two other rebellions that came out of western Côte d'Ivoire in late 2002: the Mouvement pour la Justice et la Paix (MJP) and the Mouvement Populaire Ivoirien du Grand Ouest (MPIGO). Although they represented homegrown grievances, these two groups were largely extensions of Liberian president Charles Taylor's regional security and economic interests.

The Forces Nouvelles was not always the most cohesive of rebellions, but it represented a significant enough threat to Côte d'Ivoire's incumbent regime to merit international intervention by the French, regional African militaries, and the UN. This set of interventions undergirded a series of peace talks that sought to incorporate the rebellion's political and military leaders into Ivorian state politics. But ongoing controversy and intransigence over key provisions of a series of accords drew the talks out for nearly a decade and sparked a renewed rebellion that eschewed a political settlement in favor of full-blown victory by domination. Since this turnabout, the rebel-backed government of Alassane Ouattara has been reelected (2015), and many members of the Forces Nouvelles have been integrated into Côte d'Ivoire's political and military establishment.

This section begins by showing how Ivoirité became a mechanism of exclusion that upended the status of key actors within Ivorian politics. It then follows the trajectory of the Forces Nouvelles from its inception during Côte d'Ivoire's first civil war (2002–2007), through an awkward and protracted period of political settlement implementation (2007–2010), and finally to the country's reversion to the armed rebellion that ushered in its ultimate victory by domination in 2011. The case illuminates how status reversal can galvanize rebellion, how embeddedness can facilitate political settlement, and how incumbent intransigence toward accommodation can lead to victory by domination as a feasible fate for a rebellion composed of political insiders.

Elite Politics and the Rise of Ivoirité

Although the Forces Nouvelles was a rebellion of multiple moving parts, it had at its core disgruntled soldiers, a composition that conferred a degree of organizational cohesion to the group. Many of these soldiers came from the north of the country, as did several of the political actors with whom they made alliances. This meant that their linkage to Côte d'Ivoire's political establishment was rendered vulnerable to the ongoing, deliberate attempts on behalf of incumbents to delegitimize and disenfranchise these actors through the distinct mechanism of citizenship, captured by the concept of Ivoirité. The trajectory of the Forces Nouvelles therefore reflected the tensions between its core membership, which consisted of insiders, and their having been institutionally redefined as outsiders by the state. Thus, the dynamics of political embeddedness, and attempts at disembedding key actors from Côte d'Ivoire's prevailing political establishment, accelerated along two vectors.

Along the first of these vectors was the quick unraveling of longstanding open-door immigration policies and corresponding ethnic balancing strategies that had characterized the Houphouët-Boigny era from independence until his death in 1993. Even prior to independence, especially during the 1920s and 1930s, the colonial state's creation of a plantation-based economy had laid the foundation for the initial political contours of land-based ethnic identity. This occurred by differentiating and managing relationships among landowners, planters, and what became a rather favored class of migrant laborers known collectively as "Dioula."[95] The country's postindependence politics were able to paper over some of the more contentious issues of land tenure and nationality in the service of political stability, and stability was in fact the modal pattern of politics.

Led by the philosophy that "the land belongs to those who cultivate it," the Ivorian economic model of plantation agriculture relied heavily on migrant labor from neighboring countries and inflows of foreign capital. The ensuing success of the Ivorian economy fed Houphouët-Boigny's patronage machine. With his one-party political system and the Baoulé ethnic group at its center, the Parti Démocratique de la Côte d'Ivoire-Rassemblement Démocratique Africain (PDCI-RDA) dispensed sinecures to different ethnic constituencies in order to manage their coexistence with migrant laborers, particularly those in the country's southwestern part, the ethnic Bété and Kroumen. However, economic decline in the 1980s began to strain this strategy, as a fall in global cocoa prices dried up the resources necessary to maintain the institutional status quo and to provide jobs for a swelling number of educated young men.

As political parties were legalized in 1990, President Houphouët-Boigny called snap elections and lavished all twenty-six parties with resources as a successful strategy to divide and defeat opposition to his own PDCI-RDA, which included Laurent Gbagbo's Front Populaire Ivorien (FPI).[96] Although this political strategy represented brazen co-optation of the country's fledgling democratic transition, it nevertheless repurposed preexisting modes of elite accommodation. However, after Houphouët-Boigny's death, his less savvy successor, Henri Konan Bedié, was either unwilling or incapable of implementing the necessary political and economic reforms. Instead, he focused on managing political opposition, and his restrictions on political parties led to a boycott of the country's 1995 elections and his easy victory. This move represented the first step away from his predecessor's ethnic balancing strategy and toward a fiercer national dialogue about citizenship, all against the backdrop of ongoing economic recession.

Following these broader trends, the second vector was the weaponization of Ivoirité as the basis for political exclusion. It began initially to exclude Alassane Ouattara's candidacy and his new party, the Rassemblement des Républicains (RDR) from the 1995 presidential election by claiming he was not a native Ivorian, as he grew up in Burkina Faso. Under Bedié, Ivoirité became legally institutionalized in electoral politics, an act that did not simply block Ouattara's entry into the regime but painted large swaths of northern Ivorians as having "mixed heritage," therefore disqualifying many of them from their roles in government and creating a new north-south identity cleavage.[97] Ivoirité also came to signify what some scholars have referred to as "authochtony"—in the Ivorian case, this meant that citizenship was restricted to those born to parents who were members of certain "sovereign" ethnic groups. Those born of Ivorian soil were designated as "pure" in the context of the country's status hierarchy. Although the policy was created to target Ouattara, Ivoirité began to appear in everyday practices of discrimination against those of "dubious nationality."[98]

The "Christmas coup" of 1999, led by junior officers in the Forces Armées Nationales de Côte d'Ivoire (FANCI) elevated General Robert Guéï to the presidency. Although this event may have slightly slowed overt expressions of ethnonationalism, it nevertheless upended several other features of Ivorian politics. First, an ethnic Yacouba from the west, Guéï overthrew the prevailing Baoulé ethnic clique that had occupied the upper echelons of state power since independence and replaced it with soldiers.[99] Second, although the military was now a central feature of regime politics, Guéï proved unable to manage divisions and mistrust in the ranks as they splintered into a number of unwieldy factions, prompting him to rely increasingly on an expanded gendarmerie to counter them.[100] Third, because many northerners occupied places within the military, Guéï's coup increased their relative power and thus incentivized mainstream political parties to continue to push for Ivoirité. This ongoing campaign was clearly affirmed by the supreme court's invalidation of Ouattara's candidacy for the country's 2000 elections, which Gbagbo's FPI won.

Following Gbagbo's victory and the ascendancy of his FPI political party, a revived version of Ivoirité rapidly expanded to represent a broader nativist rejection of foreigners, northerners, and Muslims. It also drove a wave of xenophobic sentiment rooted in land ownership as the country's economic crisis became further intertwined with political instability.

With Gbagbo as the self-appointed steward of territorial identity, the interests of "autochthons"—particularly those of his Bété ethnic group from the southeast—now assumed a central role in regime politics, creating a new raft of prohibitions and obstacles for those not deemed "pure" Ivorian. This key cleavage between insider and outsider was most pronounced between members of Gbagbo's FPI and Ouattara's RDR parties. Yet Ivoirité as a systematic program of national identity found purchase within a number of other institutions, including schools and, most important, the military. The implication here was that those deemed lacking in the key quality of Ivoirité, now the central, organizing principle for Ivorian society, were viewed as threats to the prevailing order and therefore deserving of economic and political dis-possession,[101] creating permissive conditions for civil war and rebellion.

The Anatomy of the Forces Nouvelles

Ivoirité was not just about assigning subordinate status to certain groups. It was a deliberate strategy of explicitly disembedding groups from state institutions—groups that had been more or less accommodated by polit-ical society in a previous era when such strategies were useful and pos-sible. The emergent discourse of insider versus outsider that was enthu-siastically embraced by regime elites following the Houphouët-Boigny era, and the associated moves toward the institutionalization of Ivoirité, cast a distinct set of politico-military actors from the political establish-ment. These actors formed the core of the Forces Nouvelles.

The MPCI formed in 2000 as an amalgam of exiled Ivorian soldiers who incubated their rebellion in the Burkinabe capital of Ouagadougou. Although this inner core was not necessarily monolithic, it nevertheless brought into the formation of the MPCI an organizational endowment and mobilizational skills. Above all, the MPCI possessed an intact net-work of cadres who shared common experiences in school during the Bedié period and during their time with the FANCI. Because they were from the north, they held the common view that they were victims of institutionalized discrimination, and most were also political supporters of Alassane Ouattara.

Institutionally, many came from distinct military factions that had formed during Guéï's junta—namely, the Cosa Nostra, Camorra, and Red Brigades.[102] Others had served in the UN Mission in Central African Republic (MINURCA) in the late 1990s.[103] Other groups within the MPCI included the Zinzin ("crazy ones"), the Bahéfoué ("sorcer-ers"), and a crop of army deserters who had fallen out with Guéï.[104] Once the MPCI seized most of the north and began its advance toward the capital, Abidjan, it fleshed out its force with sympathetic members of the FANCI[105] and gendarmerie,[106] as well as many young northerners, and traditional hunters known as Dozos.

A single galvanizing military actor for the MPCI was Sergeant-Chief Ibrahim Coulibaly, also known as IB. A man who wore several hats, he had previously served as Ouattara's bodyguard, was a key member of the 1999 coup, was a member of Guéï's Presidential Guard, and had been a military attaché to Canada.[107] Supplementing his leadership were MPCI cofounders Sergeant Souleymane Diomandé ("la Grenade") and Corpo-ral Diarrassouba ("Zaga Zaga"),[108] and colonels Michel Gueu and Ismaël

Soumalïa Bakayoko, and Boka Yapi.[109] Authority was further distributed among several key cadres: Staff Sergeant Tuo Fozié, Chérif Ousmane, Issiaka Ouattara, and Massamba Koné, each of whom had served in leadership roles within the regime security apparatus.[110]

As the MPCI took territory and consolidated its northern positions, two new rebellions emerged from the western part of the country in late 2002—the MJP and MPIGO.[111] Politically, neither group had discrete linkages to regime politics, although many claimed they fought to avenge the death of Guéï, who hailed from Côte d'Ivoire's western region. Although there were a handful of Ivorian soldiers in the mix, such as MPIGO's Felix Doh, the leadership of each group consisted largely of Liberian and Sierra Leonean fighters, among them Sam Bockarie of the Revolutionary United Front. Strategically, the MPCI saw these groups as potential allies that could provide additional muscle to help them reach the key port of San Pedro on the coast. Yet to a large extent, the MJP and MPIGO were extensions of Charles Taylor's regional security and economic interests. Disrupting the border area between Liberia and Côte d'Ivoire provided the Liberian leader with an opportunity to grab resources and to counter Ivorian support for a group of anti-Taylor rebels, the Movement for Democracy in Liberia (MODEL), which made use of Ivorian territory.[112]

This new front in the civil war generated a massive humanitarian crisis.[113] Unlike their MPCI counterparts in the north, MJP and MPIGO fighters were highly predatory against civilians. Above all, the west became a flashpoint for a complex web of politicized ethnicity that served both domestic and regional interests. Ongoing tensions between ethnic Guéré and the northwestern Yacouba and Dioula groups took on a cross-border character with the arrival of both Liberian fighters and refugees in western Côte d'Ivoire. On one side of the cleavage, many Liberian members of MJP and MPIGO were Liberian Gio, close cousins to Ivorian Yacouba. This linkage reflected the political alliance between Taylor and Guéï, and it often manifested as violence targeted toward Guéré. On the other side were Liberian refugees recruited by the Ivorian government from refugee camps, many of whom were ethnic Krahn, a subset of the Krou group that also includes the Guéré and Bété (Gbagbo's group). The resulting instability, which was occurring against the backdrop of halfhearted political negotiations, prompted the MPCI to expand its authority into the west, purge the MJP and MPIGO of its mercenary elements, and effectively absorb the remainder of the groups. Shortly thereafter, it rebranded itself as the Forces Nouvelles, which was now positioned to pursue its path toward victory by domination.

FANCI vs. Forces Nouvelles

The civil war in Côte d'Ivoire was largely symmetrical and irregular by virtue of the limited relative capacity of both the army and the rebels. In addition, France's role in physically separating the antagonists effectively froze the country into two separately administered territories, which created conditions for a durable, mutually hurting stalemate.

Historically, the FANCI had been a fairly stable feature of Ivorian politics, if not an entirely visible part of the grander project of political legitimacy through agricultural exports and ethnic balancing.[114] Rather, Houphouët-Boigny, like many African rulers, kept the army small and weak, preferring to rely on France's ongoing military presence to bolster regime security.[115] Yet under post-Houphouët governments, the FANCI soon became an unstable microcosm of sectarian divisions. Bedié stocked its upper echelons with his Baoulé coethnics, and northern officers were routinely passed over for promotion while also being required to take oaths of personal loyalty.[116] And as mentioned earlier, Guéï's coup in 1999 put the military at the center of the political establishment. Paradoxically, Guéï increased the power of the gendarmerie and his own personal guard—the Brigade Rouge—to counter an increasingly untamable and factionalizing FANCI that was unbeholden to its own hierarchy.[117] Gbagbo, who shared Guéï's mistrust of the army, increasingly relied on parallel irregular forces, which continued and expanded the pattern of "militianization" of Ivorian politics,[118] while further allowing Ivoirité to permeate state institutions. The outcome was the hollowing out of the FANCI, which created the structural conditions for some of its northern members to break off and form the Forces Nouvelles.

In squaring off against the Forces Nouvelles, the FANCI faced a rebellion with an initial resource endowment of arms stolen from Ivorian armories, as well as substantial financing from a string of successful bank robberies.[119] In addition, the group enjoyed support from neighbors, supplemented by a mixture of guerrilla and commercial war economies. In the first instance, foreign support played a key initial role in shaping the Forces Nouvelles' resource base. Burkina Faso hosted disgruntled members of the FANCI that became the core of the MPCI, providing organizational support, weapons, and territory from which the rebellion launched its first operations.[120] The MPCI's early operational successes also yielded substantial seizures of FANCI weapons.[121] In the west, the MJP and MPIGO received substantial patronage from Charles Taylor, who stocked each group with weapons and mercenaries from Liberia and Sierra Leone as part of a strategy of regional destabilization and resource acquisition.[122] This support diminished as the MJP and MPIGO folded into an expanded Forces Nouvelles, which also involved a major purge of mercenaries from their ranks by mid-2003.[123] But Liberia would remain a key player in an intersecting system of localized ethnic and cross-border conflict.[124]

Second, as the war progressed, the Forces Nouvelles developed a rudimentary state in the north, which built upon preexisting Ivorian institutions and upon striking new bargains with the local Dozo militias, which helped the Forces Nouvelles maintain order.[125] A key component of rebel governance here was establishing La Centrale, which central-ized authority and managed the flow of tax receipts collected within zones the Forces Nouvelles controlled, generating significant resources to administer territory and sustain the rebellion.[126] The mode of gover-nance, though extractive, was not always predatory—for instance, the Forces Nouvelles kept water-treatment facilities working in major towns under its control.[127] Finally, with La Centrale largely collecting and distributing the revenue, the Forces Nouvelles engaged in commer-cial trade of the key commodities of cocoa, timber, and diamonds. Indi-rectly, this meant the systematic taxation of diamond mining, cocoa har-vests, and felled hardwoods in areas under rebel control, as well as placing levies on the transport of such goods.[128]

To be sure, the political economy of the Forces Nouvelles helped level the playing field against the FANCI by providing ample resources. Yet most significant was the French military's Operation Licorne, which played a key role in establishing a buffer zone, the Zone de Confiance (ZDC) between the two rival camps. Augmented and eventually replaced by regional and UN soldiers, French troops manned checkpoints and conducted regular patrols within the ZDC. Periodically, Licorne con-ducted substantial operations to disrupt the capacity of either side, for instance, its 2004 retaliatory destruction of the Ivorian air force.[129] The symmetrical, irregular nature of the conflict was thus essentially locked in place by French intervention. This pattern largely persisted through the second phase of the country's civil war, against the backdrop of a series of cease-fires and peace agreements, a matter to which I now turn.

Peace Accords, Regime Strategies, and the Path to Victory

It was a long walk to victory by domination for the Forces Nouvelles. Yet at several key points, it seemed as though the rebellion would achieve victory via incorporation as it passed through a series of failed cease-fires and peace negotiations—the Linas-Marcoussis agreement and the Kléber Accords of 2003, three iterations of Accra agreements in 2003–2005, two Pretoria agreements in 2005, and finally the Ouagadougou Peace Agreement of 2007, which was supplemented no less than four additional times. Clearly, for most of its decade-long run, the rebellion was locked into a mutually hurting stalemate with the incumbent Gbagbo regime. Each attempt to reach an agreement, and each agreement's collapse, coincided with key strategic political recalibrations for rebels and incumbents alike that created permissive conditions for the Forces Nouvelles' eventual seizure of state power.

After the MPCI's southern advance was stopped in its tracks by French intervention, a series of cease-fires culminated in the Linas-Marcoussis accord of January 2003, the first international attempt to broker a durable political settlement. The accord sought to end the war by forming a reconciliation government with key posts designated for both rebels and opposition political parties, and by paving the way for multiparty elections by 2005. Although the accord unraveled in less than two years, it had several important politico-military effects on the trajectory of what would immediately thereafter become the Forces Nouvelles, and it hardened the incumbent regime's strategy for dealing with the rebellion.

Militarily, a tentative cease-fire brokered by the Economic Community of West African States (ECOWAS) effectively froze the country into two halves, with the northern one controlled by rebels and the southern by the government, and the ZDC patrolled by French, ECOWAS, and UN peacekeepers. To be sure, this rearrangement of territorial space effectively contained full-blown war between rebels and the FANCI. Yet it also provided the stability required for both sides to recalibrate political strategies that eventually played out within the context of drawn-out negotiations. The territorial freeze also reinforced the preexisting north-south political divide by hardening identities through the establishment and maintenance of opposing state and rebel administrations. And though the emergence of the MPIGO and MJP complicated the MPCI's military calculations, these western rebellions were nevertheless incorporated into the broader negotiations, which also marked the moment when they were folded into the MPCI.

Politically, this period signaled the elevation of Guillaume Soro as the main political representative for the rebels.[130] Formerly the leader of the student union Fédération Estudiantine et Colaire de la Côte d'Ivoire (FESCI), Soro, though not a soldier, became secretary general of the MPCI and would become a key political player in the following years.

Most important, the talks facilitated an essential political alliance between two key signatories—the Forces Nouvelles and Ouattara's RDR party. Although Ouattara had played no role in the rebellion, this alliance, dubbed the "Marcoussiste" movement,[131] fused military and political opposition to the hegemony of Gbagbo's FPI in Ivorian politics and sought to dismantle Ivoirité as an instrument of political exclusion.

By mid-2003, Linas-Marcoussis began to unravel along the key dimension of power sharing, exacerbated by intractable issues of nationality, elections, and disarmament.[132] Much of this breakdown occurred on account of a distinct regime strategy to go through the motions of reconciliation on one hand while pushing forward a range of measures to prevent it on the other.

Indeed, as Straus has observed, the modal pattern of Gbagbo's strategies for dealing with any opposition, was to "combine repression and intimidation with nominal accommodation and inclusion."[133] As such, the failure of Linas-Marcoussis very much reflected the hardening of the broader strategy of elimination and a lukewarm commitment to control. Following the collapse of Linas-Marcoussis, this dual approach dragged out promises of future reconciliation and elections against the backdrop of increasing support for government-backed militias and their violence against key categories of Ivorians.

The events of the years from 2003 were driven by three main factors. First, the country remained militarily divided in two, which allowed both sides to attempt rearming. This occurred under wavering regional support for an ECOWAS peacekeeping force,[134] and a rickety deployment of UN troops[135] that hamstrung any ability to monitor cease-fire violations,[136] leaving the French as the primary, reluctant broker.[137]

Second, the politics of reaching a durable political settlement remained a game of blowing through election deadlines and thwarting the attempts by a range of outside mediators to hold Gbagbo to a timetable while convincing the Forces Nouvelles to disarm.[138] Such conditions only worsened in October 2005, once Gbagbo's formal term officially ended, after which he insisted on remaining in power.[139]

Third, this period marked a high point for shoring up the FANCI with Gbagbo loyalists and the mobilization of progovernment militias.[140] While Gbagbo wrangled with communal politics, power to influence things on the ground increasingly fell into the hands of Charles Blé Goude and his leadership over the Jeunes Patriotes militia,[141] which played the role of the FPI's "shock troops" in urban areas.[142] The central idea was to deploy a radical, ultranationalist strategy to thwart rebel demands for a "new political order" that would dismantle Ivoirité and assure the legitimacy of Ouattara's candidacy in future elections. Yet the use of these militias, while dangerous in the short term, only betrayed the weakness of Gbagbo's overall position.

These key factors converged upon the 2007 Ouagadougou Peace Agreement, which set the scene for a victory by incorporation by handing to Guillaume Soro the post of prime minister,[143] and by placing the FANCI and Forces Nouvelles under a joint command, the Centre du Commandement Intégré.[144] The agreement also set a timetable for disarmament, the withdrawal of peacekeepers, and the closing of the ZDC. Yet the perennial sticking point of national identity remained: Who qualified as Ivorian? Who could compete and vote in national elections? Multiple delays ensued and the election timetable was extended, but in principle, Ouattara was granted permission to stand for president.[145]

After nearly a decade of pushing for political inclusion, the elections of November 2010 seemed to be the culmination of a long process of victory by incorporation for the Forces Nouvelles.[146] Ouattara, now the leader of a broad coalition of rebels and the RDR, competed and won a runoff against Gbagbo's FPI. As result of his loss, a furious Gbagbo imposed a curfew and refused to concede to the "outsider" Ouattara, despite overwhelming international support for Ouattara as the electoral victor.[147] These moves renewed underlying tensions between the rebels and the militias supporting rival political actors, sparking violence and creating permissive conditions for a rebel resurgence and Côte d'Ivoire's second civil war.

By March 2011, the Forces Nouvelles again began to mobilize for a fight. This time the rebels were not required to run the gauntlet of a French-enforced ZDC barring their advance to Abidjan. Instead, the group faced and pushed through a loosely controlled UN buffer zone and in roughly one month's time handily conquered Abidjan.[148] By April, the rebels controlled Abidjan, effectively achieving victory domination over the intransigent incumbents and installing Ouattara as the country's rightful president. Rebels soon populated the new government, which also reorganized the national army into the more integrated Forces Républicaines de Cote d'Ivoire (FRCI).

In sum, the Forces Nouvelles was a rebellion driven by the status hierarchy grievances of former insiders institutionally reconstituted as outsiders to the prevailing political establishment. Blocked from the opportunity to enter into a political settlement and achieve a victory by incorporation, the group's only alternative was to achieve victory by domination.

Conclusion

The cases in this chapter demonstrate that political embeddedness confers key benefits upon rebellions that can be translated into some variant of victory. Both the SPLA and Forces Nouvelles began with distinct organizational endowments linked to key members' roles in state institutions. Although their respective paths toward victory were far from seamless, they nevertheless followed the contours of what should be expected from political insiders.

In this light, the SPLA and Forces Nouvelles had several features in common. First, the nature of the insiders who formed the organizational core of each rebel group: in both cases, they were members of their respective counties' national army. This meant that these insurgencies began with substantial start-up costs already met in terms of leader-cadre relationships, and in terms of having had a place within each state's political establishment. The SPLA case is particularly instructive in this sense, as most portrayals of Sudan's north-south civil war do not recognize that John Garang and key cadres were insiders who were very much embedded within the Sudanese armed forces. Moreover, the embedded political organization of the MPCI, which was the heart of what became the Forces Nouvelles, was the main driver of its path to victory after having absorbed the MPIGO and the MJP groups, which were largely composed of outsiders. This military vector suggests that there may in fact be qualitative differences in the nature of political embeddedness. That is, it might be harder to argue that members of the Ministry of Finance, for instance, could have marshaled forward rebellions similar to the SPLA and Forces Nouvelles and met similar variants of victory.

Second, both the SPLA and Forces Nouvelles shared parallel experiences in having their initial forced exit from a political establishment institutionalized or nearly institutionalized. That is, the identity markers that signified each group's place within Sudan's and Côte d'Ivoire's respective political societies became vectors along which status reversal was galvanized. For the SPLA, this was the steady erosion of southern Sudanese political autonomy in the 1970s, culminating in the imposition of sharia law in 1983, which cast southern Sudanese as second-class citizens. For the Forces Nouvelles, efforts to impose Ivoirité in order to circumscribe the participation of northerners in Ivorian politics animated both its civil war and efforts to end it. Interestingly, the intractability of Sudan's identity politics nevertheless gave way to the CPA and the ultimate secession of South Sudan. Yet in the Ivorian case, Ivoirité did not take full root institutionally—it came down to the personal refusal of Gbagbo to honor elections that had been guaranteed by a political settlement. A central insight here is that in insider politics that are heavily contaminated by identity markers, the role of *individuals* associated with both rebellions and incumbents may facilitate or obviate the more conventional predictors of accommodation.

Some differences are also worth noting. First, the SPLA and Forces Nouvelles diverge fairly dramatically in terms of leadership. For most of Sudan's civil war, the political identity of the SPLA was essentially indistinguishable from the fundamental character of John Garang, who came to epitomize an African guerrilla leader and larger-than-life personality in southern Sudan. The Forces Nouvelles, however, had nothing close to a Garang analog. IB never had total control over the rebellion, and Guillaume Soro was much more of a political actor than a military one, whose significant though muted role was perhaps the result of years of the stalemate that characterized much of Côte d'Ivoire's civil war. Second, the fates of each of these rebellions were differently tempered by time. The SPLA survived for more than two decades of protracted conflict that eventually demanded some form of accommodation. In contrast, the Forces Nouvelles was able to achieve a jarringly rapid victory following the collapse of its own political settlement. Both of these factors—the role of leadership, and how time factors into rebel trajectories—merit further inquiry.

These cases generate some additional questions. First, although they show that material capacity is less predictive of rebel fates than political embeddedness, what remains to be explained is the impact of the external actors' *political imperatives* on rebel trajectories. Consider those who wish to participate in regional war making. Both the SPLA and Forces Nouvelles received substantial support from neighbors, particularly territorial sanctuary that helped incubate each group's organizational structure. Whatever the regional ambitions of these sponsor regimes, in the SPLA case, Ethiopia was instrumental in shoring up Garang's leadership, whereas Burkinabe oversight of the Forces Nouvelles was key to its organizational start-up costs. If such support can help consolidate organizational endowments of insiders, to what extent can it provide this service to outsiders? I take up this question in the following chapter. Another key question, however, is that when rebels become proxies of unfriendly neighbors, to what extent does this enter into the calculus of regime strategies beyond the logic of political embeddedness? This also merits further inquiry.

Now consider those actors who wish to participate in peacemaking. The civil war in southern Sudan dragged on for years before any regional or international efforts to end it ever took root. To many observers and peace advocates, it was the only way for rebels and incumbents to get to the CPA. In the Côte d'Ivoire case, the immediate intervention of French troops effectively froze the conflict while a more regional effort to craft a political settlement unfolded by fits and starts. The question here is: To what extent are paths to victory by incorporation a function of political embeddedness versus regional and international diplomatic pressure to make a deal? Is it an essential component for insider business? Or does peacemaking merely act as a lubricant for accommodation that might have occurred anyway? Chapter 5 provides an opportunity to consider this question in light of the fates of outsiders.

In addition, a fresh puzzle generated from these cases is the divergent nature of postwar political order in South Sudan and Côte d'Ivoire. The rapid unraveling of South Sudan shortly after its independence suggests that some rebels may be incapable of effectively ruling once they seize the mantle of state power.[149] The SPLA has transformed from a successful rebellion that achieved victory incorporation into a highly corrupt and violent regime in the new capital, Juba. In contrast, Côte d'Ivoire's postwar trajectory following the victory of the Forces Nouvelles, though certainly not without obstacles, has been much more sanguine. What explains this variation? To be sure, the structural underpinnings of these two countries are dramatically different—Côte d'Ivoire's postwar recovery builds upon a decades-long legacy of economic development and relative political stability, whereas South Sudan's leaders have had to conjure a new state from an institutionally adrift political vacuum. Further inquiry should explore the extent to which the nature of rebel organizations, their place within prewar political society, and their associated fates in civil war shape political order after meeting any variant of victory. I take up this discussion briefly in Chapter 6.

Notes

1. Multiple interviews with South Sudan officials, Juba, August 2009, August 2010, July 2011.
2. See Johnson's bibliographic essay in *The Root Causes of Sudan's Civil Wars*, pp. 181–194.
3. Poggo, *The First Sudanese Civil War*, pp. 56–58.
4. Ibid.; Johnson, *The Root Causes of Sudan's Civil Wars*, p. 29.
5. Poggo, *The First Sudanese Civil War*, pp. 52–54.
6. Beshir, *The Southern Sudan*, pp. 80–81, Poggo, *The First Sudanese Civil War*, pp. 92–96.
7. "Anya-Nya" is Madi for "snake venom" and was broadly used to refer to both political and military actors from 1963. The use of a Madi term was not embraced by other ethnic groups, which had their own names for the rebellion.
8. Rolandsen, "The Making of the Anya-Nya Insurgency in the Southern Sudan, 1961–1964."

9. A fascinating record of SANU's interpretation of events can be found in their news journals of the mid-1960s, *Voice of Southern Sudan* and *Voice of the Nile Republic*.

10. Wakoson, "The Origin and Development of the Anya-Nya Movement, 1955–1972," pp. 131–136.

11. Ibid., pp. 135–136; Poggo, *The First Sudanese Civil War*, pp. 147–149.

12. Johnson, *The Root Causes of Sudan's Civil Wars*, p. 31; Wakoson, "The Origin and Development of the Anya-Nya Movement," p. 138; Poggo, *The First Sudanese Civil War*, pp. 151–153.

13. Johnson, *The Root Causes of Sudan's Civil Wars*, p. 37; Poggo, *The First Sudanese Civil War*, pp. 157–161.

14. Poggo, *The First Sudanese Civil War*, pp. 73–89; Beshir, *The Southern Sudan*, p. 85.

15. Poggo, *The First Sudanese Civil War*, pp. 140–144.

16. Wakoson, "The Politics of Southern Self-Government, 1972–1983," in Daly and Sikainga, eds., *Civil War in the Sudan*, p. 38; Kasfir, "Southern Sudanese Politics Since the Addis Ababa Agreement."

17. Wenyin, "The Integration of the Anya-Nya into the National Army."

18. Kasfir, "Southern Sudanese Politics Since the Addis Ababa Agreement."

19. Johnson, *The Root Causes of Sudan's Civil Wars*, pp. 41–42.

20. Ibid., pp. 42–51.

21. Kasfir, "Southern Sudanese Politics Since the Addis Ababa Agreement," pp. 153–154.

22. Johnson, *The Root Causes of Sudan's Civil Wars*, pp. 42–43; Badal, "The Addis Ababa Agreement Ten Years After," p. 13.

23. Interview with Major General William Deng, Juba, August 2009.

24. Badal, "The Addis Ababa Agreement Ten Years After," p. 29; Kasfir, "Southern Sudanese Politics Since the Addis Ababa Agreement," pp. 163–164.

25. Badal, "The Addis Ababa Agreement Ten Years After," p. 24.

26. "Redivision and Reshuffle," *Africa Confidential*, 5 June 1983.

27. Arou, "Devolution"; "Lull on the Southern Front," *Africa Confidential*, 3 August 1983.

28. Badal, "The Addis Ababa Agreement Ten Years After, p. 17; "Party Games," *Africa Confidential*, 27 April 1983.

29. "Uneasy Southern Calm," *Africa Confidential*, 2 March 1983; "Civil War Brewing," *Africa Confidential*, 13 April 1983.

30. Johnson, *The Root Causes of Sudan's Civil Wars*, pp. 60–61; "Sudan: Allah and the South," *Africa Confidential*, 19 October 1983.

31. Interview with William Deng, Juba, August 2010; Johnson, *The Root Causes of Sudan's Civil Wars*, p. 61.

32. Johnson, *The Root Causes of Sudan's Civil Wars*, pp. 92–94.

33. Interview with William Deng, Juba, August 2010.

34. "The Southern Front," *Africa Confidential*, 6 July 1983.

35. These men included Riek Machar, Yusuf Kuol, Wani Igga, Lam Akol, Danny Aweet Akut, Kuol Manyang, Galario Modi, Ngachigak Ngaciluk, Gordon Kong, Martin Majer, and Aweet Akut. Interviews with Colonel Philip Aguer Panyang, SPLA spokesman, and Danny Awet Akut, deputy speaker of Parliament, Juba, August 2011.

36. Interviews with Kuol Manyang, governor of Jonglei State August 2010; and Lam Mathiang, August 2011.

37. Interview with Justice Bullen Pan Chol, August 2011.

38. See Khalid, ed., *John Garang Speaks*.

39. Mampilly, *Rebel Rulers*.

40. "Red Flows the Nile," *Africa Confidential*, 30 November 1983; "Nimeiry Under Pressure," *Africa Confidential*, 4 January 1984; "The Shadow of the Brotherhood," *Africa Confidential*, 23 April 1986.

41. "Sudan: A Tragic Stalemate," *Africa Confidential*, 18 March 1994.

42. "Sudan: Opening New Fronts in the Oil War," *Africa Confidential*, 23 March 2001.

43. "Sudan: Killing Fields," *Africa Confidential*, 21 February 2003; "Sudan: Coordinates," *Africa Confidential*, 24 January 2003.

44. "Sudan: Allah and the South," *Africa Confidential*, 19 October 1983.

45. "Sudan: SPLA Arrest," *Africa Confidential*, 22 January 1988; "Sudan: Conflict in the SPLA," *Africa Confidential*, 9 September 1988; Johnson and Prunier, "The Foundation and Expansion of the Sudan People's Liberation Army."

46. Johnson, *The Root Causes of Sudan's Civil Wars*, pp. 87–88.

47. "Sudan: Challenges All Round," *Africa Confidential*, 13 May 1988.

48. Interview with Dr. Marial Benjamin, minister of commerce, government of South Sudan, August 2009.

49. "Garang's African Offensive," *Africa Confidential*, 9 February 1990.

50. "Straining at the Edges," *Africa Confidential*, 26 October 1990; "The SPLA in Focus," *Africa Confidential*, 20 April 1988.

51. "A regional setback for the SPLA," *Africa Confidential*, 14 June 1991.

52. Gerard, "Sudan Transitional Assistance for Rehabilitation (STAR) Project"; Levine, "Promoting Humanitarian Principles."

53. Bradbury, Leader, and Mackintosh, *The "Agreement on Ground Rules" in South Sudan*, pp. 29–30.

54. Keen, *The Benefits of Famine*.

55. Johnson, *The Root Causes of Sudan's Civil Wars*, pp. 67–69.

56. Human Rights Watch, *Famine in Sudan*.

57. Johnson, *The Root Causes of Sudan's Civil Wars*, pp. 65–66.

58. "Sudan: Southern Guerrilla Factions," *Africa Confidential*, 1 February 1984; "Anyanya II," *Africa Confidential*, 18 June 1986.

59. "Lull on the Southern Front," *Africa Confidential*, 3 August 1983.

60. "Stalling Speed," *Africa Confidential*, 22 May 1985.

61. "Sudan: Conflict in the SPLA," *Africa Confidential*, 9 September 1988.

62. "General Inertia," *Africa Confidential*, 14 August 1985.

63. "Battle Lines," *Africa Confidential*, 1 October 1985.

64. Johnson, *The Root Causes of Sudan's Civil Wars*, pp. 121–126.

65. "Movement in the Minefield," *Africa Confidential*, 3 March 1995.

66. Johnson, *The Root Causes of Sudan's Civil Wars*, pp. 118–120; "Sudan: Falling Out, Falling In," *Africa Confidential*, 4 February 2000.

67. "North and South," *Africa Confidential*, 4 February 1987; "No Solution," *Africa Confidential*, 4 March, 1987.

68. "An Unholy Alliance," *Africa Confidential*, 13 February 1985.

69. "Nimeri's Last Card?" *Africa Confidential*, 15 February 1984; "Disintegration," *Africa Confidential*, 11 April 1984.

70. "The Diarchy," *Africa Confidential*, 24 April 1985.

71. "The Southern Front," *Africa Confidential*, 6 July 1983.

72. Johnson, *The Root Causes of Sudan's Civil Wars*, pp. 79–81.

73. Ann Mosely Lesch, *Sudan: Contested National Identities*.

74. "Sudan: Calling the Shots at Machakos," *Africa Confidential*, 26 July 2002.

75. "Falling Out, Falling In," *Africa Confidential*, 4 February 2000; "Whitewashing Reality," *Africa Confidential*, 12 May 2000.

76. "Sudan: Opening New Fronts in the Oil War," *Africa Confidential*, 23 March 2001; "Sudan: In a Word," *Africa Confidential*, 23 January 2002; "Sudan: Oiling the Daggers," *Africa Confidential*, 20 April 2001.

77. Johnson, *The Root Causes of Sudan's Civil Wars*, p. 76.

78. Zonal Commands were distributed as follows: Riek Machar in Western Upper Nile, Lam Akol in Northern Upper Nile, Yussef Kuwah in Southern Kordofan, James Wani in Central Equatoria, and Daniel Weid Akot in Northern Bahr el Ghazal.

79. "In the Sights of the New World Order," *Africa Confidential*, 2 April 1993.

80. Jok and Hutchinson, "Sudan's Prolonged Second Civil War and the Militarization of Nuer and Dinka Ethnic Identities."

81. Rolandsen, *Guerrilla Government*.

82. "Over the Abyss," *Africa Confidential*, 9 May 1984; "In the Balance," *Africa Confidential*, 28 March 1984.

83. Johnson, *The Root Causes of Sudan's Civil Wars*, pp. 103–105; "The Great Hunger," *Africa Confidential*, 9 November 1990; Hassan, "The Sudan National Democratic Alliance (NDA)."

84. These included Umma, the DUP, the Beja Congress, and the Sudan Communist Party.

85. "Marking Time," *Africa Confidential*, 1 May 1998.

86. "Arms Against a Sea of Troubles," *Africa Confidential*, 15 November 1996.

87. "The Countdown Begins," *Africa Confidential*, 31 January 1997; "Next Year Kadugli," *Africa Confidential*, 9 January 1998.

88. "Blow Up," *Africa Confidential*, 24 September 1999.

89. US envoy John Danforth insisted on a cease-fire in the Nuba mountains, which resulted mainly in military assets shifted to fight in other theaters. Danforth also advised against self-determination as a platform for the SPLA, which was ultimately ignored; "In a Word," *Africa Confidential*, 23 January 2002; "Unconstructive Engagement," *Africa Confidential*, 22 February 2002.

90. "Calling the Shots at Machakos," *Africa Confidential*, 26 July 2002.

91. "Peace in Our Time," *Africa Confidential*, 24 October 2003; International Crisis Group, *Dialogue or Destruction?*

92. "Joy in the South, Silence in the North," *Africa Confidential*, 21 January 2005.

93. The NDA was not a signatory to the accord, and as a result the NCP regime was able to consolidate its authority further. For a critical look at the CPA, see Young, *The Fate of Sudan*.

94. International Crisis Group, *Sudan Endgame*.

95. For more on land and identity under French colonial rule, see Marshall-Fratani, "'Who Is Who': Autochtony, Nationalism, and Citizenship in the Ivorian Crisis."

96. Decalo, "The Process, Prospects, and Constraints of Democratization in Africa."

97. Marshall-Fratani, "'Who Is Who,'" p. 23.

98. Förster, "Insurgent Nationalism."

99. "General Guëi Is Looking More Like a Presidential Candidate," *Africa Confidential*, 14 April 2000.

100. "Moving Goalposts," *Africa Confidential*, 21 July 2000.

101. Marshall-Fratani, "'Who Is Who,'" pp. 23–24.

102. Baégas and Marshall-Fratani, "Côte d'Ivoire," p. 92.

103. Ibid., p. 94.

104. "Whose Army?" *Africa Confidential*, 11 October 2002.

105. Baégas and Marshall-Fratani, "Côte d'Ivoire," p. 94.

106. Personal observation of the author in the western cities of Man and Danané, 2003.

107. Baégas and Marshall-Fratani, "Côte d'Ivoire," p. 93.

108. "A New Front Opens," *Africa Confidential,* 20 December 2002.

109. "The Nightmare Scenario," *Africa Confidential*, 27 September 2002.

110. Baégas and Marshall-Fratani, "Côte d'Ivoire," p. 94.

111. "A New Front Opens," *Africa Confidential,* 20 December 2002.

112. Baégas and Marshall-Fratani, "Côte d'Ivoire," p. 97.

113. Médecins Sans Frontières, *"Ça va en peu maintenant."*

114. Baégas and Marshall-Fratani, "Côte d'Ivoire," p. 88.

115. "Doing the Business," *Africa Confidential*, 19 December 1997.

116. "Military Mumbles," *Africa Confidential*, 24 May 1996.

117. "The Army and the OAU Are Both at Odds with the General," *Africa Confidential*, 29 September 2000.

118. Baégas and Marshall-Fratani, "Côte d'Ivoire," p. 89.

119. Hazen, *What Rebels Want*, p. 145.

120. "The Military Might?" *Africa Confidential*, 29 June 2001; International Crisis Group, *Côte d'Ivoire: The War Is Not Yet Over,* pp. 10–11; Hazen, *What Rebels Want*, pp. 147–148.

121. Hazen, *What Rebels Want*, pp. 145–146.

122. Global Witness, *The Usual Suspects*; Hazen, *What Rebels Want*, pp. 155–159.

123. Hazen, *What Rebels Want*, p. 157.

124. Baégas and Marshall-Fratani, "Côte d'Ivoire," pp. 96–99.

125. Förster, "Dialogue Direct."

126. Hazen, *What Rebels Want*, pp. 164–168.

127. Observations of author in western cities of Man and Danané, 2003.

128. Hazen, *What Rebels Want*, pp. 166–167; Global Witness, *Hot Chocolate.*

129. Carroll and Henley, "French Attack Sparks Riots in Ivory Coast," *Guardian*, 7 November 2004.

130. "Foul Play," *Africa Confidential*, 24 January 2003.

131. "After the Phoney War," *Africa Confidential*, 2 April 2004.

132. International Crisis Group, *Côte d'Ivoire: No Peace in Sight.*

133. Straus, *Making and Unmaking Nations,* p. 156.

134. "Fighting for Peace," *Africa Confidential*, 8 November 2002.

135. "Between the Wars," *Africa Confidential*, 16 April 2004.

136. "Not All Necessary Powers," *Africa Confidential*, 17 February 2006.

137. "High Noon," *Africa Confidential*, 4 February 2005.

138. "No Polls, No Peace," *Africa Confidential,* 7 October 2005.

139. "Time's Up," *Africa Confidential*, 4 November 2005.

140. "Private Coups," *Africa Confidential*, 9 September 2005.

141. "No Deal," *Africa Confidential*, 7 February 2003.

142. Baégas and Marshall-Fratani, "Côte d'Ivoire," pp. 105–109.

143. "A Do-It-Yourself Peace," *Africa Confidential,* 5 October 2007.

144. "All Their Own Work," *Africa Confidential*, 16 March 2007; "The 'Soro Ranks,'" *Africa Confidential*, 5 October 2007.

145. "It's Not Over Yet," *Africa Confidential*, 25 April 2008; "Democratic Deficit," *Africa Confidential*, 4 July 2008; "Three's a Crowd," *Africa Confidential*, 31 October 2008; "The Much-Postponed Polls," *Africa Confidential*, 8 January 2010.

146. "And Then, There Were Two," *Africa Confidential*, 5 November 2010.

147. International Crisis Group, *Côte d'Ivoire: Is War the Only Option?;* "Two Presidents, One Crisis," *Africa Confidential*, 17 December 2010.

148. "Guns, Votes, and Cocoa," *Africa Confidential*, 18 March 2011.

149. Johnson, "Briefing"; Rolandsen, "Another Civil War in South Sudan."

5

The Fates of Outsiders:
Rebel Groups in Sierra Leone
and Central African Republic

*Each generation must out of relative obscurity, discover its mission,
fulfill or betray it.*

—Franz Fanon, quoted in Revolutionary
United Front/Sierra Leone, *Footpaths to Democracy*

As the vignette in Chapter 1 illustrates, as Sierra Leone's civil war
ended in early 2002, the Revolutionary United Front (RUF) emerged
with nothing to show for it. The RUF is a flagship case of defeat by disintegration. What explains this fate? The dominant narrative portrays
the group as little more than a criminal enterprise fixated on the
exploitation of illicit alluvial diamond markets.[1] To be sure, some members of the group certainly became intoxicated by the short-term wealth
offered by commercial and predatory war economies. But tying diamonds to the RUF's fate cannot correctly identify whether it was private
gain or the material needs of rebellion that acted as the primary motiva-
tor. Alternatively, a more sympathetic view casts the RUF as a rebellion
of marginalized youth responding to a crisis of modernity.[2] This may be
partly true, but it is better at explaining why the RUF fought and not
why it met the fate that it did.

The Revolutionary United Front (RUF)

This section shows that the RUF's fate is rooted in its outsider status.
Largely established outside the country, the RUF was an inchoate group
of political strangers—to the state and to one another. Its lack of political
embeddedness meant few organizational foundations on which to build a

135

rebellion. And the low political status of its leadership meant few paths to political accommodation by successive regimes in Freetown, the seat of government. Those opportunities for incorporation were clumsily squandered, which in fact only accelerated the group's fragmentation.

Non-Embedded Rebels

Understanding the fate of the RUF begins by examining its organizational core. Having germinated far afield of Sierra Leone's state institutions, the rebellion's membership was fundamentally low status. This story begins in the 1980s, when the small knot of elites that made up Sierra Leone's incumbent All People's Congress (APC) government regularly suppressed dissent. This caused Freetown to become a bed of youth radicalism as middle-class students of Fourah Bay College merged with the urban underclass that Abdullah has described as "lumpens."[3] Together they embraced the revolutionary ideology of pan-Africanism and the radical discourse of Libyan Muammar Gaddafi's Green Book.[4]

The youth activism of Freetown soon intersected with Gaddafi's broader program of support for revolutionary movements throughout West Africa. By the end of the decade, Freetown student leader Alie Kabbah, under the banner of the People's Democratic Front (PDF), began shepherding young Sierra Leoneans to Benghazi to receive "Advanced Capacity Building in Revolutionary Ideology." Those who merely sought ideological education quickly abandoned any notion of rebellion and returned to Freetown. But others remained to receive guerrilla training—among them the three key figures Abu Kanu, Rashid Mansaray, and Foday Saybana Sankoh. Little is known about Kanu, but Mansaray allegedly fought briefly with Angola's People's Movement for the Liberation of Angola (MPLA).[5] Sankoh had been a corporal and signals officer in the Sierra Leone Army (SLA) but was jailed for failing to report an attempted coup in 1971. Released in 1978 and banned from the army, Sankoh became a wandering photographer. Sankoh, older than the rest, with his military background and natural charisma, stepped into the dominant role as the group's spokesman and "head of ideology."[6]

While in Benghazi, this trio of nominal rebel leaders made the pivotal decision to make a pact of mutual support with like-minded Liberian revolutionaries.[7] By late 1989, twenty-odd Libyan-trained Sierra Leonean "Special Forces" joined Charles Taylor's National Patriotic Front of Liberia (NPFL) as it invaded Liberia from neighboring Côte d'Ivoire. In June 1990, they participated in securing the NPFL's headquarters in the town of Gbargna.

Based in the nearby training center of Camp Naama, Sankoh (known as "Pa Morlai") began recruiting and training fighters for what would become the RUF. The first group of RUF "vanguards"—essentially the rebellion's cadre tier—was an incongruent cluster of Sierra Leoneans living in Côte d'Ivoire and Liberia. Key among them, and emblematic of the outsider nature of the RUF, were Issa Sesay, who worked as a petty trader and cobbler in Abidjan, and Sam Bockarie, a hairdresser and nightclub dancer in Liberia. Some joined willingly. Others were captured. Many Sierra Leoneans living in Liberia who had been detained in NPFL prisons entered the RUF for protection.[8] In the months that followed, Sankoh collected slightly fewer than 400 vanguards and pushed them into a hurried and untested training program at Camp Naama carried out by NPFL commandos.

In March 1991, Sankoh introduced the RUF to the world in a fiery ultimatum to the APC on *BBC Radio*.[9] Nine days later the group, heavily supported by NPFL fighters, attacked border towns in Kailahun and Pujehun Districts. In the early days of the RUF's invasion, it was in these communities that vanguards filled out their ranks and expanded the rebellion's membership. Those who identified with the RUF's emergent ideology joined as "willing revolutionaries," but most were forcibly recruited.[10] Rank and file were transferred to collection points and divided into *salon wosus*, or fighters; "stand-bys," or trainees; and fresh "recruits."[11] The savvier members of this crop would soon go on to become cadres as the RUF's "junior commandos."[12] The key observation here is that the RUF began a rebellion of non-embedded outsiders. The Sierra Leone Truth and Reconciliation Commission summarizes nicely:

> In character, this group of people stands to be considered as a highly unconventional fighting force; its members were taken on board in troubled circumstances, many of them under false pretenses, duress, or threats to their lives; and they were only loosely bound together by superficial bonds more out of a sense of common adversity than any true notion of unity. It is therefore hardly surprising that the relationships of these vanguards among themselves would fluctuate between friendly camaraderie and mutual suspicion.[13]

As such, the RUF's initial organization endowment was rooted in a social base of marginalized, rural youth of uneven educational backgrounds.[14] Although the rebellion experienced brief periods of relative cohesion, its dominant organization pattern would tend toward fragmentation largely along personal cleavages and conflict between internal rival power bases.

Bush Rebels vs. Bush Army

Sierra Leone's civil war was emblematic of symmetrical, irregular warfare, which saw largely threadbare rebellion squaring off against a chronically anemic, venal national army. The relatively low capability of rebel and incumbent alike was the dominant feature of the civil war, despite the later involvement of private security firms and both regional and international peacekeeping forces. Either way, even if the RUF managed to marshal resources in the service of eventually taking and holding territory, it did not translate into a fate beyond defeat disintegration.

A look at the RUF's capacity shows that it was limited from the onset of its rebellion, and the group was often dependent on external support. Those Sierra Leonean fighters who made up the initial invasion force from Liberia were demonstrably undertrained by virtue of their hasty mobilization.[15] More experienced Liberian and Burkinabe fighters made up four-fifths of this original force and provided ample muscle to compensate for the RUF's shortfalls. But the untamable nature of these foreign fighters, particularly their tendency to violently target civilians, set the scene for wider patterns of impunity that regularly undermined Sankoh's authority on the ground.[16] Moreover, schisms among Sankoh, Kanu, and Mansaray led to the unceremonious executions of the latter two, which sowed mistrust among their respective followers. The result was that the RUF was built upon a shaky foundation that lacked organizational cohesion, with Sankoh now firmly in charge of the rebellion and Bockarie and Sesay becoming his two main cadres.

But by 1992, many RUF fighters had tired of the Liberians in their midst and broke violently with the NPFL as Taylor also shifted his focus to dealing with his own Liberian quagmire.[17] Those Liberians who remained launched the "TOP 20" and "TOP 40" operations against the RUF "book men" who had been systematically documenting their abuses, which the RUF answered in kind with the "TOP FINAL" operation that killed nearly all the remaining Liberians by September 1992.[18] These battles with the NPFL, while purging troublesome elements from the RUF, expended most of the RUF's ammunition and eliminated much of its muscle. By late 1993, the rebels' remaining battle groups were scattered and incommunicado between Kailahun and Pujehun Districts,[19] highly disorganized and demoralized, and with only forty-five operational weapons among them.[20]

By 1994, by sheer force of luck, these two flanks found one another while moving down a common bush path. Led by a revitalized Sankoh, the group mustered the wherewithal to regroup into what they called

"RUF Phase II,"[21] which operated from an array of bush camps and from an associated decentralized command structure. Now facing the need to acquire resources locally, the RUF pursued a conventional guerrilla strategy of avoiding direct confrontation with the Sierra Leone Armed Forces, ambushing military convoys, raiding towns and villages for supplies and food, and abducting manpower for fighters and porters.

Until then, the SLA was merely a ceremonial institution, kept weak and relatively useless by previous regimes. Its inexperienced troops were now expected to go to the front lines to fight the RUF with outdated weaponry, malfunctioning equipment, and trucks borrowed from the Ministry of Works.[22] Despite being Africa's largest recipient of aid from the US Africa Security Program,[23] spending $2 million per month on the war[24] and forging defense pacts with Guinea and Nigeria,[25] the SLA remained remarkably weak.[26]

Unpaid for months and stranded in the bush with poor equipment and insufficient ammunition, the SLA suffered humiliating battlefield defeats. The neglect of the army soon prompted a group of war-front junior officers to overthrow the APC regime in 1992.[27] Hailed as "the Redeemer," coup leader Captain Valentine Strasser, who had been wounded in battle,[28] replaced the APC with the National Provisional Ruling Council (NPRC).

Despite the coup, which might have predicted a shift in state military capacity against a ragtag guerrilla outfit, the dominant pattern of symmetrical, irregular conflict persisted. Poor leadership and weak organizational capacity in the NPRC and the army produced what Kandeh has called "spoils-based collapse" as the regime proved unable to translate its populist coup into a durable regime.[29] In many ways, the NPRC was like the RUF—political outsiders who had displaced the country's long-standing political networks without developing any of their own.

The biggest problem the NPRC faced, aside from the RUF, was its inability to control its fighters. A harried and haphazard recruitment of youths of sketchy backgrounds soon turned the national army into a bloated juggernaut five times its original size.[30] Untrained and undisciplined, these new troops began to exploit, and in some cases to cause disorder for personal gain. In towns and villages throughout the country, ordinary Sierra Leoneans experienced the phenomenon widely described as "sobels"—soldiers by day and rebels by night, so that residents could not tell which side was preying on them.[31] Although it remains unclear what the depth or frequency of their coordination was, members from both the army and the RUF engaged in a "sell game."[32] In this maneuver, soldiers would tip off rebels about the timing and location of convoys, which the RUF then ambushed, and then clandestinely sold the looted goods, arms, and ammunition back to the army.[33]

The RUF was now making incursions into mining and cash-crop regions, which began to choke state revenues as the war effort siphoned off 75 percent of state spending. In response, in 1995 the NPRC turned to private security firms, beginning with the ill-fated Gurkha Security Group (GSG), and then the South African Executive Outcomes (EO), which agreed to fight the RUF in exchange for commercial mining concessions.[34] EO tightened control over the army and engaged Sierra Leone's civilian-based, ethnic militias known generically as Kamajors.[35] The Kamajors fought on the same plane as the RUF, equally as knowledgeable of the terrain while carrying nothing more than hunting rifles.

Following the brief interlude of a democratic regime (see below), a bizarre new phase of state-rebel parity continued, following a fresh 1997 coup d'état that brought the RUF into a temporary power-sharing agreement with a new military junta in Freetown called the Armed Forces Revolutionary Council (AFRC).[36] Although this short-lived coalition reduced outright conflict in the country, the nature of the combined violence had increased predation upon ordinary civilians by then. Beyond that, the low-level, symmetrical conflict continued with Nigerian troops and Kamajors who operated from neighboring Guinea at the behest of the government ousted by the AFRC.

The AFRC junta did not last long. After its fall in early 1998, the soldier-rebel coalition factionalized and scattered throughout Sierra Leone into a kaleidoscope of competitive factions. This pushed the RUF into new resource terrain. At this key juncture, RUF strongmen Bockarie and Sesay reactivated their networks with Charles Taylor. This injected fresh resources into the RUF, but they were selectively doled out to the group with the objective of seizing control over economically viable parts of Sierra Leone on Taylor's behalf.[37] Taylor began to direct cross-border trade in diamonds, gold, and cash crops, which he exchanged with the RUF for weapons, ammunition, and fuel.[38] Although these resources allowed Bockarie and Sesay to reassert control over the rebellion and supported efforts to take and hold territory, the profits often amounted to little more than "chicken change."[39] Most of Taylor's commercial goals soon took on a security imperative as he ordered the RUF to consolidate all captured weapons[40] and deploy to Guinea in a failed bid to push back his own domestic insurgency.[41]

Despite these resource links, the war remained largely symmetrical and irregular due to the weak coalition of Nigerian-led peacekeepers called the Economic Community Monitoring Group (ECOMOG), SLA loyalists, and Kamajors. Spread thin and lightly armed, this combined force was only temporarily able to extend into the countryside as territory was cyclically taken, lost, and retaken. This created permissive conditions for a reinvigorated AFRC faction to begin its march to retake Freetown. On 6 January 1999, it overwhelmed the city's defenses with ranks swollen to 10,000 strong through mass abductions.[42] After plunging Freetown into the civil war's most concentrated period of violence, by 19 January, ECOMOG had regrouped and was able to push the invaders out of the capital.[43]

From that point onward until the end of the war, Sierra Leone remained divided between territory held by the RUF and that nominally controlled by the government with the backing of external peacekeepers, turf that was largely managed by a network of roadblocks and checkpoints by rebels, militias, soldiers, and peacekeepers alike. By 2001, an expanded UN intervention effectively froze this pattern of control into place, until the RUF's disintegration gave way to formal reconstitution of the state by 2002.

Dealing with the RUF

With the RUF as non-embedded outsiders, the dominant strategy to deal with the rebellion was that of elimination, which corresponded to the relatively low threats the group posed to successive regimes, despite the broader destabilization to the country. As mentioned above, these regime counterinsurgency campaigns played out within the context of symmetrical, irregular warfare, in which the capacities of the SLA (plus its backers) and the RUF were roughly the same, and the rebellion eventually came to control large swaths of Sierra Leonean territory.

Yet also throughout the war, different regimes—either through idiosyncratic whim or international pressure—shifted to strategies of control that offered several paths to accommodation for the RUF, none of which were successful. Each failed strategy to incorporate the rebellion, maneuvers that were carried out by military juntas and democratic governments alike, illuminates the problems inherent in doing business with non-embedded outsiders such as the RUF.

The first attempt was driven by the personal agenda of a military leader. As the NPRC's rickety counterinsurgency campaign unfolded, splits between regime hard-liners and moderates prompted several attempts to talk to the RUF.[44] Yet an early offer of amnesty rang hollow when the first batch of RUF fighters to come forward were either imprisoned or executed.[45] Sankoh therefore rejected subsequent overtures, and other civil society initiatives were similarly rebuffed.[46] In early 1996, NPRC leader Valentine Strasser was overthrown in a palace coup by his second in command, Julius Maada Bio, in order to guarantee the country's election timetable. With the RUF at its weakest militarily, Bio opened talks in order to secure the release of his sister, Agnes Deen-Jalloh, from the group's political wing based in Côte d'Ivoire.[47]

These initial efforts to create dialogue gave way to further attempts by Sierra Leone's newly elected government, which was guided by its own separate set of interests. Although the 1996 elections were marred by RUF attacks, they handed victory to Ahmed Tejan Kabbah with 36.1 percent of the popular vote.[48] A reluctant peacemaker, Kabbah kept up military pressure against the RUF alongside contentious negotiations with the group's leaders. These talks culminated in the Abidjan Peace Accord on November 30, 1996.[49] In a tepid bid for incorporation, Abidjan granted the RUF amnesty, established a timetable for disarmament, and guided the group's transition into a political party.

Yet neither side was committed to the agreement, and cease-fire violations were commonplace. For Kabbah, an accord with the RUF merely secured continued donor funding, but privately he continued military action using the Kamajors, who overran the RUF bush Zogoda headquarters the day the Abidjan accord was signed. Meanwhile, Sankoh won a key concession in the negotiations that expelled EO from Sierra Leone, which opened a space for the RUF to rearm and refinance.[50] Although Bockarie was able to secure arms, other attempts were horribly botched, most notably an incident in Nigeria that led to Sankoh's apprehension and long-term house arrest at the Abuja Hilton.[51] As it turned out, the first meaningful political settlement between the Sierra Leone government and the RUF was less of an overture of accommodation and more at the behest of international pressure on Freetown, and an opportunity to regroup for the rebels.

However, the RUF still found itself confined to the country's periphery as efforts to rearm failed. Resource scarce, the rebellion was suddenly presented with a fresh opportunity to incorporate into the political establishment—albeit one now controlled by military officers. Following the 1997 coup that overthrew Kabbah's government, junta leader Major Johnny Paul Koroma reached out to the RUF with a concrete offer of accommodation. After an hourlong phone call from his hotel room in Abuja, Sankoh ordered the RUF to march to Freetown and take orders from Koroma.[52]

No doubt, this phase in regime strategies to deal with the RUF seemed to mark a turning point. Indeed, this alliance between the SLA and RUF was mutually beneficial. For Koroma, the RUF offered potential muscle to counter ongoing threats from Kamajors. For Sankoh, joining the SLA meant a boost for his ailing rebellion, presenting the possibility that Nigeria would release him to take up his office as the AFRC deputy chairman. Yet upon giving an interview on the BBC's *Focus on Africa*, Nigerian authorities cut his phone line, which removed him from further command decisions for the RUF.

And although the AFRC may have been sincere in incorporating the RUF into a new political order at the state level, the rebellion's merger was haphazard and contentious, and it eventually led to major cleavages. Although some RUF members occupied positions in the AFRC Supreme Council, which received housing, vehicles, and salaries,[53] they remained subordinate players in a regime dominated by the chief coup-makers, who maintained control over ministries, the military, and regional secretariats.[54] In fact, a full integration into the AFRC's political and military structure never occurred, and many senior RUF cadres remained without official title.

Instead, there stood two separate organizations that bred misunderstanding and ego clashes.[55] The ability to maintain a siloed command structure outside of Freetown allowed RUF strongmen to resist integration and pursue their own agendas.[56] Bockarie led this pattern by appointing himself to the rank of "Mining Commander" and relocating from Freetown to Kenema District to mine diamonds in Tongo Field's Cyborg Pit,[57] passing commands to the AFRC in the capital via Sesay. The RUF's failure to integrate into the new political environment, even one controlled by the military and guided by economic interests, reflected the awkward task of incorporating rebels with no historical linkages to state authority.

Most important, though, Kabbah's government, sitting in exile in neighboring Guinea, was not done fighting. During the short year of the AFRC, Kabbah led a regional effort to isolate and eject the junta and sought to resume a strategy of elimination against the RUF. Trade embargoes and sanctions rendered Sierra Leone ungovernable as food and fuel shortages crippled day-to-day functions, and government revenues collapsed.[58] Ultimately, the Conakry Peace Plan of 23 October 1997 presented a veneer of accommodation for the AFRC, providing a diplomatic exit by promising to hand back power to Kabbah by the following April.[59] But alongside these moves, both sides continued military preparations. Koroma received clandestine arms shipments and help from Ukrainian mercenaries.[60] Above all, RUF hard-liners in the alliance resisted negotiations because of Nigeria's refusal to release

Sankoh from house arrest.[61] In effect, then, the Conakry plan was dead in the water.

Kabbah, with robust support from ECOMOG, soon launched a strategy to return to Sierra Leone and resume his role as the head of state. Supported by Kamajors, Nigerian troops continually hounded and skirmished the AFRC,[62] which culminated in an all-out offensive in February 1998. Operation Tiger Head, the first phase of ECOMOG's broader Operation Sandstorm, moved into Freetown along three axes, capturing a series of strategic locations.[63] Within weeks the AFRC/RUF coalition was flushed from Freetown and under the hot pursuit of ECO-MOG's Operation Tiger Tail.[64]

Now restored, Kabbah's government immediately closed the path to accommodation with both the rebels and the former soldiers, issuing blanket public emergency provisions, allowing mob justice, and arbitrarily detaining AFRC and "collaborators."[65] Hasty treason trials led to the public execution of twenty-four soldiers and sixteen civilians in late 1998.[66] Nigeria soon handed Sankoh over to Sierra Leone, where he was tried and sentenced to death.[67]

The strategic pendulum, however, soon swung back toward accommodation once again, as the madness unleashed upon Freetown in January 1999 caught the attention of Western diplomats and donors, who resumed pressure on Kabbah to release Sankoh and restart talks with the RUF.[68] The ultimate result was the Lomé Peace Accord on 7 July 1999.[69] Like the Abidjan accord, the agreement gave the RUF fighters amnesty, arranged disarmament, demobilization, and reintegration (DDR), and allowed the rebellion to become a political party. Key RUF cadres were given cabinet positions in the new Government of National Unity, and Sankoh became vice president and chair of the Commission for the Management of Strategic Resources, National Reconstruction and Development (CMRRD). ECOMOG was to transition into the UN Assistance Mission in Sierra Leone (UNAMSIL), which would oversee Lomé's implementation.[70]

True to prediction, the accord quickly unraveled along both its military and political provisions.[71] Cease-fire violations were widespread, and the RUF in diamond-producing areas refused to disarm. This intransigence culminated in early May 2000, when the RUF kidnapped 500 UNAMSIL peacekeepers,[72] while a self-styled militia called the West Side Boys made up of ex-AFRC abducted several dozen foreign military observers.

In Freetown things were not much better. Although the AFRC was not a signatory to Lomé, its Commission for the Consolidation of Peace (CCP) appointed Koroma as its chairman.[73] Dragging its feet for months, the CCP starved Sankoh of resources and infrastructure, while

Kabbah, Koroma, and Kamajor leader Hinga Norman secretly plotted to arrest RUF political cadres in Freetown. A series of anti-Sankoh protests provided a chance to provoke a violent confrontation with the RUF that led to Sankoh's arrest.[74] Consequently, the RUF's path to accommodation was effectively cut, as UN peacekeepers fanned out across Sierra Leone and further choked off the RUF's ability to achieve victory by domination.

The RUF's Path to Disintegration

As a rebellion of non-embedded outsiders, the RUF disintegrated along two dimensions. First, its weak organizational endowments and loose connections between leaders and cadres set the scene for irreparable factionalization. Few prewar connections meant that the group's cadres, who rose within the RUF as a result of battlefield successes, developed independent power bases that deviated from internal rules as they pursued personal agendas. Second, although there were several paths to incorporation, the RUF fit awkwardly into state authority networks, and its few brushes with regime politics only accelerated the group's fragmentation.

Recall the RUF's rushed invasion from Liberia, where it failed to consolidate a cohesive relationship between its leaders and cadres. Any initial military gains made during this period were only modest, and the group remained confined to a belt along the Liberian border.[75] These conflict dynamics, combined with acute resource dependence on the NPFL, exacerbated a number of cleavages that undermined the group's capacity to manage fragmentation. Smaller incidents included a dispute over the selling of arms and ammunition to Liberian rebels, which led Pujehun District's "Big Four" junior commanders to kill twenty-four vanguards.[76]

But the significant split occurred with the RUF's founding members. As NPFL fighters killed Abu Kanu in a power struggle in Pujehun,[77] Sankoh ordered the execution of Mansaray and twelve RUF vanguards, whom he sentenced to death over their opposition to the overwhelming presence of NPFL commanders. These developments elevated Sankoh to the top of the RUF, while the deaths of Mansaray and Kanu sowed divisions among fighters. Finally, after a set of military setbacks,[78] Taylor pulled his support, which was followed by a cycle of revenge killings between NPFL and RUF fighters that pushed the group into a different phase of rebellion.[79]

During "Phase II" of the rebellion, the RUF retreated into a collection of bush camps where Sankoh was now free to rearrange his vanguards and junior commandos into two distinct sets of cadres. The first was politico-administrative, stocked with nominally educated "book men" and members of the group's Internal Defence Unit (IDU) that recorded violations of the RUF Code of Conduct, a key part of bush-camp indoctrination that placed strict proscriptions on the behavior of fighters. Each combat group contained administrative "G" and "S" officers in charge of overseeing a range of activities, including storage of food and munitions, political education, and liaising with civilians.[80] The second set of cadres was made up of fighters led by the last remaining member of the Libyan-trained RUF Special Forces, Mohammed Tarawalie ("Zino"). A collection of RUF vanguards populated command positions in each fighting unit. The hierarchy then branched out geographically to encompass area commanders, who fanned out throughout a network of bush camps that penetrated much of the country.[81]

For a short period, the RUF became a fleet-footed guerrilla force where bush-camp isolation became a source of cohesion for fighters who remained largely insulated from the SLA's more conventional fighting force. Peters suggests the following:

> The bush camp phase proved to be a pivotal period in the movement's history. Isolated from the wider society, the movement was consolidated [and] it became a kind of secular sect. Bonds of commitment and loyalty were forged in the militarized camps, rather than in the RUF's civilian liberated zones, resulting in a new and durable solidarity, largely among conscripts and based on meritocratic principles of seniority, egalitarian principles of redistribution and the unifying factors of a common danger and a shared fate.[82]

Yet by mid-1995, the EO and Kamajors began rescuing the NPRC's flagging counterinsurgency campaign, closing in on RUF positions and pushing Sankoh to negotiate the Abidjan Peace Accord out of desperation. Clandestinely, Sankoh continued to shop for arms, which led to his subsequent arrest in Nigeria.

His removal from the RUF hierarchy exposed two key organizational cleavages within the rebellion. The first was a deep division created by the Abidjan negotiations, which excluded combatant cadres and elevated its politico-administrative members to the accord's Commission for the Consolidation of Peace, which colluded with Kabbah to sideline Sankoh. Yet through the RUF radio operator in Danané, Côte d'Ivoire, Sankoh relayed the command to Bockarie to have them arrested.[83] The role of the RUF "book men" in any future negotiations was hence foreclosed, leaving the Sierra Leonean government to deal mainly with the group's combatant cadres, who were ill-suited for negotiations.

This period also brought into stark relief divisions that had germinated in RUF's decentralized bush camps, where key strongmen developed independent power bases through battlefield bravado. Sankoh had come to manage these cadres through sheer favoritism and fear, and he applied the RUF Code of Conduct inconsistently. The RUF's system of internal surveillance, which applied widely to the rank and file, gave several commanders a free pass, as intelligence officers ignored violations out of fear of reprisals.[84] Thus, there were few mechanisms to filter out those willing to engage in the most reckless, predatory behavior associated with the RUF. Higher status within the organization meant these cadres could deviate from the RUF Code of Conduct and enjoy privileges not afforded other commanders in the austere bush-camp environment. Most instructive was the case of Bockarie, who was responsible for widespread atrocities against civilians that went unpunished. Against regulations, he once entered the Zogoda heavily armed; and when most commanders had five bodyguards, Bockarie had twenty.

The collapse of Abidjan, Sankoh's arrest in Nigeria, the ultimate death of Zino in the Zogoda, meant that Bockarie—the RUF's most feral member—assumed command of the rebellion. The RUF's organizational structure now locked in patterns of behavior that incentivized competition among factions with few crosscutting loyalties and gave way to the pursuit of personal agendas.

The RUF's cohesion fared no better with the AFRC, and the subordinate role of its rebel cadres amplified internal divisions. Any pretense of ideology or program for political reform gave way to the pursuit of economic agendas that manifested along factional lines. Now freed from fighting the army, but not having to actually govern, strongmen such as Bockarie and Sesay could exploit the protection derived from the state to shift the RUF away from a military hierarchy and toward a commercial one centered on diamond mining. Up until then, while still in bush campus, most rank and file had adhered to the RUF's rudimentary rules. But now control had become a clear function of ruthlessness, where fighters could openly ignore the Code of Conduct.[85] Moreover, conflict arose within the AFRC-RUF alliance. Organizationally, rebels sat uncomfortably alongside soldiers and they quarreled openly. For instance, RUF commanders bristled at being called "bush colonels," and many junta leaders seemed to regret inviting them to Freetown.

Above all, joining the AFRC exposed the RUF to a military defeat by ECOMOG and Kamajors. As McGregor points out:

> The RUF decision to enter into a defined military alliance with the coup leaders brought the RUF out into the open where it could be crushed by conventional military force, a costly defiance of all traditional guerrilla strategy—RUF success had always been based on avoiding direct confrontation with government forces. The result was the elimination of much of the movement's leadership and a good portion of its arms.[86]

In the months following its ouster from Freetown, the AFRC-RUF coalition launched Operation Pay Yourself, in which cadres and rank and file alike indulged in an orgy of looting and predatory violence that further incentivized personal agendas and activated long-standing grudges. The alliance then splintered into a kaleidoscope of shifting factions that fought one another as well as ECOMOG and Kamajors throughout the country. The main RUF group consolidated control of the eastern and northern half of the country and renewed cross-border resource linkages with Charles Taylor, while the dominant SLA group repositioned in northeastern Koinadugu District to stage the attack on Freetown in January 1999.

The externally brokered Lomé Peace Accord was designed to address Sierra Leone's civil war by cobbling together a power-sharing agreement between the government and the RUF. Yet, perhaps by design, this attempt to accommodate the RUF further unraveled the group's already brittle organization. In particular, the negotiations allowed Sankoh to be released from custody and reintroduced into the RUF's politics after a lengthy absence, which created fresh divisions in the rebellion. Although Lomé's provisions incorporated Sankoh and some political cadres into the government, still Sankoh struggled to build political infrastructure in Freetown and maintain command of fighters in the field, few of whom stood to benefit directly from Lomé. Those among the RUF's emergent commercial-combatant cadres had no real ambitions to join the political establishment, and Lomé meant disarmament, disempowerment, and an end to any commercial enterprise they had created.

By December 1999, Bockarie and his followers abruptly quit the RUF and moved to Monrovia to lead Taylor's Anti-Terrorist Unit (ATU) there.[87] Sankoh's lack of authority over the RUF manifested in the group's kidnapping of 500 UN peacekeepers, led by Augustine Gbao. When civilians marched on Sankoh's Freetown house to protest the intransigence of RUF fighters, his bodyguards fired into the crowd. Sankoh was arrested and permanently removed from the RUF hierarchy.

These events signaled the Lomé agreement's dissolution by May 2000, which only further accelerated the RUF's disintegration. The rebellion, which still controlled over half of the country's territory, was nevertheless now subject to a new range of pressures it was unable to manage.[88] With Sankoh in prison, Bockarie in Liberia, and the peace process in tatters, the group's disparate factions squared off against peacekeepers, Kamajors, ex-AFRC fighters, and one another. To be sure, those factions such as Sesay's that were still connected to cross-border commercial trade in diamonds, gold, and cash crops with Taylor still continued to reap the benefits of being able to control territory and exploit resources. However, the focus on business ventures instead of any remaining political role for the RUF in state politics further incentivized spoils-based factional splits. Above all, the unraveling of its organizational order made it near impossible for RUF commanders to keep control over the group's rank and file, who now felt free to engage in widespread asset stripping of the civilian population.

At this juncture, the RUF's total disintegration required only a small push by external actors and two successive cease-fire agreements. Although these arrangements temporarily froze in place the RUF's control of northern and eastern Sierra Leone, they also required some sort of political interlocutor for the rebellion to chart a path forward. At the behest of West African leaders, Sesay became the RUF's interim leader, a man whom they viewed as politically malleable.[89]

Yet Sesay was more of a businessman than a political actor, let alone a master negotiator. By then, he had fully monopolized control over the RUF's commercial activity, largely as an instrument of Taylor, who sought to consolidate his commercial interests in the broader Mano River region by destabilizing it. Sesay shifted the RUF high command to his home region of Makeni and elevated his non-RUF Temne kinsman to important positions within what was still nominally the RUF.[90] Sesay's focus on private accumulation came at the expense of rival cadres, and that only deepened infighting and left most RUF fighters uncertain of their future.[91]

Finally, the cease-fire agreements allowed for expanded UNAMSIL presence throughout the country, especially in the diamond-producing areas of Tongo and Kono. The sheer numbers of peacekeepers provided a symbolic measure of military pressure on the RUF, choked off the day-to-day predation of fighters, and ultimately facilitated the extension of state authority to areas previously deemed no-go areas for state officials. Above all, this narrowing space for RUF commercial operations effectively cut off Sesay's source of factional dominance. As a result, Taylor soon lost interest in maintaining him as a regional capo.[92] With the mentorship of West African dignitaries, Sesay became convinced of the need for a quick political exit, and for his own protection, he began to cooperate with the UN to usher in the RUF's DDR. Within a few short months, state functions returned to territory previously held by the RUF, while its membership slotted into vocational training programs, or in Sesay's case, were arrested for war crimes and crimes against humanity. The RUF could very well have met any variant of victory over the course of its eleven-year insurgency—but it met defeat by disintegration.

The Séléka Rebellion

A look at present-day Central African Republic shows a broken state. The size of Texas but with the population of South Carolina, the country has experienced five military coups and multiple rebellions since gaining independence from France in 1960. The state in CAR has steadily hollowed out over decades, making it one of the poorest and least developed countries on earth. It ranks dead last at 188 on the 2016 UN Human Development Index.[93] The capital city, Bangui, although quite charming, bears the scars of neglect. It looks as though it has not even had a paint job in decades, which reflects the overall crippled state of the country's infrastructure.

Despite the relatively free and fair elections of early 2016, fairly robust international peace operations, and international aid, years of institutional decay have left most Central Africans at the state's margins, creating fertile ground for recurrent rebellion and violent coups. The country's civil war and its aftermath have claimed thousands of lives, generated nearly half a million refugees and an additional 400,000 internally displaced, with around half of Central Africans facing food insecurity.[94]

Decades of misrule and predation explain much of CAR's current disorder, but so does the civil war that brought the Séléka rebellion to a swift and jarring victory in March 2013.[95] Bookended by failed negotiations, the Séléka rolled over CAR's Forces Armées Centrafricaines (FACA) and South African troops in a span of only a few months to overthrow the government of François Bozizé. Shortly after their victory, Séléka fighters fanned across the country in search of plunder. In response, a range of self-defense militias collectively called "anti-Balaka" rose up to challenge them, setting off a cycle of intercommunal violence that became increasingly about religious identity. State disintegration has meant that territorial control outside Bangui continues to be held by numerous armed groups that operate in various and shifting combinations, some of which sustain their operations with illicit natural-resource trading, forced taxation, and pillage in the country's periphery.[96]

The Séléka means "alliance" in Sango, the lingua franca of CAR. Although some of its members, including its titular leader Michel Djotodia, had served as functionaries in regime politics, the Séléka should not be considered a politically embedded rebellion per se. Rather, it was a rickety coalition of armed groups that emerged from the far-flung porous borderlands with Chad and Sudan. Together these groups shared a loose identity marked by Islam's role in politics and society, which also reflected a keen sense of historical marginalization from the state. Neighboring Chad and Sudan, which had historically meddled in CAR politics, were early backers of the Séléka, and fighters from these countries played an important role in the group's victory. In this section, I examine these conditions and chart the Séléka's path as a rebellion of outsiders. I also consider the postwar collapse of the CAR's political order (such as it was) and raise key questions about rebel organization, victory, and regime consolidation.

Elite Politics in CAR

To proceed, a brief discussion of CAR's elite politics is in order, as it does much to explain the Séléka's rise and subsequent fate. The genealogy of CAR's kleptocracy has been treated in superb detail elsewhere.[97] Suffice it to say here that since the colonial period, political authority in CAR has been characterized by what Smith has called "concessionary politics," in which a small clutch of elites has served as gatekeeper of state resources, access to which has been granted to outside economic interests in exchange for rents that are in turn used to nourish patronage networks and deploy violence to demobilize rivals.[98]

Elsewhere described as the "Bangui Carousel,"[99] regime politics in CAR has long been the enterprise of a disproportionately small number of these elites, estimated at around 500.[100] Also called "La Mangeoir," or the trough, CAR's public sector has historically focused on gaining and maintaining access to power and privilege through official title.[101] Rather than having state institutions constrain their behavior, CAR's elites have systematically circumvented and manipulated institutions in their favor. But seldom do these state institutions, such as they are, extend outside the capital city, giving rise to the expression "the state in CAR stops at PK 12," the outer district of Bangui. This means that government functionaries, even those assigned duties in the provinces, rarely stray from the capital, essentially stranding most of the country's population at the far end of the state.

Centralizing power and managing rival elite networks has also relied on the expansion of parastatal organizations, the privatization of public funds generated by resource plunder, and the dismantling of institutional checks and balances, including the banning of political parties and civil society organizations. Successive rulers in CAR have not hesitated to use the state's coercive apparatus to silence opposition, reinforced by the savvy instrumentalization of external meddlers, particularly France, Libya, and Chad.

Although these patterns were largely set in motion by the country's first president, David Dacko, kleptocratic governance became institutionalized under Colonel Jean Bedel Bokassa, who ruled CAR from 1965 to 1979. Although Bokassa was initially popular, he soon resembled a caricature of an African despot, proclaiming himself emperor in 1976 and shoring up his rule with patronage from Libyan president Muammar Gaddafi.[102]

CAR's armed forces, the FACA, though comparatively weak, have long been a microcosm of elite competition. During the government of André Kolingba (1981–1993) in particular, elite competition took on an ethnic and regional dimension as the FACA was stocked with members of his own ethnic Yakoma. Elite political rivalry in Bangui had the downstream consequence of sharpening a larger cleavage between the country's southern Riverains and its northern Savaniers. Kolingba's successor, Ange-Félix Patassé, hardened identity markers further by creating a 3,000–strong praetorian guard drawn from his own northern Ouham-Pendé region, as well as 2,000 Chadian troops for his own protection.[103]

After François Bozizé toppled Patassé through a military coup in 2003, he populated his government with close friends and relatives, monopolized the diamond trade, and bolstered the Presidential Guard while keeping the bulk of the army weak, fearing military competitors from past governments. Like his predecessors, Bozizé restricted state authority to Bangui, with some control extended to his native area in the west dominated by ethnic Gbaya, while most of CAR remained on the far side of a wide gulf. Generally, politics in CAR has been both a highly incestuous and divisive affair, in which the country's elites are just as likely to be recycled through elite accommodation as they are to be replaced via coup d'état or rebellion.

Anatomy of the Séléka

Titular leader Michel Djotodia was once a low-level state official in Darfur, but most members of the Séléka rebellion came from far afield of CAR's elite networks. In fact, the Séléka has been aptly described as a "heterogeneous consortium of malcontents."[104] This means that organizationally, the group consisted of an alliance of individual strongmen, Sudanese and Chadian mercenaries, and Central African fighters from the country's far-flung northeastern prefectures of Vakaga and Bamingui-Bangoran. Because of its historical cross-border linkages to Chad and Sudan that date back to the precolonial period, and the Muslim contours of its cultural identity, many Séléka recruits from this region had long since been considered "foreigners" in CAR and faced widespread discrimination. For these reasons, the Séléka began with very few prewar organizational endowments, and certainly no preformed relationships between leaders and cadres. Although this did not prevent the group's victory, it had real consequences for the postvictory political order, examined below and further discussed in Chapter 6.

At the Séléka's core were three armed groups that emerged from localized conflicts and regional insecurity, groups that fought the Bozizé regime—and one another—before fizzling out in the face of the 2008 Libreville Peace Agreement (discussed below). At the center sat the Union des Forces Démocratiques pour le Rassemblement (UFDR), led by Michel Djotodia, Abakar Sabone, and Damane Zakaria. This was essentially a coalition of local self-defense militias, *pisteurs* (park rangers), and dispossessed Chadian "ex-liberators" who had once helped usher Bozizé into power. The Convention des Patriots pour la Justice et la Paix (CPJP), led by Abdoulaye Issène, formed another key component of the Séléka. Initially, the group splintered following disagreements over signing the 2008 Libreville Peace Agreement, creating CPJP Fondamontale, led by Nourredine Adam, and the Convention Patriotique du Salut du Kodro (CPSK), led by Mohamed Moussa Dhaffane. Initial attempts to form an alliance in Niamey, Niger, in March 2012 were hamstrung by personal rivalries and the factionalization of the CPJP. But by September, Adam and Dhaffane formally joined forces under the Séléka banner in N'Djamena, Chad, with the Djotodia's UFDR entering the alliance in the following months. Together they began operations in December 2012. As the rebellion quickly grew, the founding groups entered into fair-weather alliances with a number of other armed groups: the Chadian Front Populaire pour le Redressement (FPR) of Baba Laddé, the Front Démocratique du Peuple Centrafricain (FDPC) of Abdoulaye Miskine, and the Union des Forces Républicaines (UFR) of Florian Ndjadder.

As suggested by this bewildering kaleidoscope of acronyms, a key feature of the Séléka was the multipolar distribution of power among its key strongmen and the lack of integration of its fighting units, which created a situation where "everybody was a leader."[105] With Djotodia as the group's titular chairman, Nourredine Adam and Mohamed Moussa Dhaffane nevertheless possessed independent power bases. Foreign fighters played a significant role as the Séléka served as a conduit for ongoing cross-border linkages with "politico-military entrepreneurs" from Chad and Sudan's own conflicts.[106] As Chadian fighters coalesced around Adam, Djotodia sought to balance against him by using his previous networks in Darfur to bring in Sudanese fighters.[107] This meant that the Séléka was now flush with loot-seeking mercenaries with no fixed loyalties, and meanwhile, Dhaffane was fleshing out his power base by recruiting Central Africans as the war unfolded.[108]

Moreover, distinct ethnic contours characterized each partner in the alliance.[109] Djotodia's UFDR was largely Gula; Nourredine Adam's CPJP Fondamontale was Runga; Dhaffane's CPSK was largely Bornu. Complicating this ethnic imbalance further were fighters drawn from pastoralist groups such as the Fulani and the Peuhl. These divisions shaped the Séléka's internal politics in a way that fomented distrust between each faction leader, and by creating ethnic centers of gravity for different commanders. Meanwhile, Sudanese and Chadian fighters occupied their own self-contained units.[110]

As the rebellion quickly unfolded, it recruited fighters from different communities with promises of economic rewards. As these fighters settled under local commanders, they seldom penetrated beyond their immediate commander, so that even Séléka strongmen exercised little control over fighting units.[111] The rebellion's official demands soon expanded in tandem with the multiplying interests of its members,[112] some of which centered on lucrative diamond-mining operations in areas under their control.[113] All told, one rough, anecdotal estimate held that 20 percent of Séléka fighters were foreigners, 40 percent "true believers," and the remaining 40 percent were loot-seeking opportunists who joined as the rebellion advanced to Bangui.[114]

Weak Rebels, Weak Army

The Séléka's victory was swift, but the rebellion nevertheless operated within the broader context of symmetrical irregular warfare, in which the capacities of both the rebellion and the FACA were relatively quite low, and small arms and loose organizational structures figured prominently as key components of the technology of rebellion.

Much of the research on the Séléka's military capacity has focused on the group's resource flows since its dissolution in September 2013, which examines how its current control of territory and exploitation of natural resources have allowed its current factions continued access to small arms.[115] To be sure, the political economy of previctory Séléka certainly relied on exploiting resources within the territories it rapidly captured. But the group's initial resource endowments were very much tied to shifting networks of a range of armed actors that flowed through CAR's border region with Chad and Sudan.[116] Not only did the fluid identities and loyalties of these fighters converge on the Séléka at a key juncture, but regional political interests also aligned with the rebellion's resource needs.[117]

For both Chad and Sudan, a Séléka regime could help maintain their respective regional spheres of interests. Both provided manpower, organizational support and military advising, arms and ammunition, and territory to the Séléka. For Chad, a decision to intervene in CAR's affairs reflected a long-standing pattern of what has been described elsewhere as *vassalage*.[118] Here, Chadian ruler Idris Déby regularly meddled in Central African politics to manage the permeable border area and any associated threats to his regime that emanated from it, and attempted to preserve Chad's business interests in CAR, including oil.[119] Arguably, this logic guided Chad to flip its support from Bozizé to the Séléka by 2013. Meanwhile, Sudan's logistical and political support dovetailed with Djotodia's linkages with Khartoum-aligned militias based in Darfur, which he cultivated while serving as a CAR official in South Darfur in the 1990s. Khartoum's geopolitical and economic interests were similar to N'Djamena's, particularly in regard to Darfuri rebels potentially using CAR as a rear base, and in boosting access to regional resources. In addition, a newly independent South Sudan created a new dynamic on a new shared border region, where cooperation between Bozizé, the SPLA, and the Ugandan army against the LRA in CAR created concerns for Khartoum.[120] Nourished with these resource endowments, the Séléka rebellion rapidly faced down a rickety state army bolstered by South African troops.

This outcome fit a broader pattern of weakness on the part of the FACA, which was only able to function historically by virtue of sustained external support, particularly from France and Chad. In CAR, the FACA was just one of a range of predatory actors with deplorable human rights records.[121] Rather than serve the security interests of the state, it was often weakened deliberately by successive regimes that often used it as a reservoir of ethnic loyalty and to consolidate divisions between elite networks.[122] Small (about 5,000 members with only 1,500 operational soldiers), underequipped, and low on morale, the largely Bangui-based FACA maintained a primary focus on the

Presidential Guard, charged with protecting Bozizé and his family.[123] Years of failed security-sector reform fostered conditions upcountry such that self-identified authorities and stewards of security, often indistinguishable from *zaraguinas* (highway robbers), created webs of roadblocks in an effort to seek profit.[124] In fact, the chronic insecurity that resulted from this environment created fertile conditions for the grievances that drove many Séléka fighters in the northeastern part of CAR.

Regime Strategies and the Séléka's Path to Victory

Prior to formation of the Séléka in 2012, the regime of François Bozizé confronted a range of armed groups with a variety of grievances. Largely at the behest of regional leaders, the Bozizé regime showed a pattern of grudgingly entering into peace talks with rebels, while relying on external support to bolster the FACA's (ultimately unsuccessful) operations against them. It was the predictable failure of these negotiations to accommodate rebelling outsiders that merely galvanized successive waves of rebel challengers.

Largest among these groups was the Armée Populaire pour la Restauration de la République et la Démocratie (APRD). This group consisted of supporters of the Bozizé-deposed regime of Ange-Félix Patassé, which regrouped in the north and northwest following the presidential elections in 2005 that consolidated Bozizé's authority. Bolstered by the Central African and Chadian "ex-liberators," the APRD coalesced around Patassé's defense minister Jean-Jacques Démafouth. Also active during this period was the Front Démocratique du Peuple Centrafricain, a smaller group of Patassé loyalists led by cadre Abdoulaye Miskine that occupied the northern Ouham prefecture.

The other, more significant group at the time was the Union des Forces Démocratiques pour le Rassemblement, which came from the Vakaga prefecture. As described above, the UFDR was more of a homegrown amalgam of self-defense groups and *pisteurs* responding to localized conflicts among Gulu, Runga, and Kara ethnic groups, and cross-border encroachment of armed actors from Sudan and Chad. The arrival of Chadian ex-liberators and attacks on Gula villages by Bozizé's Presidential Guard galvanized the UFDR to fight against the Bozizé regime.

Beginning in 2007, a series of agreements between the Bozizé government and these groups unfolded by fits and starts. An accord signed in Syrte, Libya, with the FDPC and the UFDR, and a parallel accord reached in Birao with UFDR, offered vague promises of how each rebel group would participate in the "management of state affairs" and how the FACA would absorb rebel fighters.[125] These accords eventually converged in an "inclusive dialogue" that led to the Libreville Comprehensive Peace Agreement of 2008. This accord ultimately included the APRD, the Mouvement des Libérateurs Centrafricains pour la Justice (MLCJ), and the UFR. Like previous agreements, Libreville set out the conditions for amnesty, disarmament, demobilization, and reintegration (DDR), and absorption into the FACA.

True to prediction, the Libreville Agreement provided a path of accommodation to the insider-led APRD, and a handful of its leaders joined the Bozizé government, with Démafouth allowed to form a new political party. Yet the implementation of the accord stalled for the outsider-led UFDR and others, as Bozizé displayed recalcitrance about doing business with them.[126] DDR was delayed indefinitely, and the promise of 15 million CFA per fighter was broken.[127] Those political prisoners who had been promised release remained behind bars, and the UFDR's Djormo Didou received a disappointing posting as the minister of housing.[128]

Most of all, despite the rebels' gradual encroachment into the lucrative diamond-mining areas,[129] a core grievance remained, which was Bozizé's ongoing nepotism and corruption. Thus, by March 2012, three core groups (see above) overcame their own rivalries and became the Séléka. Augmented by alliances with other, smaller rebellions and bolstered by Chadian and Sudanese mercenaries, the Séléka began its attacks in mid-September 2012. After a brief lull, the coalition seized control of the key northern town of Ndélé on December 10, followed by a string of easy victories over regional centers such as Bria and Bambari. In less than a month, the Séléka moved to within forty miles of Bangui.

A second Libreville peace agreement, hastily brokered on 11 January 2013, temporarily halted the Séléka's advance toward Bangui,[130] although the group had already consolidated control over key mining towns and commercial operations. According to the latest agreement, Bozizé was to remain in power until his term expired in 2016. In addition, several Séléka cadres were granted key cabinet positions in a government of national unity, which was also expected to arrange elections for the National Assembly and to implement a number of reforms.

The Inclusive Political Dialogue that took place in Bangui provided somewhat of a homegrown anchor for the talks. Yet despite the raft of documents produced by the three-day process—a cease-fire, a declaration of principles, and a peace agreement—the new Libreville agreement suffered from similar problems as its predecessor, as it was largely cobbled together by member heads of state from the regional Communauté Économique des États de l'Afrique Centrale (CEEAC), resulting in what one observer called "peace talks without the talks."[131] Following a process marred by mistrust and a lack of credible guarantors, and with disingenuous commitment from a weakened Bozizé and rebel leaders alike, the new Libreville agreement, like the last, was never implemented.[132] By 18 March, the Séléka gave Bozizé seventy-two hours to begin implementation. The rebellion then renewed its march toward Bangui on 21 March, seizing the capital three days later and meeting the rare fate of victory domination.

Post-Victory Unraveling

The Séléka's path, although victorious, was short-lived, which raises important questions about the fate beyond rebel fates. Against the backdrop of symmetrical, irregular warfare, the Séléka rebellion was able to achieve victory domination in a shockingly short span of time. But as a rebellion of outsiders, it had neither the cohesion nor the institutional linkages to meaningfully consolidate a new regime and establish political order. After less than one year of misrule, the government led by Djotodia, which went unrecognized by member states of the African Union (AU), fragmented internally and was pushed from Bangui. Its composite of "all fighters and no politicians" was unprepared to run a government owing to lack of maturity and weak leadership.[133]

Several factors related to the organization and behavior of the Séléka, and its positionality within CAR's political establishment, might explain its postvictory fate. First, the competing interests of its strongmen meant the Séléka had "no political program" beyond the collective goal of ousting Bozizé.[134] Once the incumbent was gone and the FACA effectively disbanded, Djotodia suspended the constitution, dissolved the government and the National Assembly, and announced he would rule by decree.[135] Over a ten-month span, he issued over 500 such decrees that parceled out lucrative government sinecures to senior Séléka members and, true to prediction, several elites he recycled from previous governments.[136]

Now occupying the dual roles of CAR's head of state and minister of defense, Djotodia had to manage ongoing rivalries among Séléka leaders by granting them positions of acceptable status within the government. Nourredine Adam thus became minister of public safety, a post he abused with impunity.[137] As minister for water, forests, hunting, and fisheries, one of Dhaffane's first acts was to loot the ministry building's storage of animal skins and ivory.[138] Yet such accommodations only briefly papered over long-standing mistrust, perceptions of ethnic favoritism,[139] and chronic military and political disagreements among the three Séléka strongmen. These soon boiled over when Adam imprisoned Dhaffane, creating a deep schism that never healed.[140] All the while, Djotodia and his largely Gula entourage set about pillaging state coffers and assuming tight control over natural-resource concessions and clandestine trade networks.[141]

Second, Séléka leaders never had full control over their fighters, which had swollen to an estimated 20,000 by June 2013.[142] Whereas some were integrated into a hollow and gutted national army or hastily cantoned into camps, most were allowed to pay themselves violently and with impunity. Fighters ran rampant in Bangui and carved a westward path through towns and villages, unleashing well-documented human rights abuses, the most egregious of which were committed by Sudanese and Chadian mercenaries.[143] Yet rather than attempt to rein in their excesses, Djotodia formally disbanded the Séléka on 14 September 2013, which merely formalized the fragmentation that was already occurring.[144]

The excesses of Séléka fighters soon produced a grassroots backlash that further undermined the stability of the Djotodia government. Remnants of Bozizé's regime and the FACA[145] helped mobilize a range of local self-defense groups, collectively called the "anti-Balaka," a moniker that roughly translates into "machete-proof." The primary goal of this loose collection of militias was to avenge their communities for Séléka atrocities. Following their December attack on Bangui, the country descended into a vicious cycle of intercommunal violence that took on increasingly religious contours.[146]

The ensuing humanitarian crisis prompted international condemnation and intervention. Peacekeeping missions from CEEAC and the African Union,[147] poorly equipped and politically compromised, were soon augmented by the French Opération Sangaris, signaling a more serious international engagement with CAR as Djotodia came under increasing regional pressure.[148] By January 2014, regional heads of state from the CEEAC had convinced Djotodia to resign and seek exile. A transitional national government, led by former Bangui mayor Catherine Samba-Panza, supported by an expanded UN peacekeeping mission (UN Multidimensional Integrated Stabilization Mission in the CAR, or MINUSCA), assumed control of CAR's government. After multiple delays, relatively free and fair democratic elections in February 2016 finally marked the end of the transition as Faustin Archange Touadéra assumed the presidency.[149]

Yet CAR is far from political stability. The Séléka, now splintered into a kaleidoscope of factions, maintain control of lucrative mining regions, trade in commodities, and taxation of roads and border crossings.[150] In places like Bambari, CAR's third-largest city, the state remains absent and humanitarian conditions are severe. Even with the presence of UN peacekeepers, ex-Séléka strongman Ali Darrassa and his Unité pour la Paix en Centrafrique (UPC) taxes the lucrative trade in coffee, cattle, gold, and diamonds that runs through a corridor up to Sudan or south to Bangui. Throughout the country, hundreds of thousands of Central Africans face food insecurity and displacement as they contend with intercommunal divisions that were nurtured over the long term and hardened by the civil war.[151] Similar to the RUF's brief brush with regime authority within the AFRC alliance in Sierra Leone, the Séléka case is illustrative of what can happen when political outsiders, lacking organizational endowments, solid leader-cadre ties, and linkages to state institutions, actually win.

Conclusion

In contrast to the cases in Chapter 4, the divergent fates of the RUF and Séléka showcase the obstacles faced by political outsiders who rebel against the state. Lacking organizational cohesion or significant linkages to regime politics, both groups squandered opportunities to either incorporate into the regime they fought or maintain a hold on the regime they replaced.

The RUF and Séléka had several things in common. First, the bulk of their fighting forces consisted of marginalized youth who sat on the far side of a wide gulf between the groups they ostensibly represented and the prevailing political establishment in Sierra Leone and CAR. To be sure, the titular leaders for each group were not young men, and they each served brief stints in government jobs. Sankoh—"Pa Morlai"—had been a lowly army corporal before being cashiered and imprisoned. And Michel Djotodia had been a low-level functionary in CAR's foreign service, based in a far-flung office in Nyala, Darfur. But by and large, the membership profile of both the RUF and Séléka—leaders, cadres, and followers alike—was essentially unrecognizable to the elites who occupied regime politics in both countries. In fact, early in the RUF's rebellion, there was some question over whether or not Foday Sankoh even existed.[152] And once in power, Djotodia's efforts to cobble together a regime from the detritus of CAR elites and Séléka strongmen failed miserably. Either way, both the RUF and Séléka faced disingenuous and ultimately foreclosed opportunities to negotiate and bargain with the regimes they fought, leading to divergent fates of defeat disintegration and victory domination, respectively.

Second, likely because of their lack of prewar organizational endowments, both the RUF and the Séléka developed fundamentally multipolar distributions of power. This meant that within each insurgency, competition among rivals could not be contained by any hegemonic structure, codes of conduct, or norms. The RUF's divergent power bases developed over the course of the Sierra Leone conflict, a process set in motion early by Liberian influence, reinforced by geographical decentralization, and allowed to continue as strongmen such as Bockarie developed their own power bases without being held in check. The Séléka, however, began its rebellion as a fair-weather alliance between a range of armed movements, a structure that was never unified under a single, hegemonic command. The result of the proliferation of independent power bases was factionalization, although each group experienced this fate at different junctures. For the RUF, fragmentation followed an arc of uncoordinated political, economic, and military strategies, which led to the group's implosion once any possibility for victory via domination or incorporation was foreclosed. For the Séléka, which managed to keep its disparate factions relatively unified until the moment of victory, infighting came out into the open once the Bozizé regime was overthrown, after which the coalition rapidly unraveled.

There were also some contrasts between the RUF and Séléka. Although both were made up of marginalized outsiders, they differed along the dimension of identity. To be sure, near the moment of the RUF's implosion, cleavages developed between Sesay's hometown ethnic Temne mafia and cadres from ethnic groups such as the Mende. Otherwise, the RUF was decidedly a nonethnic rebellion. Members of the Séléka, however, had a common identity rooted in the ethnic and religious groups of CAR's borderlands with Chad and Sudan, which was the main marker of their political "outsiderness." And while both the RUF and Séléka had multipolar distributions of power, differences in identity also meant corresponding differences in communal structure. Whereas the RUF deliberately sought to integrate all fighters across fighting units irrespective of ethnic or religious backgrounds, the Séléka allowed their units to remain communally segmented among ethnic Runga, Bornu, and Gula, and created separate units of Sudanese and Chadian fighters. This dimension of rebel organization and how it undermines or supports cohesion as an alternative to political embeddedness merits further inquiry.

There are, as always, lingering questions. As touched upon in the concluding sections of Chapters 3 and 4, the roles of different types of external actors merit consideration here. That is, both the RUF and Séléka rebellions were part of regional cross-border resource networks that provided material support to their military campaigns. Sierra Leone and CAR were also loci of regional and international peace operations.

Again, a chief insight of this investigation is that material capacity is an insufficient predictor of a rebellion's fate. Yet the role of outside support in the Séléka case may very well challenge this claim—Sudan and Chad provided territorial sanctuary, weapons and ammunition, and sizable muscle, which arguably helped overwhelm the FACA in short order and achieve a rapid victory by domination. The RUF case, on the other hand, is illustrative of instances where proxy warfare can facilitate the unraveling of a rebellion.[153] At key bookends of Sierra Leone's civil war, Liberia's Charles Taylor dribbled out resources to the RUF in exchange for using the group as a blunt instrument for his wider regional security and economic imperatives—and arguably dismembered them in the process.

Consider now the role of peacemakers and peacekeepers. In both the RUF and Séléka cases, attempts to cobble together durable political settlements failed in part because the incumbent regimes in both countries were demonstrably loath to accommodate their members, despite regional and international pressure to conjure the magic bullet of a peace accord. Moreover, because the international architecture of peace operations tends to be more reactive than proactive, robust interventions only really took place toward the coda of both the RUF and Séléka's respective trajectories. For the RUF, the group met defeat disintegration in spite of a series of political settlements. For the Séléka, meaningful regional and international involvement only occurred *after* its victory, which may have accelerated its demise in the postvictory political dispensation.

This last point brings us back to earlier discussions about postwar political order. The evidence in this chapter provides an opportunity to gauge the role of non-embedded political outsiders in the contrasting cases of Sierra Leone and CAR. For instance, immediately following the RUF's disintegration, some ex-cadres attempted to repurpose it into a political party to compete in the postwar election in 2002. The RUFP managed to harvest an unimpressive 1.73 percent of votes, which declined to an even more paltry 0.6 percent a decade later, and sunk to 0.5 percent in the 2018 general election. Yet these dismal losses nevertheless occurred in elections that were largely free and fair. Although Sierra Leone remains backbreakingly poor and near the bottom of most global welfare indices, it remains relatively politically stable.

As discussed earlier in this chapter, the situation in CAR paints a much bleaker picture. The immediate aftermath of the Séléka victory was tantamount to state collapse, leading to widespread intercommunal violence, a massive humanitarian crisis, and the splintering of the country into an archipelago of fiefdoms controlled by various armed actors. Despite massive UN intervention, the imposition of a transitional government, and the relatively smooth democratic elections in 2016, the country is far from recovering from this trauma. A preliminary observation from these cases suggests that when outsiders lose, political stability is more likely. Yet when outsiders win, postwar political order is much less guaranteed.

Notes

1. Gberie, *A Dirty War in West Africa.*
2. Richards, *Fighting for the Rainforest*; Peters, *War and the Crisis of Youth in Sierra Leone.*
3. Abdullah, "Bush Path to Destruction."
4. Student groups at Fourah Bay College included the Green Book Study Group, Pan African Union (PANAFU), the Gardener's Club, and an umbrella organization called Mass Awareness and Participation.
5. Abdullah, "Bush Path to Destruction," p. 217.
6. Abdullah, "The Revolutionary United Front in Sierra Leone," p. 187.
7. Sierra Leone Truth and Reconciliation Commission (hereafter TRC), vol. 3A, "Military and Political History," p. 95.
8. Ibid., p. 103.
9. "Liberia: Taylor Goes Abroad," *Africa Confidential,* 19 April 1991.
10. TRC, "Miltary and Political History," pp. 137–140.
11. Abdullah, "The Revolutionary United Front in Sierra Leone," p. 188.
12. Interview with former RUF commander, March 2011.
13. TRC, "Miltary and Political History," p. 106.
14. Richards, *Fighting for the Rainforest.*
15. Ibid., p. 120; Ashraph, "How Things Fell Apart," p. 3.
16. Pham, *The Sierra Leonean Tragedy,* p. 85.
17. "Liberia: The Battle for Gbargna," *Africa Confidential,* 28 May 1993; "Is the Game Really Over?" *West Africa,* 8–14 March 1993; "Ecomog's Peace Offensive," *West Africa,* 19–25 April 1993.
18. TRC, "Military and Political History," pp. 170–174.
19. Interview with former RUF commander, January 2008.
20. TRC, "Military and Political History," p. 174.
21. Interview with former RUF commander, January 2009.
22. Interview with SLA colonel, January 2009; Musa and Musa, eds. *The Invasion of Sierra Leone,* pp. 66–68; Bundu, *Democracy by Force?* p. 51.
23. "Troubled Country," *West Africa,* 13–19 May 1991.
24. Zack-Williams and Riley, "Sierra Leone," p. 94.
25. "Nigeria Shows Concern," *West Africa,* 6–12 May 1991; "Checking the Advance," *West Africa,* 27 May–2 June. Note that Nigerian minister of defense Sani

Abacha was a personal friend of Momoh and viewed Nigeria's mission in Liberia as naturally including Sierra Leone.

26. "No Change?" *West Africa,* 26 April–2 May 1993.

27. "The Sierra Leone Coup," *West Africa,* 11–17 May 1992; "We Need Urgent Help," *West Africa,* 15–21 June 1992.

28. "We Need Urgent Help," *West Africa,* 15–21 June 1992.

29. Kandeh, "What Does the 'Militariat' Do When It Rules?"

30. TRC, "Miltary and Political History," pp. 159–163.

31. Ibid., p. 198.

32. Keen, *Conflict and Collusion in Sierra Leone*; Abraham, "State Complicity as a Factor in Perpetuating the Sierra Leone Civil War."

33. Interview with former RUF commander, March 2011; TRC, "Miltary and Political History," pp. 202–207.

34. Reno, *Warlord Politics and African* States, p. 130; Francis, "Mercenary Intervention in Sierra Leone"; Rubin, "An Army of One's Own."

35. Muana, "The Kamajoi Militia"; Ferme and Hoffman, "Hunter Militias."

36. "Coup in Freetown?" *West Africa,* 2–8 June 1997; "Koroma's Coup," *Africa Confidential,* 6 June 1997.

37. TRC, "Miltary and Political History," p. 230; "West Africa According to Mr. Taylor," *Africa Confidential,* 22 January 1999.

38. "Kabbah's Comeback," *Africa Confidential,* 20 February 1998.

39. Interview with former RUF commander, March 2011.

40. Ibid.

41. "The Dynamics of the Mano River Union Conflict," *West Africa,* 30 April–6 May 2001.

42. TRC, "Miltary and Political History," p. 324.

43. "No Surrender, No Deal," *Africa Confidential,* 22 January 1999; "The Madness in Sierra Leone," *West Africa,* 1–14 February 1999.

44. "Revolution in Crisis?" *West Africa,* 7–13 December 1992; "Frontline Freetown?" *Africa Confidential* 31 March 1995.

45. Interview with former RUF commander March 2011.

46. These included the Mano River Bridge Initiative (MRBI), the National Coordinating Committee for Peace (NCCP), and the civil society Contact Group, led by UK-based Conciliation Resources.

47. "Whither Sierra Leone?" *West Africa,* 29 January–4 February 1996.

48. Kandeh, "In Search of Legitimacy."

49. Gberie, "Paying the Price"; Mutwol, *Peace Agreements and Civil Wars in Africa,* pp. 216–250.

50. Interview with former RUF commander, June 2011.

51. Interview with former RUF commander, March 2011.

52. "The Rebels' Position," *West Africa,* 30 June–6 July 1997.

53. Interview with former RUF commander, March 2011.

54. Special Court for Sierra Leone (hereafter SCSL), Trial Chamber Judgment II, Part VI, "Political Structure of the AFRC Government," Freetown, SCSL, 2007, pp. 98–107.

55. SCSL Trial Chamber I Judgment, Freetown, SCSL, 2009, p. 249.

56. SCSL Trial Chamber I Judgment, Freetown, SCSL, 2009, p. 220.

57. Confidential, nonprivileged documents from the Sierra Leone Special Court.

58. "Putschists v. Putschists," *Africa Confidential,* 18 July 1997.

59. "The Conakry Peace Accord."

60. Interview with former RUF commander, March 2011; "Cracking Koroma," *African Confidential,* 21 November 1997.

61. "Jump or Be Pushed," *Africa Confidential*, 6 February 1998.
62. "The Sierra Leone Question," *West Africa*, 22–28 September 1997.
63. TRC, "Miltary and Political History," p. 290.
64. "Operation Tiger Tail," *West Africa*, 6–26 July 1998.
65. TRC, "Miltary and Political History," pp. 296–316; "Back to Square One," *West Africa*, 6–26 July 1998.
66. "24 Soldiers Executed," *West Africa*, 19 October–1 November 1998; "Death Sentences," *West Africa,* 9–22 November 1998.
67. "RUF Leader Handed to Sierra Leone for Trial," *West Africa*, 28 September–11 October 1998.
68. "Forced to Talk," *Africa Confidential*, 28 May 1999.
69. "A Deal in Lomé," *Africa Confidential*, 9 July 1999.
70. Mutwol, *Peace Agreements and Civil Wars in Africa,* pp. 283–317; Olonisakin, *Peacekeeping in Sierra Leone.*
71. "Peace Process in Disarray," *West Africa,* 13–19 March 2000.
72. "Rebels Take On the U.N." *West Africa,* 15–21 May 2000.
73. TRC, "Miltary and Political History," p. 343.
74. Ibid., pp. 364–456; "Sierra Leone in Turmoil as Sankoh Disappears," *West Africa,* 15–21 May 2000.
75. "Mounting Fears," *West Africa,* 3–9 June 1991.
76. Interview with former RUF leader, March 2011.
77. Kanu's body was recovered by the SLA and his head was placed on a stake in the village of Dandambu.
78. "Politics of Rebellion," *West Africa,* 21–27 September 1992.
79. "Fighting for Diamonds," *West Africa,* 24–30 June 1991; "Sierra Leone: Facelift for the Old Order," *Africa Confidential,* 22 November 1991; TRC, "Miltary and Political History," pp. 170–174.
80. Email correspondence with former RUF commander, April 20, 2011; SCSL I, Trial Chamber I Judgment, Part VI, "Factual and Legal Findings," p. 223.
81. Day, "Bush Path to Self-Destruction," p. 820.
82. Peters, *War and the Crisis of Youth in Sierra Leone*, pp. 100–101.
83. Interview with RUF commander, March 2011.
84. SCSL I, Trial Chamber I Judgment, Part VI, "Factual and Legal Findings," pp. 223–236.
85. Interview with former RUF commander, March 2011.
86. McGregor, "Quagmire in West Africa," p. 484.
87. TRC, "Miltary and Political History," p. 355; interview with former RUF commander, March 2011.
88. "Talking to the RUF," *West Africa*, 14–20 August 2000.
89. See *War Don Don*, a documentary film by Rebecca Richman Cohen on the Special Court of Sierra Leone, Racehorse Productions, 2010.
90. Interview with former top RUF mining commander, January 2009.
91. TRC, "Miltary and Political History," p. 333; interview with former RUF commander, March 2011.
92. Olonisakin, *Peacekeeping in Sierra Leone.*
93. United Nations Development Program (UNDP), "Human Development Report 2015," available at http://hdr.undp.org/en/composite/HDI, accessed 6 November 2017.
94. United Nations Office for the Coordination of Humanitarian Affairs (UNOCHA), "Central African Republic: Humanitarian Bulletin, Issue 17," November 2016, https://reliefweb.int/report/central-african-republic/central-african-republic-humanitarian-bulletin-issue-17-november, accessed 6 November 2017.

95. "Central African Republic: Séléka Takes Power," *Africa Confidential*, 29 March 2012.

96. Agger, *Warlord Business.*

97. International Crisis Group, *Central African Republic: Anatomy of a Phantom State.*

98. Smith, "The Elite's Road to Riches in a Poor Country."

99. Day, *The Bangui Carousel.*

100. Mehler, "Pathways to Elite Insecurity," http://culanth.org/fieldsights/549 -pathways-to-elite-insecurity.

101. "Central African Republic: Cleaning Up," *Africa Confidential*, 26 May 2000.

102. Decalo, *Psychoses of Power.*

103. "Central African Republic: Dubious Democracy," *Africa Confidential*, 22 January 1999.

104. International Crisis Group, *Central African Republic: Priorities of the Transition*, p. 6.

105. Interview with Eric Massi, July 2015.

106. Debos, "Fluid Loyalties in a Regional Crisis."

107. Interview with Eric Massi, Bangui, July 2015; also see "Central African Republic: Bozizé Back from the Brink," *Africa Confidential*, 18 January 2013.

108. Weyns, Hoex, Hilgert, and Spittaels, *Mapping Conflict Motives,* p. 16.

109. Interview, ex-Séléka commander (RPRC), Bambari, July 2015.

110. Email correspondence with NGO official, Bangui, July 2016.

111. Lombard, "Central African Republic: President Michel Djotodia and the Good Little Putschist's Tool Box," http://africanarguments.org/2013/04/02/central -african-republic-president-michel-djotodia-and-the-good-little-putchists-tool-box -by-louisa-lombard.

112. Herbert, Dukham, and Debos, *State Fragility in the Central African Republic,* p. 14.

113. Weyns, Hoex, Hilgert, and Spittaels, *Mapping Conflict Motives,* p. 21.

114. Interview with Abdoulaye Issene, Bangui, July 2015.

115. Agger, *Non-State Armed Groups in the Central African Republic.*

116. Debos, "Fluid Loyalties in a Regional Crisis"; Giroux, Lanz, and Sguaitamatti, "The Tormented Triangle."

117. Weyns, Hoex, Hilgert, and Spittaels, *Mapping Conflict Motives,* pp. 62–72.

118. For an extensive study of Chad's relationship with CAR, see Mogba and Yahoumbi, *Centrafrique.*

119. Weyns, Hoex, Hilgert, and Spittaels, *Mapping Conflict Motives,* pp. 65–66.

120. Ibid., pp. 69–71.

121. Human Rights Watch, *State of Anarchy, Rebellion, and Abuses Against Civilians.*

122. Mehler, "Why Security Forces Do Not Deliver Security."

123. Spittaels and Hilgert, *Mapping Conflict Motives.*

124. Lombard, "Navigational Tools for Central African Roadblocks."

125. Mehler, "Rebels and Parties," p. 129.

126. International Crisis Group, *Central African Republic: Untangling the Political Dialogue.*

127. Vlavonou, "Understanding the 'Failure' of the Séléka Rebellion."

128. Mehler, "Rebels and Parties," p. 130.

129. International Crisis Group, *Dangerous Little Stones*, pp. 15–19.

130. "Bozizé Back from the Brink," *Africa Confidential*, 18 January 2013.

131. Kennedy Tumutegyereize and Nicolas Tillon, "Central African Republic: Peace Talks Without the Talks," *African Arguments,* http://africanarguments.org

/2013/03/15/central-african-republic-peace-talks-without-the-talks-by-kennedy
-tumutegyereize-and-nicolas-tillon-conciliation-resources.

132. Warner, "Flawed Peace Process Leads to Greater Unrest in the Central
African Republic."

133. Interview with Mohamed Moussa Dhaffane, Bangui, July 2015.

134. Interview with former prime minister Nicholas Tiangaye, Bangui, July 2015;
Bøås, *The Central African Republic—A History of Collapse Foretold?"*

135. "CAR Rebel Head Michel Djotodia 'Suspends Constitution,'" *BBC News*,
26 March 2013.

136. Day, *The Bangui Carousel.*

137. U.N. Security Council Committee Established Pursuant to 2127 (2013) Con-
cerning the Central African Republic, "Narrative Summaries of Reasons for Listing
Nourredine Adam," May 13, 2014.

138. Agger, *Behind the Headlines.*

139. Interview with ex-Séléka commander (FRC/UPC), Bambari, July 2015.

140. Interview with Mohamed Moussa Dhaffane, Bangui, July 2015.

141. International Crisis Group, *The Central African Crisis.*

142. Interview with Abdoulaye Issene, Bangui, July 2015; Vlavonou, "Understanding the 'Failure' of the Séléka Rebellion."

143. Human Rights Watch, *I Can Still Smell the Dead;* Amnesty International,
Central African Republic.

144. Weyns, Hoex, Hilgert, and Spittaels, *Mapping Conflict Motives,* p. 23.

145. Interview, Joachim Kokate, Bangui, July 2015.

146. Day and Agger, "To Understand the Crisis in the CAR, Beware of Familiar
Narratives," *Al Jazeera America*, 10 January 2014.

147. These included CEEAC Mission de Consolidation de la Paix en République
Centrafricaine (MICOPAX), which was replaced by the AU's Mission International
de Soutien à la Centrafrique (MISCA).

148. "Central African Republic: France Wades In Again," *Africa Confidential*, 18
October 2013; "Central African Republic: On the Brink," *Africa Confidential*, 13
December 2013.

149. Al Jazeera, "Central African Republic: Touadera Wins Election," 21 February 2016, available at www.aljazeera.com/news/2016/02/central-african-republic
-touadera-wins-election-160221044730048.html.

150. Dukhan, *Splintered Warfare.*

151. Interview with Zéphirin Mogba, professor of sociology, University of Bangui, CAR, July 2015.

152. J. L. Musa, "The Enigma of Corporal Foday Sankoh."

153. Day, "Bush Path to Self-Destruction."

6

Beyond Rebel Fates

Victorious warriors win first and then go to war, while defeated warriors go to war first and then seek to win.

—Sun Tzu

Wars have outcomes. The study here has approached this phenomenon from the distinct angle of rebel fates, which clarifies these outcomes. It reconsiders the complex political interactions between rebellions and regimes, which are largely shaped by rebels' historical role in political society and regime politics. Focusing on the rebel group as the unit of analysis distinguishes this study from standard accounts of conflict duration and termination that focus on conflict dyads.

A brief review of this theoretical framework is in order. Rebel fates vary by their degree of political embeddedness in state authority structures. Some groups are composed of disparate political outsiders, and others contain key insiders from the fragmented networks of the prevailing political establishment. Politically embedded groups have organizational endowments that cohere around disenfranchised elites who once played a role in state institutions. These elites leverage prewar political networks and bring their organizational endowments into rebellion in such a way that either increases the likelihood of winning outright or facilitates their reentry into regime politics by way of a political settlement with incumbents. Alternatively, groups composed of political outsiders are already marginalized from the existing political system. These outsiders may have alternative sources of organizational cohesion, such as ethnicity or class, but they will lack access to political networks granting entry to authority structures, unless they replace them entirely. In addition, the "technology of rebellion" shapes rebel fates by considering the parity between rebels and state militaries. Rebels may fight in asymmetrical irregular wars against conventional state militaries. Or they may fight in symmetrical irregular warfare, in which rebels and state militaries are more or less unevenly matched. The key insight here is that political embeddedness mediates the effects of rebel capacity and is a better predictor of rebel fates.

By and large, the empirical record in Africa supports these claims and lends a modicum of generalizability outside the African context. However, the case studies also illuminate several dimensions of rebel fates not entirely captured by this study and suggest important implications for efforts to end conflicts and usher in political stability after they end. In this final chapter, I reflect on one key outcome omitted by the previous survey of potential fates, and that is rebel persistence. I also reexamine proxy warfare as a key causal factor illuminated by the case studies but not considered by the explanatory framework. I conclude by discussing the linkages between rebel fates and political stability in Africa.

Rebel Persistence

> *There are survivors . . . there's no winners.*
> —Haymitch Abernathy, *The Hunger Games*

This study has provided an explanation for why rebel groups meet variants of victory and defeat. But what of instances where armed groups avoid these fates and persist in spite of time, military pressure, and opportunities to lay down arms? The ADF appears to be one such group, demonstrating a remarkable durability over time.[1] In addition, though the Séléka were victorious, their fall from regime authority was followed by a proliferation of factions that continue to operate in various and shifting combinations throughout CAR, nourished by illicit natural-resource trading, forced taxation, and pillage in the country's periphery.[2] Outside Africa, northeastern India's myriad Naga rebels are decades old and have been portrayed as persistent and interminable.[3]

The question of rebel persistence is a neglected topic in the broader study of civil war and rebellion. Yet investigating the factors that enable rebel groups to persist against pressures to perish in the violent, contingent environment of civil war is nevertheless important. The focus on rebel persistence is part of the project of clarifying broader questions of conflict duration and termination and what makes some conflicts more intractable than others. Yet as was argued earlier, cross-national studies of conflict duration and termination tend to use countries or conflict dyads for their units of analysis, which obscure the puzzle of rebel persistence as its own distinct phenomenon. Approaching conflict duration through the lens of rebellion as the primary unit of analysis, and persistence as an outcome worthy of study, sheds new light on the world's more stubborn wars in countries such as DRC, South Sudan, Afghanistan, and Colombia.

To be sure, measuring persistence is problematic. How do we know if an ongoing rebellion has not yet met a more decisive fate? A persistent rebellion today could be extinct tomorrow, could win next week, or could negotiate later this year. Weinstein has helpfully described "resilience" as how rebels respond to the "shocks" of battlefield loss and success, changes in resources, and counterinsurgency.[4] Here resilience is a function of a rebellion's initial economic and social endowments, which help manage the expectations of different fighters through payoffs or promises, and broader relationships with civilian populations.[5] Alternatively, Jordan explains the resilience of terrorist groups in terms of their internal bureaucracy and levels of popular support, which allow them to persist following the decapitation of their leadership.[6]

Rebels persist when they maintain strategic control over group organization and its resources and when they successfully manage the myriad threats and contingent events found within civil war's violent environment. Somehow these rebels evade defeat over a significant amount of time, despite being outmatched militarily, and in situations where an alternative outcome should plausibly have occurred. It is not uncommon for rebels to choose to continue fighting after failed peace negotiations, in which they have either been denied or have forgone an opportunity to settle with the state.[7]

The Persistence of the Lord's Resistance Army (LRA)

Consider again the case of the Lord's Resistance Army, which remains one of the more puzzling cases of rebel persistence. Indeed, the LRA has long defied many categorizations of rebel organization and behavior.[8] There is a well-established body of scholarly work that addresses the LRA's complex origins, why it fights,[9] and the difficulties in separating objective analysis from political narratives.[10] Yet the tendency to focus on the drivers and consequences of LRA violence does not account for why the rebellion has survived for nearly three decades.

The LRA's trajectory cuts across three distinct phases, each of which suggests potential explanations for its persistence. In the first phase, the LRA emerged as an outgrowth of the Uganda People's Democratic

Army, described in Chapter 3 as a politically embedded rebellion that met the fate of victory incorporation. The LRA's organizational core consisted of the UPDA's more intransigent members and was built upon a conventional military hierarchy, while many of its fighters were drawn to Joseph Kony's more cosmological view of Acholi identity. In this form, the LRA fought a low-level insurgency from the late 1980s until the early 1990s. Peace talks in 1993 failed alongside the Ugandan government's increased militarization of northern Uganda.

This closed off the group's operational space and pushed it into a second phase, where it shifted to southern Sudan as a client of the regime in Khartoum, which intensified its rebellion.[11] This experience not only provided weapons and military training for the LRA but also sanctuary it could use to consolidate its organizational structure in lightly governed borderlands. In the late 1990s Sudan's sponsorship declined as the Ugandan military was allowed to hunt the LRA in southern Sudanese bases. These operations failed to eliminate the LRA and only caused a fresh conflict and massive humanitarian crisis in northern Uganda. Ultimately, a combination of military pressure and the extension of the new South Sudanese government in 2005 pushed the LRA from its sanctuaries, and it again relocated to the hinterlands of DRC, CAR, and Sudan.

After using the Juba peace process to regroup, the LRA has persisted in spite of having broken into several groups scattered among three states, and military pressure brought to bear by the African Union-Led Regional Task Force (AU RTF).[12] Most fighters survive through the practice of years of bush autonomy, subsisting on seasonal rivers, a network of boreholes, and temporary farms supplemented by hunting, knowledge of wild foods, and healing herbs.[13] And though Sudan no longer provides military support, it tacitly allows Kony to hide in the Kafia Kinji region that borders South Sudan and CAR. This also supplies markets for the LRA to exploit regional illicit resource networks, particularly ivory, diamonds, and gold.[14]

The LRA case suggests several things. Although it initially inherited organizational endowments from the UPDA (an insider rebellion), it most often behaved and was treated by the Ugandan government as a group of outsiders. Kony's background as a primary school dropout and one-time Catholic altar boy from rural Acholiland engendered no meaningful connection to state authority beyond fighting it.[15] Over time, any institutional linkages between the LRA and Uganda's political establishment—former army standpatters—eroded through battlefield deaths, surrenders, and executions. This left Kony—the ultimate outsider—at the apex of an intransigent rebellion unable to be fully incorporated by a regime with no intention of accommodating its members beyond amnesty for its fighters.

The explanatory framework proposed here suggests other possible fates for the LRA. Victory domination remains highly unlikely, given that the group no longer operates within Uganda. Alternatively, the LRA could meet either variant of defeat—elimination or disintegration. Yet the LRA's path has been to remain an active rebellion for nearly three decades and across multiple countries. It is a flagship case of rebel persistence, but without an adequate explanation.

Potential Explanations

What then explains rebel persistence? To manage the myriad threats and contingent events found within its broader, often violent environment, the LRA in particular seems to sit at the nexus of three key factors that have remained more or less intact against the backdrop of regional geopolitical shifts and in the face of multiple challenges. The first is an alternative form of organizational cohesion that has a high degree of flexibility to deal with shocks and adapt to shifting political conditions. The LRA's structure is built upon conventional hierarchy inherited from ex-soldiers, but it is augmented by a distinct set of beliefs in spiritual communication and cultural symbols that provide internal order and socialize fighters[16] (most of whom are renewable abductees) and guarantees the primacy of Kony's leadership.[17] In addition, though I have argued for the limits of capacity as a determinant of rebel fates, a second possible factor is the LRA's savvy resource use. Although Sudanese sponsorship bolstered the LRA, the group's access to resources was in fact intermittent, which taught its fighters how to adapt to fluctuating periods of abundance and scarcity.

Above all, the factors of organizational endowment and resource-acquisition strategies appear to influence persistence through interaction with the broader political and territorial environment. Borderlands with little penetration of state institutions, particularly those characterized by ongoing insecurity, are formidable sanctuaries that provide permissive conditions for a rebel group to nurture its organizational structure and diversify resource-acquisition strategies. Far afield from state intrusion, bush life maintains the LRA's organizational autonomy and continues to provide an identity anchor for fighters who have become both consumers and producers of violence.[18] Ongoing insurgency in bush sanctuaries is a way of life that maintains a sense of purpose, identity, group cohesion, and the legitimacy of Kony's authority. Moreover, the absence of large-scale political or social structures allows the LRA the autonomy to regulate internal control and impose hegemony over rival actors, while also reducing the burdens of governing. Upended by violence and displacement, far-flung communities in these spaces have little capacity to challenge or resist multiple armed groups in the region, thus enabling the LRA to remain historically dominant. In these ways, the LRA's survival mirrors Weber's assertion that "the existence of the war lord . . . depends solely on a chronic state of war and upon a comprehensive organization set for warfare."[19]

Without doubt, the LRA's trajectory of persistence may be idiosyncratic. Its organizational structure and use of resources have been well suited to particular regional political conditions. The LRA in particular, however, has demonstrated a remarkable ability to situate itself in environments with little or no penetration of state institutions as these spaces become available, then relocating when they become unavailable. This suggests that rebel motivations might actually matter. That is, rebels who do not necessarily fit the conventional definition here— "rebels rebel"—and instead seek alternative paths to survival beyond joining or replacing an incumbent regime, may be subject to different sets of political incentives that would otherwise influence more conventional armed groups. As such, the LRA reflects changes in the broader patterns of conflict in Africa, where full-scale civil wars have given way to fragmented armed groups with decentralized power bases that sprawl across remote border regions.[20]

Circling back to the ADF and ex-Séléka cases can offer some additional comparative leverage. Both groups share with the LRA a broader regional, geopolitical environment, devoid of state structures that could put institutional checks on rebel persistence. Such patterns are certainly evident with other armed groups such as Nigeria's Boko Haram and the myriad militias of South Sudan and Somalia. In terms of resource acquisition strategies, the ADF, like the LRA, was a former client of Sudan and was left to its own devices on the DRC-Uganda borderlands, which suggests a certain adaptation to resource self-reliance. Yet the ex-Séléka groups that currently operate in CAR appear not to have had matching experience with dramatic fluctuations in resource access. In fact, the drivers of the Séléka rebels, both before and after their short stint as rulers of CAR, seem to be economic incentives and maintaining access to resources. What is key here is that neither group shares with the LRA a comparable organizational story. Although the anatomy of the LRA has evolved over time, key elements of the group's initial organizational endowments have facilitated its survival. In contrast, the perennial outsider status of the ADF and ex-Séléka do little to predict their persistence. Taken together, these cases seem to remain outliers, and a generalizable explanation of rebel persistence may require additional research.

Either way, these observations dovetail with Olson's distinction between roving bandits and stationary bandits, the latter of which require a degree of political order to guarantee the "rational monopolization of theft" of territory under its control.[21] Although groups such as the LRA have been periodically semisedentary, seldom have they sought to directly govern people or territory. And though resource plunder has always been part of the LRA's resource-acquisition strategy, it has now become central to its roving banditry, and ongoing political disorder in its borderland sanctuaries continues to enable the group's persistence.

Proxy Warfare

I want you to be concerned about your next-door neighbor. Do you know your next-door neighbor?

—Mother Teresa

Proxy warfare, or state sponsorship of rebellion, is neither new nor an uncommon phenomenon in Africa, and it has been a common feature of several cases examined in this study. Uganda's WNBF, UNRF II, and ADF groups received resources in varying degrees from the Sudanese government. In the 1980s, Ethiopia provided territory, arms, and organizational inputs to the SPLA. This arguably narrowed the path to a political settlement as the SPLA was required to align its political priorities with its Ethiopian sponsors, as peace would remove a blunt instrument in the Derg's regional foreign policy.[22] And during the bookends of Sierra Leone's civil war, the RUF was largely an extension of Liberia's Charles Taylor, for better or worse. I have been explicit in minimizing rebel capacity as a predictor of rebel fates. However, many of the empirical observations here point to an alternative approach to proxy warfare that examines the distinct political relationships between rebels and their state sponsors. To be sure, a rebellion's political linkages matter to its fate, as my central argument claims. It remains plausible, however, that proxy warfare has the potential to alter a rebellion's trajectory, not by virtue of increased capacity, but by how regional political linkages extend into rebel organization when sponsors use rebels as blunt instruments to pursue their wider regional interests in a wider, geopolitical context via "war by other means" against rival states.[23]

A look at the prevailing literature on proxy warfare indicates there is already a road map to understanding this phenomenon, which can be repurposed in the service of further understanding conflict outcomes. As a common starting point, many works provide conceptual frameworks with largely atheoretical, empirical analyses.[24] Many scholars focus on Africa during the Cold War, for instance, during the 1980s when the Soviet Union and Cuba assisted Angola's Marxist Movimento Popular de Libertação de Angola (MPLA) against União Nacional para a Independência Total de Angola (UNITA), an American and South African–supported insurgency.[25] Other scholars have looked at state-to-state relations within Africa. Prunier, for instance, details Sudan's support for armed movements in Uganda from 1986 to 1999,[26] and Abbink describes how Eritrea and Ethiopia used proxies against one another before, during, and after fully going to war in 1999.[27]

The more theoretical approaches to proxy war generally slot into three baskets. The first considers the interests of sponsors as a major factor in shaping proxy wars and analyzes why it is a preferable form of military intervention, despite its potentially negative consequences.[28] Tamm, for instance, examines "transnational alliances" between Congolese rebels and rulers alike and their myriad supporters, finding that the likelihood of proxy warfare increases when there is a confluence of factors facing a potential sponsor: transnational threats, resource opportunities, and affinities such as cross-border ethnic linkages.[29] Alternatively, Bapat and Carter have independently observed that larger geopolitical interests of sponsors can lead them to constrain their proxies or even give them up in order to avoid future costs.[30]

The second theoretical approach grows out of the political economy of conflict, focusing on the relationship between resource flows and rebel organization. Staniland correctly points out the tension within this literature:[31] On the one hand, external support helps sustain armed campaigns and deprives target states of rapid victory over rebel challengers,[32] but on the other hand, can be destructive to rebel groups.[33] Staniland squares this circle by arguing that variation in preexisting political networks that constitute rebel organization determine how resources are used, an approach that dovetails well with my theoretical intuition but stops short of considering the nature of political linkages between sponsor and rebel.

A final category examines the strategic interaction between sponsors and rebels, and some of its consequences. Salehyan, for instance, applies principal-agent theory to proxy warfare and correctly observes that when sponsors "delegate" to rebel organizations, it decreases costs.

Yet sponsors still lose a degree of control over their foreign policy, which can bring unseen costs if their rebel agents are hard to tame. In another approach to strategic interaction, Tamm circles back to the circumstances that predict when sponsorship undermines insurgent cohesion, arguing that sponsors can leverage resources to deliberately alter the distribution of power within rebel organization.[34] This suggests then that prewar organizational endowments matter, which I argue is linked to political embeddedness.

Proxy Wars and Rebel Fates

Taken together, this broader literature on proxy warfare and some of the cases presented here in earlier chapters lead to several key observations. First, Africa's regional political and institutional context provides permissive conditions for proxy warfare. As we know, African boundaries and state institutions are not historical by-products of warfare[35] but were externally fixed by European colonial occupiers to avoid wars on the continent.[36] The agreement among independent African states to maintain colonial boundaries has resulted in virtual borders that are legally intact but beyond the state's capacity to fully control, with no real pressing security need to do so. Jackson argues that these "quasi-states" have "negative" or "juridical" sovereignty, enjoying universal international recognition but failing in "empirical sovereignty," or lacking the capacity to extend authority within their territory and to secure their borders.[37]

Conventional theories about interstate warfare therefore fit uncomfortably into the African context.[38] On the one hand, African states are seen as lacking the capacity to protect against international threats in an anarchic international system. On the other hand, juridical strength bolsters territorial inviolability and has reduced interstate warfare on the continent. The logic of fixed boundaries ensures there is no dominant, externally oriented security dilemma for African states. Yet, as Atzili ably argues, the boundary norms that divide weak African states cause them to become weaker and thus produce internal wars that spill over borders, creating intervention opportunities for neighbors.[39] These states belong to a distinct state system that shapes how regimes pursue their interests and how they perceive threats to their security, both internally and externally.[40]

In this context, African national security corresponds to the fragmented forces within the state. This "insecurity dilemma" means that "the assumptions of the traditional security dilemma metaphor are violated: States are preoccupied with internal rather than external security, and weak states have a guaranteed existence in what is supposedly an anarchic international environment."[41] Hence, national security is "not defined in terms of protecting specific pieces of real estate" but in terms of protecting the state apparatus and its operators. National security thus becomes a question of regime security, the threats to which do much to help us understand cycles of intervention and counterintervention in Africa's intercontinental relations.[42]

This insight exposes the paradoxical nature of proxy warfare in Africa. Whereas robust boundary control is normally an imperative of domestic security, African regimes that face their own domestic threats can sponsor proxies to destabilize and weaken neighbors' territorial control over border regions in order to undermine that rebellion's operations. Moreover, in many cases sponsors deploy their proxies directly on their own home battlefield against their domestic rivals. Rather than be at cross-purposes with a regime's security interests, the disorder of proxy warfare becomes a means of control, as Chabal and Daloz argue, where "the point of organized violence is to regulate that part of society which can usefully be marshaled for the pursuit of [its] aims."[43]

State sponsors seek informal alliances with rebels to carry out clandestine cross-border warfare. On the surface, their interests and motivations appear compatible, if not identical.[44] Yet rebel agendas may diverge from those of the sponsor, particularly in a context where there are incentives and opportunities to mask the nature of the relationship.[45] Rebels ostensibly seek to either overthrow incumbents or join established authority networks through rebellion. Sponsors, however, may not share this objective.

Either way, as principal-agent theory suggests, a sponsor creates a low-cost, specialized division of labor between itself and its rebellion, which in turn provides local knowledge and a range of viable military possibilities for destabilizing a neighbor while costing less and posing fewer risks of direct interstate confrontation. The sponsor rewards its client through resource provision, thus increasing its capacity for fighting the target regime, perhaps offering a promise of future relations, should the rebellion succeed.[46]

Thus, relations between sponsor and rebel are instrumental, conditional, and based on reciprocity. Sponsors allow a range of operational discretion required in order to accomplish their strategic ends.[47] Strategic commands are given at times but the nuts and bolts of operations are left up to the rebel group. Yet these relations are ultimately asymmetrical, as a sponsor uses its resources to provide protection and material aid in exchange for a special service—a readiness to act militarily when asked to do so, which may also include fighting on the sponsor's own battlefield. Rebels are then beholden to a sponsor that expects not only tangible results but also "non-tangible" services—a certain degree of loyalty and deference, and the surrendering of strategic autonomy.[48] Moreover, rebels have few guarantees that sponsors will not pull the plug when the costs of sponsorship exceed the benefits, or when the sponsor is satisfied with the outcome, which may not necessarily be rebel victory.

As this pertains to the fates of African rebels, the strategic interactions surrounding resource acquisition and use can extend into rebel organization and impact the autonomy of rebels' decisionmaking. Dependence on cross-border resource networks may provide resources that are independent of domestic political networks but also create obligations to external patrons. This plays out quite differently among different types of groups.

Sponsoring a rebellion of politically embedded insiders has relatively lower start-up costs because of prewar organizational endowments. And though such groups are beholden to sponsors, they tend to be more independent as they have a potential exit from the relationship with the sponsor if necessary. The range of strategic options available to such insider groups includes the possibility of entering into a political settlement with the incumbent regime. Alternatively, groups of outsiders that rely on foreign backing risk accelerated fragmentation because of higher incentives for rival leaders or ambitious cadres to gain a larger share of resources by exiting the coalition and acting independently. Because they come into rebellion with few prewar institutional networks, it is easier for sponsors to control them through resource provision, which can entail denial of support, the shifting of resources to more savvy actors and their own networks from within the group, or the elimination of troublesome actors.

In sum, in Africa's state system, the permissive duality of formal legality and of limited enforceability provides rebels with opportunities for supply and sanctuary with neighbors. Permeable border regions provide refuge for rebels because official state boundaries are not easily used by target regimes to keep insurgents out. Above all, proxy warfare in Africa is paradoxical because robust boundary control should normally be considered an imperative of domestic security. Yet incumbent regimes must consider threats to their security from both internal and neighboring actors, who can cooperate. However, it is not the resources per se that shape rebel fates but the political imperatives behind them that do, as rebel groups may become beholden to the interests of sponsors in ways that undermine a rebellion's strategic autonomy and truncate its possible trajectories.

Rebel Fates and Political Stability in Africa

> *Fate is never fair. You are caught in a current much stronger than you are; struggle against it and you'll drown not just yourself but those who try to save you. Swim with it, and you'll survive.*
>   —Cassandra Clare

It should come as no surprise that the countries featured in this study do not have stellar performances on political-stability indexes. The World Bank puts them all in the red with negative scores, with the exception of South Sudan, where no data was even available.[49] Despite the SPLA's victory by incorporation that paved the way for secession, South Sudan currently ranks first on the Fragile State Index.[50] CAR's ongoing political implosion, which only accelerated following the Séléka's victory by domination, puts it not far behind in third place. Côte d'Ivoire, once a beacon of regional stability, clocks in at twenty-first and falling. And though Sierra Leone and Uganda have been rebel free for some time, they nevertheless sit comfortably within the index's top twentieth percentile.

Such indexes seek to distill ongoing observations of political stability and provide increasingly fine-grained measures that are bundled in helpful categories of indicators that capture institutional and elite cohesion, economic development, political legitimacy, and social pressure.[51] And obviously, there is a correlation between armed conflict and political instability—although perhaps the causal direction is not clear. A more conventional view holds that political instability results from the breakdown of institutionalized patterns of authority.[52] If Huntington is correct, then Africa's patterns of political instability flow from the weak institutionalization of political authority, and its inability to manage emergent societal mobilization and intergroup conflict.[53] This assumes that institutions provide the arena in which political and societal actors manage political conflict through strategic interaction.[54]Thus, weak institutionalization creates strategic interaction problems between competing political networks where there are high levels of uncertainty and low capacity to arbitrate between groups or provide credible protection guarantees where there are lower costs for organizing rebellion.[55]

Yet do such conditions of political stability hold in the African context? How do they work in systems where patronage is the primary mechanism of authority, and where weak institutionalization is a deliberate political strategy by elites to maintain stability? It turns out that African states are remarkably resilient,[56] and their operators are quite capable of maintaining patterns of power distributions. As Chabal and Daloz have argued, Africa's "instrumentalization of disorder" demobilizes potential rivals as it chokes off the institutional channels that might serve as independent power bases. In this way, the logic of weak institutionalization keeps the prevailing establishment "working," as it were. To be sure, civil unrest, political violence, and instability occur, but more as a result of dwindling external resource bases that rulers may use to co-opt rivals through patronage and thus lower the opportunity costs to issue challenges.[57] Viewed another way, then, instability in Africa can occur when there is simply a violation of political norms or a disruption in the regularity of flow of political exchanges.[58] Otherwise, the dispensing of patronage remains a viable mechanism of political stability.[59]

With this in mind, a final implication leads to considering whether or not, or how, rebel fates matter to the political stability of African states. That is, where do the fates of rebels fit into how African politics resume after wars end? To date, the mechanisms of conflict termination seldom consider the broader political context in which rebellion occurs. Indeed, international mobilization to solve wars can often marginalize some political actors and elevate others. In the case of CAR, for instance, established political parties played almost no role in early political settlements with pre-Séléka armed groups, creating a situation where outsiders crowded out insiders,[60] thus incentivizing armed rebellion as a way to penetrate political barriers to the prevailing regime. A closer look at how conventional conflict-management mechanisms engage in such a context can help illuminate how rebel fates and political stability are or are not related.

Mechanisms of Stability in Civil War Termination

A direct contribution of this study is to provide a framework from which policymakers and third-party mediators can devise more effective responses to civil wars, with the intention of ushering in political stability in Africa. Research into the inner workings of multiple rebel groups shows how international responses, such as peacekeeping interventions and counterinsurgency operations, can influence very different outcomes, depending on the nature of their targets. Yet often, outsiders misunderstand where armed groups sit within regime politics and pursue counterproductive strategies. For instance, NATO's 2010 intervention in Libya helped remove a troublesome regime but did not consider the capacity of Gaddafi's successors to govern, a strategic lapse that perhaps violated the "do no harm" principle of intervention.[61]

The comparative framework offered herein challenges the dual conventional notions that peace operations that bring together opposing parties are always desirable, and that counterinsurgency is always an effective means to eliminate rebel challengers. Actors seeking to intervene in conflicts to square this circle might well pay attention to the complex dynamics of armed actors they hope to either contain or bolster. In some cases, picking sides can be problematic, peace without victory or defeat can be unattainable, and failure to consider structural factors may lead to protracted conflicts or unintended consequences.

As I have argued, a political settlement is only one of a range of potential outcomes experienced by rebel groups in civil wars. To be sure, it is the preferred outcome for international conflict managers, who, through the mechanisms of third-party peacemaking, peacekeeping, and peace building, urge civil war antagonists to move from violent to spoken conflict and, if they are lucky, to transform conflict to durable peace by addressing "root causes."

Indeed, there is a deep cache of case studies from over several decades of international peace operations that provide "lessons learned" for would-be interveners.[62] These experiences have also generated scholarly and policy analysis preoccupied with multiple dimensions of intervention, such as DDR, post-settlement elections, and refugee repatriation.[63] A corresponding body of work addresses the multiple challenges of peace operations and seeks to understand why they succeed or fail. Here, successes often hinge on the capacities of negotiators or on the vague concept of "ripeness."[64] A range of explanations is offered to account for failures, including breakdowns in bargaining, "spoilers,"[65] or the reluctance of rebels to disarm during postnegotiation settlement.[66] And though research has shown that peacekeeping is, on balance, successful,[67] some more recent approaches have examined the institutional dysfunctions of the interveners themselves, who create an alternative universe of "Peaceland," where their everyday practices and habits can render interventions inefficient or ineffective at best, or counterproductive at worst.[68]

Another way to approach the question of why peace operations succeed or fail is to consider the structural characteristics of armed groups and their prewar relationships to state institutions. Indeed, the impetus to "railroad peace"[69] by reconciling insiders with outsiders through intervention and internationally brokered peace accords may breed political instability. As shown in the RUF and Séléka cases, the external engineering of political accommodation can be problematic. And although the FN and SPLA had a significant degree of political embeddedness, their long respective walks to victory domination and incorporation had to navigate shifting political definitions of who was considered an insider or an outsider.

Would-be interveners would do well to understand that political embeddedness matters to efforts to end conflict—those rebellions that have a historical institutional relationship with regime politics are more likely to settle. This insight can help forestall "off-the-path" strategies that do not correspond to the nature of the rebel group without addressing the structural factors themselves. In other words, peacemakers should be wary of forcing the incorporation of outsiders into a political establishment that only shows a disingenuous interest in doing so, only to maneuver to reject the outsiders once the fighting stops. In such cases, counterinsurgency might be the most efficient path to ending civil wars.

Yet the militarized flip side to "conflict management" also has its own pitfalls. Dominant approaches to counterinsurgency often assume that incumbents seek to "outgovern" rebel challengers as part of a broader strategy of elimination.[70] Much of this thinking is based upon experiences from past wars and across armies, in particular, the development of counterinsurgency "doctrine" developed from the nineteenth- and twentieth-century campaigns of colonial armies to "pacify" local populations, or the US interventions in Vietnam and the Philippines.[71] Even contemporary critiques of these classical approaches, which put insurgent threats in the context of localized threats becoming extensions of "global insurgency," still assume that rebels are always somehow separate and distinct from regime politics.[72]

In the African context, however, counterinsurgency can be viewed much more as a function of the political relationships between incumbents and rebel challengers that exist beyond the battlefield clashes over territory and populations, and therefore often beyond the reach of outside interventions. Yet standard prescriptions nevertheless continue to focus on "state-building" measures such as training local armies, building up state institutions to provide services to noncombatants, and limiting government corruption.[73] Such approaches also rest on the presumption that successful counterinsurgency taps into noncombatant networks for information in order to sever rebels from local communities. This misses two interlinked observations: incumbents often lack the institutional capacity to launch extensive counterinsurgency programs to outgovern rebels; and they instead pursue patronage-based regime strategies for exercising authority outside of warfare.

Although coercive, militarized counterinsurgency strategies often target for elimination rebels who are political outsiders, foreign counterinsurgents would do well to devote more attention to how the strategies that regimes use to keep themselves in power are extended to dealing with insiders, and to consider how incumbents might use the mechanism of patronage to manage rebel threats that emanate from within the familiar confines of a state's political society. Attempting to eliminate politically embedded insiders with sizable constituencies can lead to protracted conflicts and prolonged political instability.

Conclusion

In the African context, political stability seems to persist in spite of civil war and rebellion, so long as, to follow Dahl's formulation, the costs of repression borne by incumbent elites do not exceed the costs of toleration.[74] This would explain the divergent strategies in Africa deployed between insiders and outsiders, which are seamless extensions of noninstitutional means of maintaining stability in the politics of the ordinary. To be sure, regimes are not always successful at keeping insurgents at bay or co-opting them, and the organizational capacity and political positionality of rebellions can sometimes send them on unexpected trajectories that upend political stability.

The victory domination of Uganda's NRA, alongside others such as the Rwandan Patriotic Front (RPF) and the Ethiopian People's Revolutionary Democratic Front, whose ouster and replacement of ancien regimes led to strong political systems, are among the few cases where "letting the rebels win" is a strong argument for those who wish to see political stability.[75] But not all victories result in such outcomes. As shown in the Séléka case, CAR is a long way from political stability. And the government of South Sudan, which grew out of the SPLA, has never fully consolidated authority, and Africa's newest state has been violently unraveling since its independence in 2011.[76]

What becomes clear here is that studying the linkage between rebels, their fates, and postconflict stability in Africa is an avenue for future research. In other words, we should ask, what happens to political order when rebels meet their respective fates? Addressing this question can support existing research on the durability or breakdown of negotiated political settlements that bring an end to civil wars.[77] Looking at the fates of rebels, which may include successful or failed attempts to consolidate authority, can give further insight into other substantive outcomes such as regime type,[78] economic development, and the roots of emergent democratic institutions.[79]

In sum, the cases in this study suggest an unsettling possibility: that political stability is a game played primarily by politically embedded insiders, by those beneficiaries of the historical institutional legacies of African states. Short of organizing and waging rebellion, there appears to be very little outsiders can do to have their interests taken seriously by the elite networks that dominate Africa's political institutions. Of course, outsiders like the Séléka might win from time to time, but even for such groups, the possibilities for political change through armed rebellion ultimately make the prospects of political stability even more distant. Those who make efforts to respond to armed conflict, and take broader measures to address political and economic development in Africa, would do well to consider the distinctions between political insiders and outsiders. To date, the overwhelming focus on postconflict reconstruction tries to create or transfer state institutions in an environment where they play a lesser role than interveners expect.[80] A possible focus could be on expanding access to more groups by enhancing cross-cutting identities that do not necessarily correspond to hard divisions of political society. This is not to say that elite politics in Africa should be abolished. Rather, a possible way forward would be to encourage the expansion of the base of elites and simply acknowledge that they operate within a noninstitutionalized context for strategic interaction and contestation.[81] Political violence may very well still occur, but the fates of rebels within an expanded domain of consensus and accommodation among groups of equal or similar status may result in more positive-sum bargains rather than more zero-sum wars.

Notes

1. Scorgie, "Peripheral Pariah or Regional Rebel?"; Titeca and Vlassenroot, "Rebels Without Borders?"

2. Agger, *Behind the Headlines.*

3. Franke, *War and Nationalism in South Asia*; Suykens, "Comparing Rebel Rule Through Revolution and Naturalization."

4. Weinstein, *Inside Rebellion*, pp. 260–265.

5. Ibid., p. 261.

6. Jordan, "Attacking the Leader."

7. Day, "'Survival Mode.'"

8. Allen and Vlassenroot, eds., *The Lord's Resistance Army.*

9. Lomo and Hovil, "Behind the Violence"; Doom and Vlassenroot, "Kony's Message"; Gersony, *The Anguish of Northern Uganda.*

10. Titeca and Costeur, "An LRA for Everyone."

11. "War in the North," *Africa Confidential*, 24 May 1996; "Why Has NRA Failed to Finish Off Kony?" *Daily Monitor*, 12 May 1995.

12. Brubacher, Damman, and Day, "The AU Task Force."

13. "Report on Kony War," *New Vision*, 1 January 2006.

14. The Enough Project, The Resolve, and Invisible Children, *Kony to LRA;* Agger and Hutson, *Kony's Ivory.*

15. Doom and Vlassenroot, "Kony's Message," pp. 20–21; for more on Kony's rural background, see Green, *The Wizard of the Nile.*

16. Titeca, "The Spiritual Order of the LRA."

17. Interviews with ex-LRA fighters, July and August 2011, December 2013.

18. Vinci, "Existential Motivations in the Lord's Resistance Army's Continuing Conflict."

19. Gerth and Mills, eds., *Max Weber*, p. 252.

20. Straus, "Wars Do End!"

21. Olson, "Dictatorship, Democracy, and Development."

22. "The SPLA in Focus," *Africa Confidential*, 20 April 1988.

23. Byman, Chalk, Hoffman, Rosenau, and Brannan, *Trends in Outside Support*, p. 32.

24. Checkel, ed., *Transnational Dynamics of Civil War*; Mumford, *Proxy Warfare.*

25. Gleijeses, *Conflicting Missions*; Laidi, *The Superpowers and Africa.*

26. Prunier, "Rebel Movements and Proxy Warfare."

27. Abbink, "Eritrea-Ethiopia."

28. Hughes, *My Enemy's Enemy.*

29. Tamm, "The Origins of Transnational Alliances."

30. Bapat, "State Bargaining with Transnational Terrorist Groups"; Carter, "A Blessing or a Curse?"

31. Staniland, "Organizing Insurgency."

32. Byman, Chalk, Hoffman, Rosenau, and Brannan, *Trends in Outside Support.*

33. Weinstein, *Inside Rebellion*, p. 10.

34. Tamm, "Rebel Leaders, Internal Rivals, and External Resources."

35. Tilly, *Coercion, Capital and European States.*

36. Herbst, *States and Power in Africa*, pp. 103–106.

37. Jackson, *Quasi-States*, pp. 67–70.

38. Dunn and Shaw, eds., *Africa's Challenge to International Relations Theory.*

39. Atzili, "When Good Fences Make Bad Neighbors."

40. Zartman, "Africa as a Subordinate State System in International Relations," p. 548.

41. Job, *The Insecurity Dilemma*, p. 18.

42. Clark, "Realism, Neo-Realism and Africa's International Relations in the Post-Cold War Era," p. 96.

43. Chabal and Daloz, *Africa Works*, pp. 77–78.

44. Bar-Siman-Tov, "The Strategy of War by Proxy," p. 269.

45. Dunér, "Proxy Intervention in Civil Wars."

46. Bar-Siman-Tov, "The Strategy of War by Proxy," p. 269.

47. Hawkins, Lake, Nielson, and Tierney, eds., *Delegation and Agency in International Organizations*, pp. 8, 27–28.

48. Bar-Siman-Tov, "The Strategy of War by Proxy," p. 270.

49. www.theglobaleconomy.com/rankings/wb_political_stability, accessed 16 December 2017.

50. http://fundforpeace.org/fsi, accessed 16 December 2017.

51. http://fundforpeace.org/fsi/indicators, accessed 16 December 2017.

52. Morrison and Stevenson, "Political Instability in Independent Black Africa," p. 348.

53. Huntington, *Political Order in Changing Societies.*

54. Przeworski, *Democracy and the Market.*

55. Fearon and Laitin, "Ethnicity, Insurgency, and Civil Wars."

56. Englebert, *Africa*, p. 41.

57. Reno, *Warlord Politics and African States.*

58. Ake, "A Definition of Political Stability."

59. Arriola, "Patronage and Political Stability in Africa."

60. Mehler, "Rebels and Parties."

61. Kuperman, "A Model Humanitarian Intervention?"

62. Crocker, Hampson, and Aall, *Herding Cats.*

63. Stedman, Rothchild, and Cousens, *Ending Civil Wars.*

64. Hampson, *Nurturing Peace.*

65. Stedman, "Spoiler Problems in Peace Processes"; Greenhill and Major, "The Perils of Profiling."

66. Walter, "The Critical Barrier to Civil War Settlement."

67. Fortna, "Does Peacekeeping Keep Peace?"

68. Autesserre, *Peaceland.*

69. Tanner, "Liberia."

70. Cassidy, *Counterinsurgency and the Global War on Terror.*

71. Nagl, *Learning to Eat Soup with a Knife,* pp. 24–29.

72. Kilcullen, "Counter-Insurgency *Redux,*" p. 111; Kilcullen, "Countering Global Insurgency"; Hoffman, "Small Wars Revisited."

73. US Army and Marine Corps, *Counterinsurgency Field Manual.*

74. Dahl, *Polyarchy.*

75. Toft, "Ending Civil Wars."

76. Johnson, "Briefing"; Rolandsen, "Another Civil War in South Sudan."

77. Licklider, "The Consequences of Negotiated Settlements in Civil Wars, 1945–1993."

78. Lyons, "The Importance of Winning."

79. Riedl, *Authoritarian Origins of Democratic Party Systems in Africa.*

80. Englebert and Tull, "Postconflict Reconstruction in Africa."

81. Gupta, "Roots of Political Instability in Africa."

Acronyms

ADF	Allied Democratic Front
ADM	Allied Democratic Movement
AFRC	Armed Forces Revolutionary Council
ANC	African National Congress
APC	All People's Congress
APRD	Armée Populaire pour la Restauration de la République et la Démocratie (Popular Army for the Restoration of the Republic and Democracy)
AROPIC	Aringa-Obongi Peace Initiative Committee
ATU	Anti-Terrorist Unit
AU	African Union
AU RTF	African Union-Led Regional Task Force
CAR	Central African Republic
CCP	Commission for the Consolidation of Peace
CDF	Civil Defense Force
CEEAC	Communauté Économique des États de l'Afrique Centrale (Economic Community of Central African States)
CLF	Caprivi Liberation Front
CMRRD	Commission for the Management of Strategic Resources, National Reconstruction and Development
CPA	Comprehensive Peace Agreement
CPJP	Convention des Patriots pour la Justice et la Paix (Convention of Patriots for Justice and Peace)
CPSK	Convention Patriotique du Salut du Kodro (Patriotic Convention for Saving the Country)
CWP	Correlates of War Project

DDR	disarmament, demobilization, and reintegration
DoP	Declaration of Principles
DRC	Democratic Republic of Congo
DUP	Democratic Unionist Party
ECOMOG	Economic Community Monitoring Group
ECOWAS	Economic Community of West Africa States
EO	Executive Outcomes
EPRDF	Ethiopian People's Revolutionary Democratic Front
FACA	Forces Armées Centrafricaines (Central African Armed Forces)
FANCI	Forces Armées Nationales de Côte d'Ivoire (National Armed Forces of Côte d'Ivoire)
FARDC	Forces Armées de la République Démocratique du Congo (Armed Forces of the Democratic Republic of Congo)
FDPC	Front Démocratique du Peuple Centrafricain (Democratic Front of the Central African Republic)
FEDEMO	Federal Democratic Movement
FESCI	Fédération Estudiantine et Colaire de la Côte d'Ivoire
FMLN	Farabundo Martí para la Liberación Nacional (Farabundo Martí National Liberation Front)
FPI	Front Populaire Ivorien (Ivorian Popular Front)
FPR	Front Populaire pour le Redressement (Popular Front for Recovery)
FRCI	Forces Républicaines de Côte d'Ivoire (Republican Forces of Côte d'Ivoire)
FRELIMO	Frente de Libertação de Moçambique (Mozambique Liberation Front)
FRONASA	Front for National Salvation
FUNA	Former Uganda National Army
GNU	Government of National Unity
GSG	Gurkha Security Group
HEC	High Executive Council
HSMF	Holy Spirit Mobile Forces
IDU	Internal Defence Unit
IGAD	Intergovernmental Authority on Development
INC	Interim National Constitution
LDU	Local Defense Unit
LRA	Lord's Resistance Army
LTTE	Liberation Tigers of Tamil Elam
LURD	Liberians United for Reconciliation and Democracy

MICOPAX	Mission de Consolidation de la Paix en République Centrafricaine (Mission for the Consolidation of Peace in the Central African Republic)
MINURCA	Mission des Nations Unies en République Centrafricaine (United Nations Mission in the Central African Republic)
MINUSCA	Mission Multidimensionnelle Intégrée des Nations Unies pour la Stabilisation en Centrafrique (United Nations Multidimensional Integrated Stabilization Mission in the Central African Republic)
MISCA	Mission International de Soutien à la Centrafrique (African-led International Support Mission to the Central African Republic)
MJP	Mouvement pour la Justice et la Paix (Movement for Justice and Peace)
MLCJ	Mouvement des Libérateurs Centrafricains pour la Justice (Movement of Central African Liberators for Justice)
MODEL	Movement for Democracy in Liberia
MONUSCO	Mission de l'Organisation des Nations Unies pour la Stabilisation en République Démocratique du Congo (United Nations Organization Stabilization Mission in the Democratic Republic of the Congo)
MPCI	Mouvement Patriotique de Côte d'Ivoire (Patriotic Movement of Côte d'Ivoire)
MPIGO	Mouvement Populaire Ivoirien du Grand Ouest (Ivorian Popular Movement of the Great West)
MPLA	Movimento Popular de Libertação de Angola (People's Movement for the Liberation of Angola)
MSF	Médecins Sans Frontières (Doctors Without Borders)
NALU	National Army for the Liberation of Uganda
NCP	National Congress Party
NDA	National Democratic Alliance
NDA	National Democratic Army
NDF	National Democratic Front
NGO	Nongovernmental organization
NIF	National Islamic Front
NOA	Ninth of October Army
NPFL	National Patriotic Front of Liberia
NPRC	National Provisional Ruling Council
NRA	National Resistance Army

OLS	Operation Lifeline Sudan
PAF	People's Armed Forces
PAIGC	Partido Africano da Independência da Guiné e Cabo Verde (African Party for the Independence of Guinea and Cape Verde)
PC	political commissar
PDCI-RDA	Parti Démocratique de la Côte d'Ivoire-Rassemblement Démocratique Africain (Democratic Party of Côte d'Ivoire—African Democratic Rally)
PDF	People's Defense Forces
PDF	People's Democratic Front
PLO	Palestinian Liberation Organization
PMHC	Political Military High Command
PRA	People's Resistance Army
PRC	People's Redemption Council
RC	Resistance Council
RDR	Rassemblement des Républicains (Rally of the Republicans)
RENAMO	Resistência Nacional Moçambicana (Mozambican National Resistance)
RPF	Rwandan Patriotic Front
RUF	Revolutionary United Front
RUFP	Revolutionary United Front Party
SAF	Sudanese Armed Forces
SANU	Sudan African National Union
SF	Southern Front
SLA	Sierra Leone Army
SPDF	Sudan Popular Defence Forces
SPLA	Sudan People's Liberation Army
SRG	Southern Regional Government
SSDF	South Sudan Defense Force
SSIA	South Sudan Independence Army
SSLM	South Sudan Liberation Movement
SSU	Sudan Socialist Union
SWAPO	South West African People's Organization
TMC	Transitional Military Council
TPDF	Tanzania People's Defence Force
TRC	Truth and Reconciliation Commission
UA	Uganda Army
UA-WNF	Uganda Army –West Nile Front
UCDP	Uppsala Conflict Data Program

UDCA	Uganda Democratic Christian Army
UDSF	United Democratic Salvation Front
UFDR	Union des Forces Démocratiques pour le Rassemblement (Union of Democratic Forces for Unity)
UFM	Uganda Freedom Movement
UFR	Union des Forces Républicaines (Union of Republican Forces)
UHSA/F	United Holy Salvation Army/Front
ULIMO	United Liberation Movement of Liberia for Democracy
UMLA	Uganda Muslim Liberation Army
UN	United Nations
UNAMSIL	UN Assistance Mission in Sierra Leone
UNITA	União Nacional para a Independência Total de Angola (National Union for the Total Independence of Angola)
UNLA	Uganda National Liberation Army
UNLF	Uganda National Liberation Front
UNRF	Uganda National Rescue Front
UNRF II	Uganda National Rescue Front II
UPA	Uganda People's Army
UPC	Uganda People's Congress
UPC	Unité pour la Paix en Centrafrique (Union for Peace in Central Africa)
UPDA	Uganda People's Democratic Army
UPDF	Uganda People's Defence Forces
UPDM	Uganda People's Democratic Movement
UPF	Uganda People's Front
UPM	Uganda Patriotic Movement
USAP	United Sudan African Parties
WNBF	West Nile Bank Front
ZANU	Zimbabwe Africa National Union
ZDC	Zone de Confiance (Zone of Confidence)

Bibliography

Abbink, Jon. "Eritrea-Ethiopia: Proxy Wars and Prospects of Peace in the Horn of Africa." *Journal of Contemporary African Studies* 21, no. 3 (September 2003): 407–425.

Abdullah, Ibrahim. "Bush Path to Destruction: The Origin and Character of the Revolutionary United Front/Sierra Leone." *Journal of Modern African Studies* 36, no. 2 (June 1998): 203–235.

———. "The Revolutionary United Front in Sierra Leone." In *African Guerrillas,* edited by Christopher Clapham, pp. 172–193. Bloomington: Indiana University Press, 1998.

———, ed. *Between Democracy and Terror: The Sierra Leone Civil War.* Dakar: CODESRIA, 2004.

Abraham, Arthur. "State Complicity as a Factor in Perpetuating the Sierra Leone Civil War." In *Between Democracy and Terror,* edited by Ibrahim Abdullah, pp. 104–120.

Adunbi, Omolade. *Oil Wealth and Insurgency in Nigeria.* Bloomington: Indiana University Press, 2015.

African Rights. *Avoiding an Impasse: Understanding the Conflict in Western Uganda.* London: December 2001.

Agger, Kasper. *Behind the Headlines: Drivers of Violence in the Central African Republic.* Washington, DC: The Enough Project, May 2014.

———. *Non-State Armed Groups in the Central African Republic.* London: Conflict Armament Research, January 2015.

———. *Warlord Business: CAR's Violent Armed Groups and Their Criminal Operations for Profit and Power.* Washington, DC: The Enough Project, June 2015.

———, and Jonathan Hutson. *Kony's Ivory: How Elephant Poaching in Congo Helps Support the Lord's Resistance Army.* Washington, DC: The Enough Project, June 2013.

Ake, Claude. "A Definition of Political Stability." *Comparative Politics* 7, no. 2 (June 1975): 271–283.

Alison, Miranda. "Cogs in the Wheel? Women in the Liberation Tigers of Tamil Eelam." *Civil Wars* 6, no. 4 (Winter 2003): 37–54.

Allen, Tim. "Understanding Alice: Uganda's Holy Spirit Movement in Context." *Africa* 61, no. 3 (July 1991): 370–399.

———, and Koen Vlassenroot. *The Lord's Resistance Army: Myth and Reality.* London: Zed Books, 2010.

Amaza, Ondoga Ori. *Museveni's Long March: From Guerrilla to Statesman*. Kampala: Fountain, 1998.

Amnesty International. *Central African Republic: Time for Accountability*. London: Amnesty International, July 2014.

Arjona, Ana. *Rebelocracy: Social Order in the Colombian Civil War*. New York: Cambridge University Press, 2017.

———, Nelson Kasfir, and Zachariah Mampilly, eds. *Rebel Governance in Civil War*. New York: Cambridge University Press, 2016.

Arou, Mom K. N. "Devolution: Decentralization and the Division of the Southern Region into Three Regions in 1983." In *Conference on North-South Relations Since the Addis Ababa Agreement*, edited by Mom K. N. Arou and B. Yongo-Bure, pp. 166–188. Khartoum: Institute of African and Asian Studies, University of Khartoum, 1985.

Arou, Mom K. N., and B. Yongo-Bure, eds. *Conference on North-South Relations Since the Addis Ababa Agreement*. Khartoum: Institute of African and Asian Studies, University of Khartoum, 1985.

Arriola, Leonardo R. "Patronage and Political Stability in Africa." *Comparative Political Studies* 42, no. 10 (October 2009): 1339–1362.

Ashraph, Sareta. "How Things Fell Apart: A History of Sierra Leone and the Conflict." *Review* (February–June 2010).

Atkinson, Ronald R. *The Roots of Ethnicity: The Origins of the Acholi in Uganda Before 1800*. The Ethnohistory Series. Philadelphia: University of Pennsylvania Press, 1994.

Atzili, Boaz. "When Good Fences Make Bad Neighbors: Fixed Borders, State Weakness, and International Conflict." *International Security* 31, no. 3 (Winter 2006–2007): 139–173.

Autesserre, Séverine. *Peaceland: Conflict Resolution and Everyday Politics of International Intervention*. New York: Cambridge University Press, 2014.

Badal, Raphael Koba. "The Addis Ababa Agreement Ten Years After: An Assessment." In *Conference on North-South Relations Since the Addis Ababa Agreement*, edited by Mom K. N. Arou and B. Yongo-Bure. Khartoum: Institute of African and Asian Studies, University of Khartoum, 1985.

Baégas, Richard, and Ruth Marshall-Fratani. "Côte d'Ivoire: Negotiating Identity and Citizenship." In *African Guerrillas: Raging Against the Machine*, edited by Morten Bøås and Kevin C. Dunn, pp. 81–111. Boulder: Lynne Rienner, 2007.

Bakke, Kristin M., Kathleen Gallagher Cunningham, and Lee J. M. Seymour. "A Plague of Initials: Fragmentation, Cohesion, and Infighting in Civil Wars." *Perspectives on Politics* 10, no. 2 (June 2012): 265–283.

Balcells, Laia. *Rivalry and Revenge: The Politics of Violence During Civil War*. New York: Cambridge University Press, 2017.

———, and Stathis N. Kalyvas. "Did Marxism Make a Difference? Marxist Rebellions and National Liberation Movements." Paper presented at the Annual Meeting of the American Political Science Association, Washington, DC, 2–5 September 2010.

Bapat, Navin A. "State Bargaining with Transnational Terrorist Groups." *International Studies Quarterly* 50, no. 1 (March 2006): 213–229.

Bar-Siman-Tov, Yaacov. "The Strategy of War by Proxy." *Cooperation and Conflict* 19, no. 4 (November 1984): 263–273.

Baumeister, Roy F., Ellen Bratslavsky, Catrin Finkenauer, and Kathleen D. Vohs. "Bad Is Stronger than Good." *Review of General Psychology* 5, no. 4 (January 2001): 323–370.

Bayart, Jean-François. *The State in Africa: The Politics of the Belly.* Cambridge: Polity Press, 2009.

Behrend, Heike. *Alice Lakwena and the Holy Spirits: War in Northern Uganda, 1985–1997.* Athens: Ohio University Press, 2000.

Bennet, Huw. *Fighting the Mau Mau: The British Army and Counter-Insurgency in the Kenya Emergency.* Cambridge: Cambridge University Press, 2012.

Benoit-Smullyan, Emile. "Status, Status Types, and Status Interrelations." *American Sociological Review* 9, no. 2 (April 1944): 151–161.

Berdal, Mats, and David M. Malone. *Greed and Grievance: Economic Agendas in Civil Wars.* Boulder: Lynne Rienner, 2000.

Beshir, Mohamed Omer. *The Southern Sudan: Background to Conflict.* London: C. Hurst, 1968.

———, ed. *Southern Sudan: Regionalism and Religion.* Khartoum: Graduate College, University of Khartoum, 1984.

Biddle, Stephen. *Military Power: Explaining Victory and Defeat in Modern Battle.* Princeton: Princeton University Press, 2004.

Bøås, Morten. *The Central African Republic—A History of Collapse Foretold?* Norwegian Peacebuilding Resource Center, January 2014.

———, and Kevin C. Dunn, eds. *African Guerrillas: Raging Against the Machine.* Boulder: Lynne Rienner, 2007.

Boix, Carles, and Susan S. Stokes, eds. *The Oxford Handbook of Comparative Politics.* Oxford: Oxford University Press, 2007.

Boone, Catherine. *Political Topographies of the African State: Territorial Authority and Institutional Choice.* New York: Cambridge University Press, 2003.

Bradbury, Mark, Nicholas Leader, and Kate Mackintosh. *The "Agreement on Ground Rules" in South Sudan.* Humanitarian Policy Group Report 4. London: Overseas Development Institute, 2000.

Bratton, Michael, and Nicholas van de Walle. "Neopatrimonial Regimes and Political Transitions in Africa." *World Politics* 46, no. 4 (July 1994): 453–489.

Breton, Albert, Gianluigi Galeotti, Pierre Salmon, and Ronald Wintrobe, eds. *Nationalism and Rationality.* New York: Cambridge University Press, 1995.

Brooker, Paul. *Modern Stateless Warfare.* New York: Palgrave Macmillan, 2010.

Brooks, Risa A., and Elizabeth A. Stanley, eds. *Creating Military Power: Sources of Effectiveness.* Stanford: Stanford University Press, 2007.

Brown, Michael. *The International Dimensions of Internal Conflict.* Cambridge, MA: MIT Press, 1996.

Brubacher, Matthew, Erin Damman, and Christopher Day. "The AU Task Force: An African Response to Transnational Armed Groups." *Journal of Modern African Studies* 55, no. 2 (2017): 275–299.

Brubaker, Rogers, and David D. Laitin. "Ethnic and Nationalist Violence." *Annual Review of Sociology* 24 (August 1998): 423–452.

Bundu, Abass. *Democracy by Force? A Study of International Military Intervention in the Conflict in Sierra Leone from 1991–2000.* London: Universal Publishers, 2001.

Burton, Michael, Richard Gunther, and John Higley. "Introduction: Elite Transformations and Democratic Regimes." In *Elites and Democratic Consolidation in Latin America and Southern Europe,* edited by Michael Burton, Richard Gunther, and John Higley, pp. 1–37. New York: Cambridge University Press, 1992.

———. *Elites and Democratic Consolidation in Latin America and Southern Europe.* New York: Cambridge University Press, 1992.

Bwambale, Bamusede. *The Faces of the Rwenzururu Movement.* Kampala: N.p., 2001–2002.

Byman, Daniel, Peter Chalk, Bruce Hoffman, William Rosenau, and David Brannan. *Trends in Outside Support for Insurgency Movements*. Santa Monica, CA: RAND, 2001.

Cabral, Amilcar. *Revolution in Guinea: Selected Texts by Amilcar Cabral*. Translated by Richard Handyside. New York: Monthly Review Press, 1969.

Carayannis, Tatiana, and Louisa Lombard, eds. *Making Sense of the Central African Republic*. London: Zed Books, 2015.

Carroll, Bernice A. "How Wars End: An Analysis of Some Current Hypotheses." *Journal of Peace Research* 6, no. 4 (December 1969): 295–321.

Carter, David B. "A Blessing or a Curse? State Support for Terrorist Groups." *International Organization* 66, no. 1 (January 2012): 129–151.

Cassidy, Robert M. *Counterinsurgency and the Global War on Terror: Military Culture and Irregular War*. Westport, CT: Praeger Security International, 2006.

Chabal, Patrick, and Jean-Pascal Daloz. *Africa Works: Disorder as Political Instrument*. Bloomington: Indiana University Press, 1999.

Checkel, Jeffrey T., ed. *Transnational Dynamics of Civil War*. New York: Cambridge University Press, 2013.

Clapham, Christopher. *Africa in the International System: The Politics of State Survival*. Cambridge: Cambridge University Press, 1996.

———, ed. *African Guerrillas*. Bloomington: Indiana University Press, 1998.

———. *Private Patronage and Public Power: Political Clientelism in the Modern State*. New York: St. Martin's Press, 1982.

Clark, John, ed. *The African Stakes of the Congo War*. Cambridge: Palgrave, 2002.

Clark, John F. "Realism, Neo-Realism and Africa's International Relations in the Post-Cold War Era." In *Africa's Challenge to International Relations Theory,* edited by Kevin C. Dunn and Timothy M. Shaw, pp. 85–102. London: Palgrave, 2001.

Cohen, Dara Kay. *Rape During Civil War*. Ithaca, NY: Cornell University Press, 2016.

Collier, Paul. *Economic Causes of Civil Conflict and Their Implications for Policy*. Washington, DC: World Bank, June 2000.

———. "Rebellion as a Quasi-Criminal Activity," *Journal of Conflict Resolution* 57, no. 1 (2003): 839–853.

———, and Anke Hoeffler. "Greed and Grievance in Civil War." *Oxford Economic Papers* 56, no. 4 (2004): 563–595.

———, Anke Hoeffler, and Måns Söderbom. "On the Duration of Civil War." *Journal of Peace Research* 41, no. 3 (May 2004): 253–273.

"The Conakry Peace Accord." In *Peace Agreements and Civil Wars in Africa: Insurgent Motivations, State Responses, and Third-Party Peacemaking in Liberia, Rwanda, and Sierra Leone,* edited by Julius Mutwol, pp. 251–281. Amherst, NY: Cambria Press, 2009.

Connable, Ben, and Martin C. Libicki. *How Insurgencies End*. Santa Monica, CA: RAND National Defense Research Institute, 2010.

Crocker, Chester A., Fen Osler Hampson, and Pamela Aall. *Herding Cats: Multiparty Mediation in a Complex World*. Washington, DC: United States Institute of Peace Press, 1999.

———. *Taming Intractable Conflicts: Mediation in the Hardest Cases*. Washington, DC: United States Institute of Peace Press, 2004.

Cunningham, David E. "Veto Players and Civil War Duration." *American Journal of Political Science* 50, no. 4 (October 2005): 875–892.

———, Kristian Skrede Gleditsch, and Idean Salehyan. "It Takes Two: A Dyadic Analysis of Civil War Duration and Outcome." *Journal of Conflict Resolution* 53, no. 4 (August 2009): 570–597.

Dahl, Robert. *Polyarchy: Participation and Opposition.* New Haven, CT: Yale University Press, 1971.

Daly, M. W., and Ahmad Alawad Sikainga, eds. *Civil War in the Sudan.* London: British Academic Press, 1993.

David, Stephen R. "Internal War: Causes and Cures." *World Politics* 49, no. 4 (July 1997): 552–576.

Day, Christopher. *The Bangui Carousel: How the Recycling of Political Elites Reinforces Instability and Violence in the Central African Republic.* Washington, DC: The Enough Project, August 2016.

———. "Bush Path to Self-Destruction: Charles Taylor and the Revolutionary United Front." *Small Wars and Insurgencies* 26, no. 5 (November 2015): 811–835.

———. "Civil War and Rebellion." *Studies in Conflict and Terrorism* 41, no. 11 (2018): 1–17.

———. "'Survival Mode': Rebel Resilience and the Lord's Resistance Army." *Terrorism and Political Violence* (March 2017): 1–21.

———, and William Reno. "In Harm's Way: African Counterinsurgency and Patronage Politics." *Civil Wars* 16, no. 2 (June 2014): 125–146.

Day, Christopher R. "The Fates of Rebels: Insurgencies in Uganda." *Comparative Politics* 43, no. 4 (July 2011): 439–458.

Debos, Marielle. "Fluid Loyalties in a Regional Crisis: Chadian 'Ex-Liberators' in the Central African Republic." *African Affairs* 107, no. 427 (April 2008): 225–241.

Decalo, Samuel. "The Process, Prospects, and Constraints of Democratization in Africa." *African Affairs* 91, no. 362 (January 1992): 27–28.

———. *Psychoses of Power: African Personal Dictatorships.* Boulder: Westview Press, 1989.

de Rouen, Karl R. Jr., and David Sobek. "The Dynamics of Civil War Duration and Outcome." *Journal of Peace Research* 41, no. 3 (May 2004): 303–320.

Doom, Ruddy, and Koen Vlassenroot. "Kony's Message: A New Koine? The Lord's Resistance Army in Northern Uganda." *African Affairs* 98, no. 390 (January 1999): 5–36.

Doornbos, Martin. "Understanding the Rwenzururu Movement: An Autobiographical Account." *Australian Review of African Studies* 26, no. 2 (December 2004): 48–53.

Dukhan, Natalia. *Splintered Warfare: Alliances, Affiliations, and Agendas of Armed Factions and Politico-Military Groups in the Central African Republic.* Washington, DC: The Enough Project, August 2017.

Dunér, Bertil. "Proxy Intervention in Civil Wars." *Journal of Peace Research* 18, no. 4 (1981): 353–361.

Dunn, Kevin C. *Imagining the Congo: The International Relations of Identity.* New York: Palgrave Macmillan, 2003.

———, and Timothy M. Shaw, eds. *Africa's Challenge to International Relations Theory.* London: Palgrave, 2001.

Duyvesteyn, Isbelle, and Jan Angstrom, eds. *Understanding Victory and Defeat in Contemporary War.* London: Routledge 2007.

Eisenstadt, S. N. *Traditional Patrimonialism and Modern Neopatrimonialism.* Beverly Hills, CA: Sage, 1973.

Elbadawi, Ibrahim A., and Nicholas Sambanis. "External Interventions and the Duration of Civil Wars." Paper presented at the World Bank's Development Economic Research Group, Princeton University, 18–19 March 2000.

Englebert, Pierre. *Africa: Unity, Sovereignty, and Sorrow.* Boulder: Lynne Rienner, 2009.

———, and Kevin C. Dunn. *Inside African Politics.* Boulder: Lynne Rienner, 2013.

————, and Denis Tull. "Postconflict Reconstruction in Africa: Flawed Ideas About Failed States." *International Security* 32, no. 4 (Spring 2008): 106–139.

Epelu-Opio, J. *Teso War, 1986–1992: Causes and Consequences.* Kampala: Fountain, 2009.

Fearon, James, and David Laitin. "Ethnicity, Insurgency, and Civil Wars." *American Political Science Review* 97, no. 1 (February 2003): 75–90.

Fearon, James D. "Fighting Rather than Bargaining." Unpublished paper, Stanford University, 2007.

————. "Why Do Some Civil Wars Last So Much Longer than Others?" *Journal of Peace Research* 41, no. 3 (May 2004): 275–301.

Ferme, Mariane C., and Danny Hoffman. "Hunter Militias and the International Human Rights Discourse in Sierra Leone and Beyond." *Africa Today* 50, no. 4 (Summer 2004): 73–95.

Figueiredo Jr., Rui, and Barry Weingast. "The Rationality of Fear." In *Civil Wars, Insecurity, and Intervention,* edited by Barbara Walter and Jack Snyder, pp. 261–302. New York: Columbia University Press, 1999.

Findley, Michael G. "Bargaining and the Interdependent Stages of Civil War Resolution," *Journal of Conflict Resolution* 57, no. 5 (October 2013): 905–932.

Förster, Till. "Dialogue Direct." In *Rebel Governance in Civil War,* edited by Ana Arjona, Nelson Kasfir, and Zachariah Mampilly, pp. 203–225. New York: Cambridge University Press, 2016.

————. "Insurgent Nationalism: Political Imagination and Rupture in Côte d'Ivoire." *Africa Spectrum* 48, no. 3 (2013): 3–31.

Fortna, Virginia Page. "Does Peacekeeping Keep Peace? International Intervention and the Duration of Peace After Civil War." *International Studies Quarterly* 48, no. 2 (June 2004): 269–292.

————. *Does Peacekeeping Work? Shaping Belligerents' Choices After Civil War.* Princeton, NJ: Princeton University Press, 2008.

Francis, David J. "Mercenary Intervention in Sierra Leone: Providing National Security or International Exploitation?" *Third World Quarterly* 20, no. 2 (April 1999): 319–338.

Franke, Marcus. *War and Nationalism in South Asia: The Indian State and the Nagas.* London: Routledge, 2009.

Gates, Scott. "Recruitment and Allegiance: The Microfoundations of Rebellion." *Journal of Conflict Resolution* 46, no. 1 (February 2002): 111–130.

Gberie, Lansana. *A Dirty War in West Africa: The RUF and the Destruction of Sierra Leone.* Bloomington: Indiana University Press, 2006.

————. "Paying the Price: The Sierra Leone Peace Process." Online series, "First Stages on the Road to Peace: The Abidjan Process (1995–96)," *Conciliation Resources* 9 (2000): 18–25.

Gerard, Antoine. "Sudan Transitional Assistance for Rehabilitation (STAR) Project." Internal paper, Doctors Without Borders/Médecins Sans Frontières USA, May 2000.

Gersony, Robert. *The Anguish of Northern Uganda: Results of a Field-Based Assessment of the Civil Conflicts in Northern Uganda.* Kampala: USAID Mission, August 1997.

Gerth, H. H., and C. Wright Mills, eds. *Max Weber: Essays in Sociology.* New York: Oxford University Press, 1946.

Gibson, Edward L. "Boundary Control: Subnational Authoritarianism in Democratic Countries." *World Politics* 58, no. 1 (October 2005): 101–132.

Gilley, Bruce. "Against the Concept of Ethnic Conflict." *Third World Quarterly* 25, no. 6 (2004): 1155–1166.

Giroux, Jennifer, David Lanz, and Damiano Sguaitamatti. "The Tormented Triangle: The Regionalization of the Conflict in Sudan, Chad, and the Central African Republic." Working paper no. 47, Crisis States Research Centre, April 2009.

Gleijeses, Piero. *Conflicting Missions: Havana, Washington, and Africa, 1959–1976.* Chapel Hill: University of North Carolina Press, 2002.

Global Witness. *Hot Chocolate: How Cocoa Fueled the Conflict in Côte d'Ivoire.* London: Global Witness, June 2007.

———. *The Usual Suspects: Liberia's Weapons and Mercenaries in Côte d'Ivoire and Sierra Leone.* London: Global Witness, March 2003.

Government of Uganda Amnesty Commission. *The Peace Agreement Between the Government of the Republic of Uganda and the Uganda National Rescue Front II.* 24 December 2002.

———. *Reconciliation in Action.* Report 2007–2008.

Green, Matthew. *The Wizard of the Nile: The Hunt for Africa's Most Wanted.* London: Portobello Books, 2008.

Greene, Thomas H.. *Comparative Revolutionary Movements.* Englewood Cliffs, NJ: Prentice Hall, 1974.

Greenhill, Kelly M., and Solomon Major. "The Perils of Profiling: Civil War Spoilers and the Collapse of Intrastate Peace Accords." *International Security* 31, no. 3 (Winter 2006–2007): 7–40.

Gupta, Anrudha. "Roots of Political Instability in Africa." *Economic and Political Weekly* 2, no. 23 (June 1967): 1041–1046.

Gurr, Ted Robert. "On the Outcomes of Violent Conflict." In *Handbook of Political Conflict,* edited by Ted Robert Gurr, pp. 238–294. New York: Free Press, 1980.

———. *Why Men Rebel.* Princeton, NJ: Princeton University Press, 1970.

———, ed. *Handbook of Political Conflict.* New York: Free Press, 1980.

Hall, Peter, and Rosemary Taylor. "Political Science and the Three New Institutionalisms." *Policy Studies* 44 (1996): 936–957.

Hampson, Fen Osler. *Nurturing Peace: Why Peace Settlements Succeed or Fail.* Washington, DC: US Institute of Peace Press, 1996.

Hansen, Holger Bernt, and Michael Twaddle, eds. *Changing Uganda.* Kampala: Fountain, 1991.

Harbeson, John, ed. *The Military in African Politics.* New York: Praeger, 1988.

Harrell-Bond, Barbara. *Imposing Aid: Emergency Assistance to Refugees.* Oxford: Oxford University Press, 1986.

Hassan, Salah. "The Sudan National Democratic Alliance (NDA): The Quest for Peace, Unity, and Democracy." *Journal of Opinion* 21, no. 1–2 (1993): 14–25.

Hawkins, Darren G., David A. Lake, Daniel L. Nielson, and Michael J. Tierney, eds. *Delegation and Agency in International Organizations.* New York: Cambridge University Press, 2009.

Hazen, Jennifer M. *What Rebels Want: Resources and Supply Networks in Wartime.* Ithaca, NY: Cornell University Press, 2013.

Hegre, Håvard. "The Duration and Termination of Civil War." *Journal of Peace Research* 41, no. 3 (May 2004): 243–252.

Herbert, S., N. Dukham, and M. Debos. *State Fragility in the Central African Republic: What Prompted the 2013 Coup?* Rapid literature review. Birmingham, UK: GSDRC, University of Birmingham, 2013.

Herbst, Jeffrey. *States and Power in Africa: Comparative Lessons in Authority and Control,* 2nd ed. Princeton, NJ: Princeton University Press, 2014.

Hoffman, Frank G. "Small Wars Revisited: The United States and Nontraditional Wars." *Journal of Strategic Studies* 28, no. 6 (December 2005): 913–940.

Horowitz, Donald. *Ethnic Groups in Conflict*. Berkeley: University of California Press, 1985.

Hovil, Lucy, and Eric Werker. "Portrait of a Failed Rebellion: An Account of Rational, Sub-Optimal Violence in Western Uganda." *Rationality and Society* 17, no. 1 (February 2005): 5–34.

Howard, Lise Morjé, and Alexandra Stark. "How Civil Wars End: The International System, Norms, and the Role of External Actors." *International Security* 42, no. 3 (Winter 2017–2018): 127–171.

Howard, M. "When Are Wars Decisive?" *Survival* 41, no. 1 (1999): 126–135.

Hughes, Geraint. *My Enemy's Enemy: Proxy Warfare in International Politics.* Brighton, UK: Sussex Academic Press, 2014.

Human Rights Watch. *Famine in Sudan: The Human Rights Causes.* New York, February 1999.

———. *I Can Still Smell the Dead.* New York: September 2013.

———. *State of Anarchy, Rebellion, and Abuses Against Civilians.* New York: September 2007.

Humphreys, Macartan, and Jeremy Weinstein."Who Fights? The Determinants of Participation in Civil War." *American Journal of Political Science* 52, no. 2 (April 2008): 436–455.

Huntington, Samuel P. *Political Order in Changing Societies*. New Haven, CT: Yale University Press, 1968.

International Crisis Group. *The Central African Crisis: From Predation to Stabilisation.* Africa Report no. 219. Brussels: International Crisis Group, 17 June 2014.

———. *Central African Republic: Anatomy of a Phantom State.* Africa Report no. 136. Brussels: International Crisis Group, 13 December 2007.

———. *Central African Republic: Priorities of the Transition.* Africa Report no. 203. Brussels: International Crisis Group, 11 June 2013.

———. *Central African Republic: Untangling the Political Dialogue.* Africa Briefing no. 55. Brussels: International Crisis Group, 9 December 2008.

———. *Côte d'Ivoire: Is War the Only Option?* Africa Report no. 171. Brussels: International Crisis Group, 3 March 2011.

———. *Côte d'Ivoire: No Peace in Sight.* Africa Report no. 82. Brussels: International Crisis Group, 12 July 2004.

———. *Côte d'Ivoire: The War Is Not Yet Over.* Africa Report no. 72. Brussels: International Crisis Group, 9 November 2003.

———. *Dangerous Little Stones: Diamonds in the Central African Republic.* Africa Report no. 167. Brussels: International Crisis Group, 6 December 2010.

———. *Eastern Congo: The ADF-NALU's Lost Rebellion.* Africa Briefing no. 93. Brussels: International Crisis Group, 19 December 2012.

———. *Sudan Endgame.* Africa Report no. 66. Brussels: International Crisis Group, 7 July 2003.

Jackson, Robert H. *Quasi-States: Sovereignty, International Relations and the Third World*. New York: Cambridge University Press, 1990.

Jentzsch, Corinna, Stathis N. Kalyvas, and Livia Isabella Schubiger. "Militias in Civil Wars." *Journal of Conflict Resolution* 59, no. 5 (April 2015): 755–769.

Job, Brian L. *The Insecurity Dilemma: National Security of Third World States.* Boulder: Lynne Rienner, 1992.

Johnson, Douglas H. "Briefing: The Crisis in South Sudan." *African Affairs* 113, no. 451 (April 2014): 300–309.

———. *The Root Causes of Sudan's Civil Wars: Peace or Truce,* rev. ed. Bloomington: Indiana University Press, 2013.

————, and Gerard Prunier. "The Foundation and Expansion of the Sudan People's Liberation Army." In *Civil War in the Sudan*, edited by M. W. Daly and Ahmad Alawad Sikainga, pp. 117–141. London: British Academic Press, 1993.

Johnston, Patrick. "The Geography of Insurgent Organization and Its Consequences for Civil Wars: Evidence from Liberia and Sierra Leone." *Security Studies* 17, no. 1 (January–March 2008): 107–137.

Jok, Jok Madut, and Sharon Elaine Hutchinson. "Sudan's Prolonged Second Civil War and the Militarization of Nuer and Dinka Ethnic Identities." *African Studies Review* 42, no. 2 (September 1999): 125–145.

Jordan, Jenna. "Attacking the Leader: Why Terrorist Groups Survive Decapitation Strikes." *International Security* 38, no. 4 (Spring 2014): 7–38.

Kainerugaba, Muhoozi. *Battles of Ugandan Resistance: A Tradition of Maneuver.* Kampala: Fountain, 2010.

Kalyvas, Stathis. "Civil Wars." In *The Oxford Handbook of Comparative Politics,* edited by Carles Boix and Susan S. Stokes, pp. 416–434. Oxford: Oxford University Press, 2007.

————. *The Logic of Violence in Civil War.* New York: Cambridge University Press, 2006.

————. "'New' and 'Old' Civil Wars: A Valid Distinction?" *World Politics* 54, no. 1 (October 2001): 99–118.

————, and Laia Balcells. "International System and Technologies of Rebellion: How the End of the Cold War Shaped Internal Conflict." *American Political Science Review* 104, no. 3 (August 2010): 415–429.

Kandeh, Jimmy. "In Search of Legitimacy: The 1996 Elections." In *Between Democracy and Terror: The Sierra Leone Civil War,* edited by Ibrahim Abdullah, pp. 123–143. Dakar: CODESRIA, 2004.

————. "What Does the 'Militariat' Do When It Rules? Military Regimes: The Gambia, Sierra Leone and Liberia." *Review of African Political Economy* 23, no. 69 (September 1996): 387–404.

Kasfir, Nelson. "Guerrillas and Civilian Participation: The National Resistance Army in Uganda, 1981–1986." *Journal of Modern African Studies* 43, no. 2 (June 2005): 271–296.

————. "Southern Sudanese Politics Since the Addis Ababa Agreement." *African Affairs* 76, no. 303 (April 1977): 143–166.

Kasozi, A. B. K. *Social Origins of Violence in Uganda, 1964–1985.* Kampala: Fountain, 1999.

Kaufman, Stuart. *Modern Hatreds: The Symbolic Politics of Ethnic War.* Ithaca, NY: Cornell University Press, 2001.

Kayunga, Sallie Simba. "Islamic Fundamentalism in Uganda: A Case Study of the Tabligh Youth Movement." Working paper no. 37, Kampala, Uganda, Center for Basic Research, September 1993.

Keen, David. *The Benefits of Famine: A Political Economy of Famine and Relief in Southwestern Sudan, 1983–1989.* Princeton, NJ: Princeton University Press, 1994.

————. *Conflict and Collusion in Sierra Leone.* London: Palgrave Macmillan, 2005.

————. "The Economic Functions of Violence in Civil Wars." *Adelphi Papers* 38, no. 320 (1998).

Khalid, Mansour, ed. *John Garang Speaks.* London: KPI, 1987.

Kilcullen, David. "Counter-Insurgency *Redux.*" *Survival* 48, no. 4 (Winter 2006–2007): 111–130.

Kilcullen, David J. "Countering Global Insurgency." *Journal of Strategic Studies* 28, no. 4 (August 2005): 597–617.

Kirschner, Shanna. *Trust and Fear in Civil Wars: Ending Intrastate Conflicts.* London: Lexington Books, 2015.

Korpi, Walter. "Power Resources Approach vs. Action and Conflict: On Causal and Intentional Explanations in the Study of Power." *Sociological Theory* 3, no. 2 (Autumn 1985): 31–45.

Krause, Peter. *Rebel Power: Why Nationalist Movements Compete, Fight, and Win.* Ithaca, NY: Cornell University Press, 2017.

Kriger, Norma J. *Zimbabwe's Guerrilla War: Peasant Voices.* New York: Cambridge University Press, 1992.

Kuperman, Alan J. "A Model Humanitarian Intervention? Reassessing NATO's Libya Campaign." *International Security* 38, no. 1 (Summer 2013): 105–136.

Kutesa, Pecos. *Uganda's Revolution, 1979–1986: How I Saw It.* Kampala: Fountain, 2006.

Laidi, Zaki. *The Superpowers and Africa: The Constraints of a Rivalry 1960–1990.* Chicago: University of Chicago Press, 1990.

Leites, Nathan, and Charles Wolf Jr. *Rebellion and Authority: An Analytic Essay on Insurgent Conflicts.* Chicago: Markham, 1970.

Leopold, Mark. *Inside West Nile: Violence, History, and Representation on an African Frontier.* Oxford: James Curry, 2005.

Lesch, Ann Mosely. *Sudan: Contested National Identities.* Bloomington: Indiana University Press, 1999.

Levine, Iain. "Promoting Humanitarian Principles: The Southern Sudan Experience." Relief and Rehabilitation Network paper no. 21, May 1997.

Lichbach, Mark. "What Makes Rational Peasants Revolutionary? Dilemma, Paradox, and Irony in Peasant Collective Action." *World Politics* 46, no. 3 (April 1994): 383–418.

Licklider, Roy. "The Consequences of Negotiated Settlements in Civil Wars, 1945–1993. *American Political Science Review* 89, no. 3 (September 1995): 681–690.

———. *Stopping the Killing: How Civil Wars End.* New York: New York University Press, 1993.

Lombard, Louisa. "Navigational Tools for Central African Roadblocks." *Political and Legal Anthropology Review* 36, no. 1 (May 2013): 157–173.

Lomo, Zachary, and Lucy Hovil. "Behind the Violence: The War in Northern Uganda." Institute for Security Studies Monograph Series, no. 99, March 2004.

Lucima, Okello, ed. *Protracted Conflict, Elusive Peace: Initiatives to End the Violence in Northern Uganda.* London: Accord/Conciliation Resources, 2002.

Lyall, Jason, and Isaiah Wilson III. "Rage Against the Machines: Explaining Outcomes in Counterinsurgency Wars." *International Organization* 63 (Winter 2009): 67–106.

Lyons, Terence. "The Importance of Winning: Victorious Insurgent Groups and Authoritarian Politics." *Comparative Politics* 48, no. 2 (January 2016): 167–184.

Mahoney, James. "Path Dependence in Historical Sociology." *Theory and Society* 29, no. 4 (August 2000): 507–548.

Mamdani, Mahmood. "Beyond Settler and Native as Political Identities: Overcoming the Political Legacy of Colonialism." *Comparative Studies in Society and History* 43, no. 4 (October 2001): 651–664.

———. *Citizen and Subject: Contemporary Africa and the Legacy of Late Colonialism.* Princeton, NJ: Princeton University Press, 1996.

———. *When Victims Become Killers: Colonialism, Nativism, and the Genocide in Rwanda.* Princeton, NJ: Princeton University Press, 2002.

Mampilly, Zachariah Cherian. *Rebel Rulers: Insurgent Governance and Civilian Life During War.* Ithaca, NY: Cornell University Press, 2011.

Mandel, Robert. "Defining Postwar Victory." In *Understanding Victory and Defeat in Contemporary War*, edited by Jan Angstrom and Isabelle Duyvesteyn, pp. 13–18. London: Routledge, 2007.

Marshall-Fratani, Ruth. "'Who Is Who': Autochtony, Nationalism, and Citizenship in the Ivorian Crisis." *African Affairs* 49, no. 2 (September 2006): 9–43.

Mason, T. David, and Patrick J. Fett. "How Civil Wars End: A Rational Choice Approach." *Journal of Conflict Resolution* 40, no. 4 (December 1996): 546–568.

Mason, T. David, Joseph P. Weingarten Jr., and Patrick J. Fett. "Win, Lose or Draw: Predicting the Outcome of Civil Wars." *Political Research Quarterly* 52, no. 2 (June 1999): 239–268.

Maynard, Kimberly A. *Healing Communities in Conflict: International Assistance in Complex Emergencies.* New York: Columbia University Press, 1999.

Mazrui, Ali. *Soldiers and Kinsmen in Uganda: The Making of a Military Ethnocracy.* Beverly Hills, CA: Sage, 1975.

McGowan, Patrick. "African Military Coups d'État, 1956–2001: Frequency, Trends and Distribution." *Journal of Modern African Studies* 41, no. 3 (September 2003): 339–370.

McGregor, Andrew. "Quagmire in West Africa." *International Journal* 54, no. 3 (Summer 1999): 482–501.

Médecins Sans Frontières. *"Ça va en peu maintenant": The Collapse of Healthcare, Malnutrition, Violence and Displacement in Western Ivory Coast.* Amsterdam: Médecins Sans Frontières, July 2003.

Mehler, Andreas. "Pathways to Elite Insecurity." Hot Spots, *Cultural Anthropology*, 11 June 2014. https://culanth.org/fieldsights/549-pathways-to-elite-insecurity.

———. "Rebels and Parties: The Impact of Armed Insurgency on Representation in the Central African Republic." *Journal of Modern African Studies* 49, no. 1 (March 2011): 115–139.

———. "Why Security Forces Do Not Deliver Security: Evidence from Liberia and the Central African Republic." *Armed Forces and Society* 38, no. 1 (January 2012): 49–69.

Migdal, Joel, ed. *State in Society: Studying How States and Societies Transform and Constitute One Another.* New York: Cambridge University Press, 2001.

Millet, Allan R., and Wiliamson Murray. *Military Effectiveness.* 3 vols. Boston: Unwin Hyman, 1988.

Mogba, Zéphirin, and Lydie Solange Yahoumbi. *Centrafrique: La vassalisation de l'état et du pouvoir à l'hégémonie militaro-politique du Tchad.* Saarbrücken: Éditions Universitaires Européennes, 2014.

Morrison, Donald G., and Hugh Michael Stevenson, "Political Instability in Independent Black Africa: More Dimensions of Conflict Within Nations." *Journal of Conflict Resolution* 15, no. 3 (September 1971): 347–368.

Muana, Patrick K. "The Kamajoi Militia: Civil War, Internal Displacement, and the Politics of Counter-Insurgency." *African Development* 22, no. 3–4 (1997): 77–100.

Mukherjee, Bumba. "Why Political Power-Sharing Agreements Lead to Enduring Peaceful Resolution of Some Civil Wars, but Not Others?" *International Studies Quarterly* 50, no. 2 (June 2006): 479–504.

Mumford, Andrew. *Proxy Warfare.* Cambridge: Polity Press, 2013.

Musa, John Lansana. "The Enigma of Corporal Foday Sankoh: Is He a Phantom?" *Sierra Leone Review* 2 (1993): 108–112.

Musa, Sorie, and John Lansana Musa, eds. *The Invasion of Sierra Leone: A Chronicle of a Nation Under Siege*. Freetown: Sierra Leone Institute for Policy Studies 1993.

Museveni, Yoweri. "Fanon's Theory on Violence." In *Essays on the Liberation of Southern Africa*, edited by Nathan M. Shamuyarira, pp. 1–24. Dar es Salaam: Tanzania Publishing House, 1971.

———. *Sowing the Mustard Seed: The Struggle for Freedom and Democracy in Uganda*. Oxford: Macmillan, 2007.

Mutwol, Julius. *Peace Agreements and Civil Wars in Africa: Insurgent Motivations, State Responses, and Third-Party Peacemaking in Liberia, Rwanda, and Sierra Leone*. Amherst, NY: Cambria Press, 2009.

Nagl, John. *Learning to Eat Soup with a Knife: Counterinsurgency Lessons from Malaya and Vietnam*. Westport, NY: Praeger 2002.

Ngoga, Pascal. "Uganda: The National Resistance Army." In *African Guerrillas*, edited by Christopher Clapham, pp. 91–106. Bloomington: Indiana University Press, 1998.

O'Connor, Raymond G. "Victory in Modern War." *Journal of Peace Research* 6, no. 4 (1969): 295–321.

Ofcansky, Thomas P. "Warfare and Instability Along the Sudan-Uganda Border: A Look at the 20th Century." In *White Nile, Black Blood: War, Leadership, and Ethnicity from Khartoum to Kampala*, edited by Jay Spaulding and Stephanie Beswick, pp. 195–208. Asmara, Eritrea: Red Sea Press, 2000.

Olonisakin, 'Funmi. *Peacekeeping in Sierra Leone: The Story of UNAMSIL*. Boulder: Lynne Rienner, 2008.

Olson, Mancur. "Dictatorship, Democracy, and Development." *American Political Science Review* 87, no. 3 (September 1993): 567–576.

Omara-Otunnu, Amii. *Politics and the Military in Uganda, 1890–1985*. New York: St. Martin's Press, 1987.

Pearlman, Wendy, and Kathleen Gallagher Cunningham. "Nonstate Actors, Fragmentation, and Conflict Processes." *Journal of Conflict Resolution* 56, no. 1 (February 2012): 3–15.

Peters, Krijn. *War and the Crisis of Youth in Sierra Leone*. Cambridge: Cambridge University Press, 2011.

Petersen, Roger D. *Resistance and Rebellion: Lessons from Eastern Europe*. New York: Cambridge University Press, 2001.

———. *Understanding Ethnic Violence: Fear, Hatred and Resentment in Twentieth-Century Eastern Europe*. New York: Cambridge University Press, 2002.

Pham, J. Peter. *The Sierra Leonean Tragedy: History and Global Dimensions*. New York: Nova Science, 2006.

Pierson, Paul. *Politics in Time: History, Institutions, and Social Analysis*. Princeton, NJ: Princeton University Press, 2004.

Pillar, Paul R. *Negotiating Peace: War Termination as a Bargaining Process*. Princeton: Princeton University Press, 1983.

Poggo, Scopas S. *The First Sudanese Civil War: Africans, Arabs, and Israelis in the Southern Sudan, 1955–1972*. New York: Palgrave Macmillan, 2009.

Posen, Barry. "The Security Dilemma and Ethnic Conflict." *Survival* 35, no. 1 (Spring 1993): 27–47.

Powell, Robert. "Bargaining Theory and International Conflict." *Annual Review of Political Science* 5 (2002): 1–30.

———. "War as a Commitment Problem." *International Organization* 60, no. 1 (Winter 2006): 169–203.

Prunier, Gerard. *From Genocide to Continental War: The "Congolese" Conflict and the Crisis of Contemporary Africa*. London: Hurst, 2009.

————. "Rebel Movements and Proxy Warfare: Uganda, Sudan and the Congo (1986–1999)." *African Affairs* 103, no. 412 (July 2004): 359–383.

Przeworski, Adam. *Democracy and the Market: Political and Economic Reforms in Eastern Europe and Latin America.* New York: Cambridge University Press, 1991.

Refugee Law Project. "Negotiating Peace: Resolution of Conflicts in Uganda's West Nile Region." Working paper no. 12, Kampala, Uganda, Refugee Law Project, June 2004.

Regan, Patrick M. "Third-Party Interventions and the Duration of Intrastate Conflicts," *Journal of Conflict Resolution* 46, no. 1 (February 2002): 55–73.

Reiter, Dan. "Exploring the Bargaining Model of War." *Perspectives on Politics* 1, no. 1 (March 2003): 27–43.

Reno, William. *Corruption and State Politics in Sierra Leone.* New York: Cambridge University Press, 1995.

————. *Warlord Politics and African States.* Boulder: Lynne Rienner, 1998.

Reno, William S. *Warfare in Independent Africa.* New York: Cambridge University Press, 2011.

Revolutionary United Front/Sierra Leone. *Footpaths to Democracy: Toward a New Sierra Leone.* www.fas.org/irp/world/para/docs/footpaths.htm.

Richards, Paul. *Fighting for the Rainforest: War, Resources and Youth in Sierra Leone.* Oxford: James Currey, 1996.

Riedl, Rachel Beatty. *Authoritarian Origins of Democratic Party Systems in Africa.* New York: Cambridge University Press, 2016.

Roessler, Philip. *Ethnic Politics and State Power in Africa: The Logic of the Coup–Civil War Trap.* New York: Cambridge University Press, 2016.

Rolandsen, Øystein H. "Another Civil War in South Sudan: The Failure of Guerilla Government." *Journal of Eastern African Studies* 9, no. 1 (January 2015): 163–174.

————. "A False Start: Between War and Peace in Southern Sudan, 1956–1962." *Journal of African History* 52 (2011): 105–123.

————. *Guerrilla Government: Political Changes in the Southern Sudan During the 1990s.* Uppsala: Nordiska Afrikainstitutet, 2005.

————. "The Making of the Anya-Nya Insurgency in the Southern Sudan, 1961–1964." *Journal of East African Studies* 5, no. 2 (May 2011): 211–232.

Rosen, Stephen Peter. *Societies and Military Power: India and Its Armies.* Ithaca, NY: Cornell University Press, 1996.

Ross, Michael. "A Closer Look at Oil, Diamonds, and Civil War." *Annual Review of Political Science* 9 (2006): 265–300.

————. "What Do We Know About Natural Resources and Civil Wars?" *Journal of Peace Research* 41, no. 3 (Summer 2004): 337–356.

Rubin, Elizabeth. "An Army of One's Own." *Harper's Magazine* 294, no. 176 (February 1997).

Rwehururu, Bernard. *Cross to the Gun: The Fall of Idi Amin and the Ugandan Army.* Kampala: Netmedia, 2008.

Sambanis, Nicholas. "What Is Civil War? Conceptual and Empirical Complexities of an Operational Definition." *Journal of Conflict Resolution* 48, no. 6 (December 2004): 814–858.

Schelling, T. C. *The Strategy of Conflict.* Cambridge, MA: Harvard University Press, 1960.

Schlichte, Klaus. "With the State Against the State? The Formation of Armed Groups." *Contemporary Security Policy* 30, no. 2 (August 2009): 246–264.

Schomerus, Mareike. "The Lord's Resistance Army in Sudan: A History and Overview." Human Security Baseline Assessment working paper, Small Arms Survey, Geneva, Switzerland, September 2007.

Schraeder, Peter J. *African Politics and Society: A Mosaic in Transformation*. Belmont, CA: Cengage Learning, 2004.

Scorgie, Lindsay. "Peripheral Pariah or Regional Rebel? The Allied Democratic Forces and the Uganda/Congo Borderland." *Round Table* 100, no. 412 (2011): 79–93.

Shamuyarira, Nathan M., ed. *Essays on the Liberation of Southern Africa*. Dar es Salaam: Tanzania Publishing House, 1971.

Shirkey, Zachary C. *Joining the Fray: Outside Military Intervention in Civil Wars*. New York: Routledge, 2016.

Sierra Leone Truth and Reconciliation Commission. *Witness to Truth: Report of the Sierra Leone Truth and Reconciliation Commission*. Accra: GPL Press, 2004.

Sinno, Abdulkader H. *Organizations at War: In Afghanistan and Beyond*. Ithaca, NY: Cornell University Press, 2008.

Smith, Stephen W. "The Elite's Road to Riches in a Poor Country." In *Making Sense of the Central African Republic,* edited by Tatiana Carayannis and Louisa Lombard, pp. 102–122. London: Zed Books, 2015.

Snyder, Jack. *From Voting to Violence: Democratization and Nationalist Conflict*. New York: W. W. Norton, 2000.

Sobek, David, and Caroline L. Payne. "A Tale of Two Types: Rebel Goals and the Onset of Civil Wars." *International Studies Quarterly* 54, no. 1 (March 2010): 213–240.

Spaulding, Jay, and Stephanie Beswick, eds. *White Nile, Black Blood: War, Leadership, and Ethnicity from Khartoum to Kampala*. Asmara, Eritrea: Red Sea Press, 2000.

Spittaels, Steven, and Filip Hilgert. *Mapping Conflict Motives: Central African Republic*. Antwerp: International Peace Information Service, February 2009.

Staniland, Paul. *Networks of Rebellion: Explaining Insurgent Cohesion and Collapse*. Ithaca, NY: Cornell University Press, 2014.

———. "Organizing Insurgency: Networks, Resources, and Rebellion in South Asia." *International Security* 37, no. 1 (Summer 2012): 145–148.

———. "States, Insurgents, and Wartime Political Orders." *Perspectives on Politics* 10, no. 2 (June 2012): 243–264.

Stedman, Stephen, and Fred Tanner, eds. *Refugee Manipulation: War, Politics, and the Abuse of Human Suffering*. Washington, DC: Brookings Institution Press, 2003.

———. "Refugees as Resources in War." In *Refugee Manipulation: War, Politics, and the Abuse of Human Suffering,* edited by Stephen Stedman and Fred Tanner, pp. 1–16. Washington, DC: Brookings Institution Press, 2003,

Stedman, Stephen John. "Spoiler Problems in Peace Processes." *International Security* 22, no. 2 (Autumn 1997): 5–53.

———, Donald Rothchild, and Elizabeth M. Cousens. *Ending Civil Wars: The Implementation of Peace Agreements*. Boulder: Lynne Rienner, 2002.

Straus, Scott. *Making and Unmaking Nations: War, Leadership, and Genocide in Modern Africa*. Ithaca, NY: Cornell University Press, 2015.

———. "Wars Do End! Changing Patterns of Political Violence in Sub-Saharan Africa." *African Affairs* 111, no. 443 (April 2012): 179–201.

Suykens, Bert. "Comparing Rebel Rule Through Revolution and Naturalization." In *Rebel Governance in Civil War,* edited by Ana Arjona, Nelson Kasfir, and Zachariah Mampilly, pp. 138–157. New York: Cambridge University Press, 2016.

Syahuka-Muhindo, A. "The Rwenzururu Movement and the Democratic Struggle." Working paper no. 15, Kampala, Uganda, Center for Basic Research, June 1991.

Tamm, Henning. "The Origins of Transnational Alliances: Rulers, Rebels, and Political Survival." *International Security* 41, no. 1 (Summer 2016): 147–181.

————. "Rebel Leaders, Internal Rivals, and External Resources: How State Sponsors Affect Insurgent Cohesion." *International Studies Quarterly* 60, no. 4 (December 2016): 599–610.

Tanner, Victor. "Liberia: Railroading Peace." *Review of African Political Economy* 25, no. 75 (1998): 133–147.

Terry, Fiona. *Condemned to Repeat? The Paradox of Humanitarian Action.* Ithaca, NY: Cornell University Press, 2002.

The Enough Project, The Resolve, and Invisible Children, *Kony to LRA: Bring Me Ivory, Gold, and Diamonds.* Washington, DC: The Enough Project, November 2014.

Thelen, Kathleen. "Historical Institutionalism in Comparative Politics." *Annual Review of Political Science* 2 (June 1999): 369–404.

Thyne, Clayton L. "Information, Commitment, and Intra-War Bargaining: The Effect of Governmental Constraints on Civil War Duration." *International Studies Quarterly* 56 (2012): 307–321.

Tilly, Charles. *Coercion, Capital and European States.* Cambridge: Blackwell, 1990.

Titeca, Kristof. "The Spiritual Order of the LRA." In *The Lord's Resistance Army: Myth and Reality,* edited by Tim Allen and Koen Vlassenroot, pp. 59–73. London: Zed Books, 2010.

————, and Theophile Costeur. "An LRA for Everyone: How Different Actors Frame the Lord's Resistance Army." *African Affairs* 114, no. 454 (January 2015): 92–114.

————, and Koen Vlassenroot. "Rebels Without Borders in the Rwenzori Borderland? A Biography of the Allied Democratic Forces." *Journal of Eastern African Studies* 6, no. 1 (2012): 154–176.

Toft, Monica Duffy. "Ending Civil Wars: A Case for Rebel Victory?" *International Security* 34, no. 4 (Spring 2010): 7–36.

————. *Securing the Peace: The Durable Settlement of Civil Wars.* Princeton, NJ: Princeton University Press, 2010.

Uganda National Rescue Front II. *Agenda for Peace Talks with the Government of the Republic of Uganda.* September 2002.

US Army and Marine Corps. *Counterinsurgency Field Manual.* Chicago: University of Chicago Press, 2007.

Vinci, Anthony. "Existential Motivations in the Lord's Resistance Army's Continuing Conflict." *Studies in Conflict and Terrorism* 30, no. 4 (2007): 337–352.

Viterna, Jocelyn. "Pulled, Pushed, and Persuaded: Explaining Women's Mobilization into the Salvadoran Guerrilla Army." *American Journal of Sociology* 112, no. 1 (July 2006): 1–45.

Vlavonou, Gino. "Understanding the 'Failure' of the Séléka Rebellion." *African Security Review* 23, no. 3 (September 2014): 318–326.

Wagner, Harrison, R. "Bargaining and War." *American Journal of Political Science* 44, no. 3 (July 2000): 469–484.

Wakoson, Elias Nyamiel. "The Origin and Development of the Anya-Nya Movement, 1955–1972." In *Southern Sudan: Regionalism and Religion,* edited by Mohamed Omer Beshir, pp. 131–136. Khartoum: Graduate College, University of Khartoum, 1984.

————. "The Politics of Southern Self-Government, 1972–1983." In *Civil War in the Sudan,* edited by M. W. Daly and Ahmad Alawad Sikainga. London: British Academic Press, 1993.

Walter, Barbara. "The Critical Barrier to Civil War Settlement." *International Organization* 51, no. 3 (Summer 1997): 335–364.

Walter, Barbara, and Jack Snyder, eds. *Civil Wars, Insecurity, and Intervention.* New York: Columbia University Press, 1999.

Walter, Barbara F. "Bargaining Failures and Civil War." *Annual Review of Political Science* (June 2009): 243–261.

———. *Committing to Peace: The Successful Settlement of Civil Wars.* Princeton, NJ: Princeton University Press, 2002.

Warner, Lesley Anne. "Flawed Peace Process Leads to Greater Unrest in the Central African Republic." *World Politics Review* 26 (March 2013).

Weber, Max. "The Sociology of Charismatic Authority." In *Max Weber: Essays in Sociology.* edited by H. H. Gerth and C. Wright Mills. New York: Oxford University Press, 1946.

Weinstein, Jeremy. *Inside Rebellion: The Politics of Insurgent Violence.* New York: Cambridge University Press, 2007.

Wenyin, D. A. "The Integration of the Anya-Nya into the National Army." In *Conference on North-South Relations Since the Addis Ababa Agreement,* edited by Mom K. N. Arou and B. Yongo-Bure, pp. 57–119. Khartoum: Institute of African and Asian Studies, University of Khartoum, 1985.

Weyns, Yannick, Lotte Hoex, Filip Hilgert, and Steven Spittaels. *Mapping Conflict Motives: The Central African Republic.* Antwerp: International Peace Information Service on Central African Republic, November 2014.

Wickham-Crowley, Timothy P. *Guerrillas and Revolution in Latin America: A Comparative Study of Insurgents and Regimes Since 1956.* Princeton, NJ: Princeton University Press, 1992.

Williams, Paul D. *War and Conflict in Africa.* Cambridge: Polity, 2011.

Woldemariam, Michael. *Insurgent Fragmentation in the Horn of Africa: Rebellion and Its Discontents.* New York: Cambridge University Press, 2018.

Wood, Elisabeth Jean. *Insurgent Collective Action and Civil War in El Salvador.* New York: Cambridge University Press, 2003.

Woodward, Peter. "Uganda and Southern Sudan, 1986–1989." In *Changing Uganda,* edited by Holger Bernt Hansen and Michael Twaddle. Kampala: Fountain, 1991.

Wucherpfennig, Julian, Nils W. Metternich, Lars-Erik Cederman, and Kristian Skrede Gleditsch, "Ethnicity, the State, and the Duration of Civil War." *World Politics* 64, no. 1 (January 2012): 79–115.

Young, Crawford. *The African Colonial State in Comparative Perspective.* New Haven, CT: Yale University Press, 1994.

———. *The Postcolonial State in Africa.* Madison: University of Wisconsin Press, 2012.

Young, Eric T. "The Victors and the Vanquished: The Role of Military Factors in the Outcome of Modern African Insurgents." *Small Wars and Insurgencies* 7, no. 2 (Autumn 1996): 178–195.

Young, John. *The Fate of Sudan: The Origins and Consequences of a Flawed Peace Process.* London: Zed Books, 2012.

Zack-Williams, A., and Stephen Riley. "Sierra Leone: The Coup and Its Consequences." *Review of African Political Economy* 20, no. 56 (March 1993): 91–98.

Zartman, William. "Africa as a Subordinate State System in International Relations." *International Organization* 21, no. 3 (Summer 1967): 545–564.

———. *Collapsed States: The Disintegration and Restoration of Legitimate Authority.* Boulder: Lynne Rienner, 1995.

Zartman, William I. *Ripe for Resolution: Conflict and Intervention in Africa.* New York: Oxford University Press, 1989.

Index

Abidjan Peace Accord, 142
Abud, Juma, 39
Acak, Smith Opon, 58
Accommodation. *See* Political accommodation
Accra Comprehensive Peace Agreement, 22, 125
Acholi, 21, 24, 35, 36, 58–62, 67, 172
Addis Ababa Agreement, 105–106, 109, 112–113
ADF. *See* Allied Democratic Front
Adjallo, 65
ADM. *See* Allied Democratic Movement
AFRC. *See* Armed Forces Revolutionary Council
Africa: Fragile State Index and, 180; insecurity dilemma of, 177–178; number of rebel groups in modern, 19; rebel fates and political stability in, 180–184
Africa Confidential, 14
African National Congress (ANC), 110
African rebels. *See* Rebels, African
African states (regimes): conceptualization of "state" and, 23–24; fragmented politics of, 24–26; hierarchies of, 29; institutional limits of rebel fates and, 37–39; political embeddedness and, 34–39, 39*tab*; proxy wars and, 177–180; rebel fates linked to, 23; structures, 11. *See also* Political embeddedness
African Union (AU), 40, 158, 159, 172
African Union-Led Regional Task Force (AU RTF), 40, 172
Ali, Moses, 68, 73
Alier, Abel, 104, 105
All People's Congress (APC), 136, 137

Allied Democratic Front (ADF), 54; disintegration fate of, 84–86, 91; fates of Uganda rebels including, 53*tab*; rebel persistence and, 170, 174–175; rebirth of, 86–89; as unusual case, 77, 91–92
Allied Democratic Movement (ADM), 84
Alur, 71
Amara, Gaskin, 2
Amaria, William, 64
Amin, Idi, 51, 63, 66–70
Amnesty Act, 52, 65–66
ANC. *See* African National Congress
Anti-Balaka militias, 20–21
Antinov aircraft, 109
Anya-Nya rebellion, 91, 103, 104, 107, 108
APC. *See* All People's Congress
APRD. *See* Armée Populaire pour la Restauration de la République et la Démocratie
Arab-Israeli war, 60
Arabization, 103
Aringa, 68, 71, 73–75
Aringa-Obongi Peace Initiative Committee (AROPIC), 75, 76
Armed Forces of the Democratic Republic of Congo (FARDC), 87–88
Armed Forces Revolutionary Council (AFRC), 140, 141, 143–145
Armée Populaire pour la Restauration de la République et la Démocratie (APRD), 157
AROPIC. *See* Aringa-Obongi Peace Initiative Committee
Arrow boys, 20
Asmara Declaration, 115
Asymmetrical irregular war, 44*tab*, 45, 54, 74
Atamvaku, Zubairi, 69, 70

About the Book

What determines the outcome for rebels in contemporary African civil wars? How are "victory" and "defeat" measured? Is there any connection between a rebel group's organization and its fate? What implications do the answers to these questions have for policymakers concerned with ongoing armed conflicts? Addressing these issues and more, Christopher Day explores the relationship between rebel groups and regime politics in Africa.

Christopher Day is associate professor of political science at the College of Charleston.